# A BRIDGE TO NOWHERE

## Temporalities of Abandonment in Rural Canada

Artfully written and meticulously crafted, *A Bridge to Nowhere* explores the lives of men and women in isolated settlements across Canada, examining how their experiences are shaped by memory, precarity, and poverty. Following men abandoned at remote rail sidings in Western Canada and women left in rural settlements in northern New Brunswick, Donna Young presents a powerful and unflinching Canadian story that critically analyses how poverty is represented in anthropological studies.

Based on research conducted in the 1980s and 1990s, this innovative ethnography centres each chapter on a specific place or individual, developing an analysis anchored in memory and relationality. Young deftly connects the precariousness of these communities to the extraction of primary resources in the twentieth century, while also addressing the gendered spaces and labour conditions that define their lives. In navigating the complex and often contradictory forces at play, the book engages with a storied loneliness set against rural landscapes and regional sensibilities.

Weaving together social history, memory studies, and the anthropology of performance, *A Bridge to Nowhere* honours the emotional and social structures embedded in the landscape, capturing the intensity of precarious living.

DONNA YOUNG is a professor emeritus of anthropology at the University of Toronto.

## ANTHROPOLOGICAL HORIZONS

Editor: Michael Lambek, University of Toronto

This series, begun in 1991, focuses on theoretically informed ethnographic works addressing issues of mind and body, knowledge and power, equality and inequality, the individual and the collective. Interdisciplinary in its perspective, the series makes a unique contribution in several other academic disciplines: women's studies, history, philosophy, psychology, political science, and sociology.

For a list of the books published in this series see p. 179.

# A Bridge to Nowhere

*Temporalities of Abandonment in Rural Canada*

DONNA YOUNG

UNIVERSITY OF TORONTO PRESS
Toronto Buffalo London

© University of Toronto Press 2025
Toronto  Buffalo  London
utppublishing.com
Printed in Canada

ISBN 978-1-4875-6446-9 (cloth)    ISBN 978-1-4875-6449-0 (EPUB)
ISBN 978-1-4875-6447-6 (paper)    ISBN 978-1-4875-6448-3 (PDF)

---

**Library and Archives Canada Cataloguing in Publication**

Title: A bridge to nowhere : temporalities of abandonment in rural
    Canada / Donna Young.
Names: Young, Donna Jean, 1956– author
Series: Anthropological horizons.
Description: Series statement: Anthropological horizons | Includes
    bibliographical references and index.
Identifiers: Canadiana (print) 20250210657 | Canadiana (ebook) 20250210681 |
    ISBN 9781487564469 (cloth) | ISBN 9781487564476 (paper) |
    ISBN 9781487564483 (PDF) | ISBN 9781487564490 (EPUB)
Subjects: LCSH: Poverty – Canada. | LCSH: Poor men – Canada. |
    LCSH: Poor women – Canada. | LCSH: Precarious employment – Canada. |
    LCSH: Ethnology – Canada. | LCSH: Canada – Rural conditions.
Classification: LCC HC120.P6 Y58 2025 | DDC 362.50971 – dc23

---

Cover design: Val Cooke
Cover image: iStock.com/Joe_Potato

We wish to acknowledge the land on which the University of Toronto
Press operates. This land is the traditional territory of the Wendat, the
Anishnaabeg, the Haudenosaunee, the Métis, and the Mississaugas of the
Credit First Nation.

University of Toronto Press acknowledges the financial support of the
Government of Canada, the Canada Council for the Arts, and the Ontario
Arts Council, an agency of the Government of Ontario, for its publishing
activities.

Canada Council    Conseil des Arts
for the Arts      du Canada

ONTARIO ARTS COUNCIL
CONSEIL DES ARTS DE L'ONTARIO
an Ontario government agency
un organisme du gouvernement de l'Ontario

Funded by the    Financé par le
Government       gouvernement
of Canada        du Canada

Canada

# Contents

# Acknowledgments

I want to thank my colleagues, friends, and family for their generous support and involvement in the research and revisions involved in writing this book. I feel certain that the following will be incomplete, but please know that I am deeply grateful. My work on the railroad was encouraged by my professors at the University of New Brunswick. I want to acknowledge the late Charles Ackerman, the late William Dalton, the late Vincent Erikson, Peter Lovell, Frances Stewart, and especially Gail Pool, all of whom introduced me to the discipline of anthropology. They were dedicated and inspiring teachers and greatly influenced the way I approach the world. I continue to be indebted to them. While at the University of New Brunswick in the 1980s, I joined an interdisciplinary Critical Studies reading group, and members of that collective came to shape my understanding of the Atlantic region. I am thankful to that amazing cadre of students, some of whom would inherit the mantle of the Acadiensis School. I owe a debt to the scholarship of historians Danny Samson, James Kenny, and especially the late William Parenteau. Also present in that group was the astute literary critic of the region, the late Herb Wyile. Their combined scholarship deepens our understanding of Atlantic Canada. Returning briefly to UNB in the early 1990s, I met Heidi MacDonald, who shares my interest in the lives and work of communities of Roman Catholic women religious in the region. Heidi, thank you for your insights and ongoing support, and generous doses of laughter.

The opportunity to pursue my doctoral work at the University of Toronto introduced me to new ideas and I enjoyed studying with an especially dynamic and thoughtful cohort of students, two of whom have remained lifelong friends. My thanks to Jennifer Lund and Anna de Aguayo for their percipience and friendship. I was fortunate to enjoy the company of fellow travellers while teaching courses at Dalhousie

University in the 1990s. I want to acknowledge Lindsay Dubois, Pauline Barber, Tania Lee, Kregg Heatherington, and Alexandra Widmer, with whom I could think aloud as my ideas were just beginning to take shape. At that time, Danyelle Karis Allen accompanied me on many long walks in which we discussed the trials and pleasures of fieldwork close to home. In more recent years, my dear friends Jill Watson and Heidi MacDonald indulged my need to read whole chapters of this book out loud, for which I am deeply thankful. They are both astute readers of the region and times I explore in this book. Anne Meneley has encouraged various iterations of this project. I treasure her prodding, intellectual acuity, and outrageous sense of humour. She is also a wonderful travel and writing companion. I thank Don Handelman for his ongoing encouragement and belief in this book. His work on ritual, play, and proto-events informs my analyses.

I have had the pleasure of working with smart, thoughtful, and incredibly decent colleagues at the University of Toronto. A few deserve special mention. I treasure the thoughtful comments and camaraderie of Maggie Cummings and Lena Mortensen. Katie Kilroy-Marac read the entire manuscript at a critical point in the book's utter unravelling and her insights helped me to reconceive the book in fresh ways. Connie Gagliardi and Kassandra Spooner-Lockyer brought creative energy to old research and helped with various tedious editorial tasks. Sandra Bamford is a constant source of support and I cherish her kindness and guidance. Michael Lambek is an inspiring mentor and colleague. I want to thank Michael for his generous and inclusive scholarship, which has opened conversations far and wide, from which I have benefited immensely. Michael's scholarship on memory and ordinary ethics has been inspirational.

I thank my editors at the University of Toronto Press: Jodi Lewchuk inherited this volume from Doug Hildebrand, and both have been encouraging and extremely patient with me. I also want to thank Anne Laughlin for her careful copy-editing. The reviewers of this volume gave me thoughtful comments that helped me to reconsider and reshape different parts of this book. Thank you for taking the time to engage with my scholarship.

I am truly indebted to the people I met while carrying out the research for this book, both on rail gangs in Western Canada, and in communities along the North Shore of Eastern New Brunswick. This is a brief glimpse into their lives at the close of the twentieth century, although the interpretations remain mine alone, simply another point of view among the many that flourished at that time. I have lost touch with the men who once worked on the railroad, but they have never been forgotten. I fondly recall time spent with people in northeastern New Brunswick and I remain friends with the woman I call Joan. I want to thank her for all the ways in which she made this book possible. I consider the brief time spent with elderly Filles de Jésus a gift. They challenged me to think about the past from a very unique perspective. Finally, I want to thank my sister-in-law Gloria Guitard for her knowledge of the North Shore. She has been a constant source of information, and I am grateful for her ongoing encouragement.

My entire family passed away over the course of writing this book. My parents, Norman Arthur and Dorothy Jean Young (née Ferris), and my siblings, Nancy Ann Beyeler (née Young), John Norman Young, and Bettie June Young, find their way into this book in surprising ways. Memories of childhood picnics with my family beside the Bridge to Nowhere that once crossed the Tay River are sweet. May *A Bridge to Nowhere* be a testament of my love for my kin, the landscapes, and people of New Brunswick.

# A BRIDGE TO NOWHERE

# A Bridge to Nowhere

> Requiring neither extended analysis nor rational justification, sense of place rests its case on the unexamined premise that being from *somewhere* is always preferable to being from *nowhere*.
>
> Keith Basso, *Wisdom Sits in Places*[1]

This book is composed of six linked ethnographic essays that attend to the lives of people who have lived on the economic, cultural, and social margins of Canadian society for many decades, if not centuries. A combination of geographical isolation and neoliberal economic restructuring[2] hovers in the ethnographic present of the places, times, lives, and stories I portray. And yet this is not a depiction of an underclass completely at the mercy of social and historical processes. A multitude of opinions and deeds vie for attention as people respond to the circumstances and situations that emerge in their lives. They do so while struggling with an overwhelming sense of dwelling in, coming from, or belonging to a nowhere place. This book is devoted to plumbing the depths of particular nowhere places – by-products of the railway and forestry industries – as affective landscapes that give rise to particular forms of attachment and subjectivity.

In each essay, I linger in a particular time/place saturated by affect and atmosphere, trying to capture the ways in which people live their lives and make sense of their worlds. The analytic poles of subject and structure are exposed by recalling the gritty objects, the unfolding of events, and the stories and turns of phrase that make mood and atmosphere palpable. Often, I focus on the canny abilities of people to outmanoeuvre circumstance and ingeniously occupy spaces of nowhere. Unbridled creativity and a sense of freedom flourish when there really is nothing left to lose, because you and your way of life have already been relegated to the dustbin of national or global imaginaries and concerns.[3] But the uncanny remnants of the past also hover in these places, fuelling ways of remembering, and ways of creating and telling stories.

This book contributes to a comparative study of Western nowhere places, which I understand to be actively created through patterns of colonial settlement, settler nation-building and modernization, and more recently, neoliberal restructuring and neglect. Historically, the key ethnographic moments I attend to span the final two decades of the twentieth century, which we have since come to recognize as nascent neoliberal times. But none of us – the key players in these essays – could really see that at the time, although an edginess, a sense of waiting for the other shoe to drop, was always in the air. Being on edge is a tacit way of acknowledging one's precarious situation, of understanding that your life is under the heel of powerful forces little understood. As Susan Lepselter notes, "[this] makes sense; this is what power feels like. In the many small cuts of everyday life, you see the effects of power, but you don't see the workings of an invisible hand" (2016: 90).

While each essay dwells on a particular present-time lifted from field notes and memory, in their entirety the chapters track an unravelling of modernity's promises; the essays probe the various ways people I knew internalized a sense of abandonment. Together they help me trace the many small indignities and ways of responding to neglect that have fuelled the current moment, in which political rhetoric and realities are being contested by those who were largely ignored in the heady days of neoliberal restructuring. The disinherited do so in ways I certainly did not anticipate; but the overwhelming edginess, despair, melancholy, anger, resentment, and rancour I found in those isolated times/places has now bled into mainstream political realities and right-wing populism far and wide. And I catch glimpses of the same troubling mood and sense of things having come undone in the writing of other anthropologists who spent time living with people in *other* Western nowhere places at the close of the twentieth century. Whether it is the melancholic despair of Hispano heroin addicts in New Mexico (Garcia 2010), a suicide epidemic among Canadian Inuit (Stevenson 2014), or the alien sensibilities of conspiracy theorists living in the American Southwest (Lepselter 2016), attention is drawn to that troubling space on the side of the road (Stewart 1996). King's (2014) account of the eruption of violence in the lobster fishery in the community of Burnt Church, just down the coast from my field site in northern New Brunswick, highlights a similar troubling space in the Miramichi Bay. State interventions and actors with ecological and economic concerns cared little for Mi'kmaq and settler attachments to place, revealed in the stories they told as they moved through the countryside and along the shore. Stewart (1996) argued that those spaces on the side of the road were intensely storied places, where ruination and rumination combined to produce sensibilities, poetics, and back-talk (a critical diacritics) that shaped encounters between people in particular ways. Lepselter similarly notes: it's the 'knowledge' of living in a western 'nowhere' that makes a texted *metanowhere* into the most intensely imagined somewhere" (2016: 94).

The resonances between these ethnographies of Western nowhere places canot, however, collapse into a generalizable mass of unwashed, nowhere people. As the ethnographers above make clear, each nowhere place has its own history and historicity; each is situated in very specific waves of colonial settlement, and in layers of expropriation of land and resources, chains of capitalist expansion and withdrawal, state formations and national projects, and all the ethnic and racialized practices that attend Western attachments to landscape and place. To what extent are the poetics and stories created by Canadians living on the edge of Crown lands[4] in Eastern Canada (King 2014) similar to, yet different from, those found on the edges of American military zones (Lepselter 2016), or those harvesting mushrooms in the wake of deforestation of the Pacific Northwest (Tsing 2015)? How do the settler histories of material and cultural dispossession for the Hispano of New Mexico (Garcia 2010) compare to those of the Acadians in the Maritime provinces? There are particular social and political histories at work in all of these places and they haunt the landscape in specific ways.

In the 1980s, I worked as a cook in Western Canada for Canadian Pacific Railway maintenance-of-way crews fixing track, first from 1981to 1983, and then again in 1986 as a graduate student, working as a part-time cook and full-time participant-observer; in other words, as an ethnographer of men who for a period of their lives called a rusted chain of boxcars home. Then, off and on throughout the early 1990s, I lived on the northeastern shore of New Brunswick, carrying out doctoral fieldwork in small coastal communities, and in the bedraggled settlements that lay just inland from the Atlantic coast. With surprising symmetry I returned briefly to both field sites twenty-five years after having left them, and only then did I fully realize the consequences of decades of neoliberal policies and neglect for the people I knew and the places they inhabited. On both return visits, it came as a complete shock to discover that places I thought timeless had been so completely altered. I found it difficult to get my bearings. Time waits for no one, certainly not for anthropologists, and ethnography quickly becomes history.[5]

Still, much can be gained from revisiting those ethnographic moments at the close of the last century when people were making valiant efforts to carve out meaningful lives for themselves, even if all the signs looked bleak. I have been struck by some recent ethnographic attempts to make sense of twenty-first century America by focusing on the debris and rubbish in a countryside ravished by the past century, as if the work of imagining the lives of those who once lived and worked there had already been relegated to the realm of archaeology.[6] In these texts, the anthropologists are left ruminating over objects in a blighted landscape. What was most startling to me, when I returned to both of my Canadian research sites, was not the remaining debris, but the complete obliteration of the objects, sights, and smells that had been so present at the time of my ethnographic fieldwork. For instance, the rail gang on which I worked had been parked in a rail yard in the middle of Lethbridge, Alberta, when I departed from the life of a railway cook for the first time in 1983. Twenty-five years later, I returned to give a talk in the Department of Anthropology at Lethbridge University to find the rail yard was completely gone. A large box store stood in its place, on land that had been completely levelled. These changes occurred prior to the arrival at Lethbridge of American professors fleeing the collapsing American economy. Academics were moving north in droves to fill positions in Canadian anthropology departments.[7] I stumbled about, feeling lost, wondering what had happened to the various seedy hotels and bars that had once abutted the track, places redolent with the smell of stale beer and cigarettes, for which there is so little tolerance in the twenty-first century. I felt I had truly reached the end of the line.[8]

Then again, twenty-five years after leaving the north shore of New Brunswick, I retraced the trip that launched my doctoral fieldwork, which I write about in chapter 2. The acrid smell of sulphur – my father called it the smell of money, when as children we would hold our noses and complain – was no longer hanging thick in the air. An entire pulp and paper industry, the lifeblood of a provincial economy, had been completely erased from the landscape. Locals had already carefully marked time by posting videos online of millworks and smokestacks being blown up for removal. On my return, few material traces remained of abandoned industries in the one-time mill towns of central and northern New Brunswick. Perhaps, in carefully removing the evidence of an industrial past, the provincial government hoped the people of New Brunswick would forget the catastrophic political and economic blunders that allowed international industries to profit from the timber on Crown lands without asking for jobs in return. Fat chance: Memory runs deep in the Maritimes.[9]

Does this deliberate obliteration of industrial ruins signify something distinctively Canadian? I think so. Most of the international industries that benefited from the resources on Crown lands enjoyed provincial and federal government support and enticements. When I talk to friends and family from New Brunswick about second-growth forests swallowing up the abandoned farms and industrial lands of my youth, they tell me it is nature gradually reclaiming a landscape once settled. It is an old Canadian trope. Margaret Atwood notes that "Canadian writers as a whole do not trust Nature, they are always suspecting some dirty trick" (1972: 59). But my kin, who work their woodlots, welcome nature's return and care little for the abandoned communities. They do not share my nostalgic memories of a more pastoral landscape now returned to wilderness, or of small hubs of working-class productivity, now erased. What remains hidden behind both ways of sensing the changing landscape are the political and economic transformations managed by government and industry.

## Creating and Occupying Spaces of Nowhere

In Canada, both railway and forest industries were key modernist projects in the late nineteenth and early twentieth centuries; federal and provincial governments invested heavily in building the infrastructure intended to develop a nation. Both industries required large reserves of labour willing to work cheaply in the middle of nowhere, whether laying track or extracting primary resources.[10] The industries were also heavily dependent on access to managed Crown lands – Indigenous lands appropriated first by the British and then the Canadian state – lands and resources that fell under the control of the new nation and were leased to the giants of international industry.[11] Wolfgang Schivelbusch (1986) brilliantly captures the sense in which railways created a new modernist sense of time and place in Europe, as the spaces in between key destinations – villages and communities not connected to the new grid put down by the railways – were destroyed.[12] But in Canada, the railway was used to open up a frontier and to put new places on the map, creating destinations, but also places in the hinterland for the rural labouring classes (Lower 1936), such as the lumberjacks of northern New Brunswick, who spent long seasons in work camps extracting timber, and the men who lived in the makeshift shanties of Western Canada while they built the railways. The process of settlers turning hinterland places – rarely acknowledged as home to First Nations – into nowhere places, is tied to both modernity's successes and its failures, failures that picked up speed and intensified as mechanization and neoliberal globalization took hold in the latter part of the twentieth century.

In my twenties, I spent several years living in a boxcar on railway sidings in Western Canada, often located miles from the closest town, in the middle of a prairie, or on a forested mountainside. Even when we parked in towns and cities, we were relegated to industrial lands not intended for domestic dwelling. We were always outliers. As for the rural settlement in New Brunswick that became the primary research site for my doctoral work, it lay a few kilometres inland from the Atlantic coast, down a backwoods road through black spruce and scraggly poplars clinging to the sides of the ditch, part of a rough network of roads connecting several small settlements. This is the sort of road you find in the fiction of David Adams Richards, a road which the locals know like the back of their hands. In *Blood Ties*, pensive young Orville is seen "walking close to the drenched woodlot … the road deserted except for him" with "his head down and hands in his pockets" (1976: 6). But note that he is seen, for those who live on these back roads rarely miss a thing, and the ties that bind those who live in these rural communities run deep. In the heat of a summer's day, I have stooped with my friend Joan on such a road to pick the wild strawberries that push through the rough gravel thrown along the side of the ditch, as deer flies buzzed about, irritating our dogs. It always came as a surprise to me that our outings were observed by others, remembered by people I barely knew and commented on at a later date.

Outsiders rarely find themselves in such places. Certainly not on the often difficult-to-reach railway sidings where a gang would be dropped for a matter of weeks; or on the back roads that lead only to the settlements and the deep woods. In these places there are no clinics, no libraries, no grocery stores, no post offices, no pubs or coffee shops. Just a lonely railway siding, or a road with tiny homes strung along it, in the middle of the woods, miles off the beaten track. They are the sorts of rural places about which Maritimers jokingly remark, "He lived so deep in the woods he had to come out to hunt." Still, railway workers and rural Maritimers are often closely attached to these middle-of-nowhere landscapes, topographies, and environments, places that twist their way into the core of their being. Ernestine, one of my elderly informants from northern New Brunswick, once told me she had a lonely nature. I have spent years pondering that odd pairing of terms, which so poignantly captures the internalization of an isolated, brutal, and, by turns, heart-breaking and breathtakingly beautiful landscape. I recognize in her self-portrayal a tender and at times frightening loneliness. But a *lonely nature* also alludes to her comfort with forms of solitude that are a consequence of having survived all those frigid winters and buggy summers without a nickel to rub between her fingers; it also alludes to her independence and resourcefulness in having stacked enough wood to get through the winter, and grown the potatoes and turnips, preserved the berries, and killed the moose or deer needed to keep food on her family's table when work was scarce, and times were tough.

The settlement of which I write did have a church, a graveyard, and a school parked midway along the road, thanks to the work of the Acadian Roman Catholic clergy who historically tried to bring relief to the impoverished settlers during and after the Great Depression. They were committed to the ideals of Catholic subsidiarity[13] and worked tirelessly to create self-sufficient rural communities. Over the years, fewer and fewer people go to mass, unless to attend a baptism, wedding, or funeral, and the school has been closed since I briefly worked there in the 1990s. Administrators hoped to introduce the wilful and unruly children to a wider – dare I say civilizing – world by busing them to regional schools, or so I was told on my return journey. I suspect administrators were seeking "efficiencies" in the delivery of services to the region. When I was in the field in the early 1990s, the regional social and cultural history of the Acadian clergy was shrouded in memories of abuse. I do not question the veracity of abuse stories, but I do want to draw attention to the rewriting of a religious past little understood in the present. If the Roman Catholic interventions of an earlier era had been toward building self-sufficient rural communities, modern efforts on the part of regionalized political bodies concerned with cost-benefit efficiencies and standardization have helped to turn the rural settlements into bedroom communities at best, impoverished rural ghettos at worst.

In the settlement where I worked, a small fire hall was built after there was a rash of house fires (which industry linked to insurance fraud); a local college student was later hired there in the summers to keep watch. There were no public places where one might run into one's neighbours to chat, unless you count the local gas station. And yet the population in this bleak settlement had not only remained constant over the last century, it actually expanded throughout the 1990s, completely bucking the trend found in the little communities on the scenic coast, or in the pulp and paper towns nearby, where out-migration was steady. Indeed, more people lived in the settlement than in the scenic coastal village where I resided, which had a fishing wharf, a post office, a grocery store, and an AlcoolNBLiquor[14] outlet, a bank, a Canadian Legion branch, a small takeout restaurant, a community hall, organized bingo, an ice rink, and a baseball diamond. Nowhere places were growing in the 1990s.

Garcia (2010), Lepselter (2016), Stewart (2007), Tsing (2015), and Pine (2016) track the growth of nowhere places in the United States during the same period. This growth occurred in response to global neoliberal trends and deindustrialization. Still, there remain significant differences. Canada's universal social programs (always under threat) and the management of Crown lands by provincial and federal governments attempt to respond to these economic and social shifts more directly,[15] although they are also affected by the logic of late capitalist rhetoric and management practices. Particularly troubling is the re-emergence of right-wing populism in Canada, strongly influenced by political ideas from our southern neighbour, ironically resulting in governments espousing a cost-means logic that serves industries resting in the hands of a few. That this way of thinking ignores the major issues of the day (climate change that threatens future generations, deindustrialization, and mechanization leading to fewer jobs, and the growing numbers of people with precarious employment) has not lessened the appeal of a rhetoric that imagines a return to the extractive industries of the past and notions of freedom closely tied to the market place and radical individualism.

### The Temporalities of Nowhere

The two nowhere places described in the chapters that follow are marked by two distinct, but related, orientations to time. The rootless railroaders are decidedly present-oriented, committed to living in the moment, while the deeply rooted settlers are tied to a melancholic past that never managed to deliver prosperity. I observe the same rootlessness of the railroaders in Lepselter's descriptions of the restless Americans who wander into the desert seeking freedom, choosing to live "in the middle of nowhere" because "they want to be left alone" (2016: 94), before moving on to the next trailer park in another nowhere place up the road. Lepselter's descriptions (2016: 140–7) of her intense interactions with one of her interlocuters, Tina, who eventually packs up her camper and moves on without a word of goodbye, produced a jolt of recognition, as I recalled those rootless people with whom I spent time in my early twenties. All of them disappeared from my life in a flash.

Then again, the deep attachment to lands historically lost in colonial wars, in which one group of settlers replaces another, produces a haunting melancholy among both the disinherited Hispano of rural New Mexico (Garcia 2010), and the descendants of both the French-Acadian and Irish settlers of the Maritimes, who put down new roots after earlier dislocations of an epic scale. Garcia describes melancholia as "unfinished grief" and "wonders how Freud's conception of melancholia can be extended to address such material losses, losses such as lands that remain present but out of reach, especially in a context in which land is constituent to cultural identity and economic survival" (2010: 84). Garcia remains attentive to the historical specificity of the Hispano addicts who "keep vigil" in culturally informed ways (2010: 71–3). I too explore the ways in which melancholy is tied to a troubled rootedness, in which colonial displacements and resentment pass from one generation to the next, turning previous losses into unremitting grief. I explore a gothic sensibility in which a sense of both loss and entrapment prevails. Maritime gothic concerns itself with the intimate memories of families entangled in repressed histories and forms of religiosity that belong to the near past but have been eclipsed by more empirical ways of making sense in the world.

I argue there is a very real connection between the two senses of being-in-time: that of the rootless track workers, already cut adrift from nowhere places that could no longer provide them with a livelihood, and that of the rooted rural dwellers in the Maritimes, descendants of the disinherited of an earlier era, who are determined to hold on to their land come hell or high water. Two distinct temporalities are at play in both of the nowhere places I describe: The first concerns "a common commitment to the present" that at moments can achieve a "transcendent escape from time itself" (Day et al. 1999: 2; Desjarlais 1997: 87–95); the second involves a form of remembering haunted by ghostly presences (Gordon 1997; Edwards 2005).[16] Neither of these temporalities is especially forward-looking or future-oriented, which can make those who appear to obstinately resist taking responsibility for their own futures the object of derision. It was perhaps the very inability of those I knew to imagine, anticipate, or effectively produce a plan that conformed to reigning ideals of restructuring and knowledge-based economies that led to a sense of their being nowhere, and hence out-of-time, in the first place. It was this anachronistic aspect and "stuckness" that most frustrated those such as teachers, social workers, game wardens, and police, who felt a need to educate or discipline these railway workers and rural inhabitants, so that they would obediently leave these places to pursue different forms of work elsewhere. The people I knew lacked the material resources and raw capital upon which such neoliberal self-fashioning depends; in any event, promises of work in the "new economy" (in tech, Green, digital, service industries, etc.) failed to materialize.

In northern New Brunswick, those who had once been so integral to the forest industry were faulted for their unrealistic attachment to places that no longer needed their labour. Indeed, their continued presence on the edge of Crown lands was sometimes said to threaten the very environment itself, an environment preserved largely for industry and wealthy sportsmen (Parenteau and Judd 2005; Parenteau 1998, 2004). In this way, the idea of the commons was long ago turned into "uncommon ground" (Cronon 1995). Some of my friends on the north shore cared passionately about the environment, but their modest forms of living reflected an ethics of care for the land little appreciated by big industry, or by the professional foresters who manage Crown lands.

On my return visit, I discovered that even modest means of employment, like seasonal tree-planting, had dried up. Instead, a few independent contractors with sophisticated machinery were harvesting trees in a checkerboard pattern, a method intended to allow the forest to regenerate on its own. As even seasonal work disappeared, no amount of gumption could turn the tide for those struggling to make ends meet on the edge of Crown lands. Nevertheless, the rural poor continue to be blamed for bankrupting the welfare state in New Brunswick. It was as if their desire to remain at home was an affront to progress itself. And while many continued to reluctantly leave home for work elsewhere, the thought of pulling up stakes and leaving home for good was deeply distressing, or simply inconceivable, to others. Some were simply too poor to leave. Railroaders, on the other hand, who had already pulled up stakes and moved on, were faulted for their troubling peripatetic and itinerant ways. Damned if you stay, damned if you go.

The literary critic Herb Wyile argues that the entire Atlantic region is represented as a cash-strapped "have not" region made up of people who need to move on. As such, the fiction of the entire region has become "speculative fiction" for the rest of Canada: "an advance glimpse of what life is like when one of the only things that you have left to sell is your past" (2011: 243). Together, gothic, and present-oriented temporalities attend to the resurfacing of repressed histories and to ongoing struggles to survive in the moment that can, as Benjamin noted, "manifest themselves as courage, humour, cunning, and fortitude" (1969: 254–5). In both orientations, time is decidedly out of joint with the hegemonic, historical unfolding of time that undergirds notions of progress and the advancement of humankind.[17] The dispossessed I knew were often blamed not only for their own poverty, but also for undermining nationalist projects that had assumed a march toward the future. Track workers and rural settlers never managed to be properly in step with the time.

*Being Oriented to the Present*

I was powerfully affected by the two years I spent as a railroad cook, years that predate my time as a graduate student, but which share many of the hallmarks of ethnographic fieldwork, except for the fact that they were years without academic purpose. For those two years, which coincided with the recession of the early 1980s, I stepped away from my family and friends and all the typical aspirations of my peers. Joining a rail gang took me far off the beaten track and, for a period of time, looking backward and looking forward were suspended. I was committed to living in the rough and tumble of the present, especially appealing when prospects for meaningful work looked grim for recent university graduates in the Maritimes. It was a relief to be freed from the pressures of trying to figure out what to do next, especially if you lacked an entrepreneurial spirit.[18] The neoliberal politics of the day seemed to me unassailable. In this regard, at least for a while, I was not so different from the railroaders with whom I spent that period of my life. But then again, when things got really bad, I did leave. I didn't drop out of the middle class entirely because I had a family that could provide for me while I stopped to regroup. The option of going home to recover from various physical and psychological assaults that were part of daily life on the railroad did not exist for most of the men with whom I worked.

Both the rootless and the rooted pay a high price for the sorts of freedom they claim in deciding to either go look for work elsewhere or to hold on to a way of life that is increasingly untenable. Those who leave almost always end up drifting from one nowhere place to another, all the while avoiding hegemonic understandings of time well spent that underlie modernist notions of personal achievement. They can appear shiftless, undisciplined, and anachronistic to those who are busy trying to get ahead, start a family, or accomplish something with their lives according to the conventional rules, the ones that tell you to get a solid education, a career, a mortgage, a spouse and kids. But they certainly are not lazy; they do hard physical labour, and they do it for very little financial reward.

To a large extent, poverty and dispossession had already denied both groups – the rootless and the rooted – the luxury of planning for a future. Those few who tried to play by the rules rarely found a brighter future. The chapters in this book document the tragic realization, among groups and individuals, that an escape from nowhere grew steadily more unlikely in the final decades of the twentieth century, as earlier promises of modernity (especially as they were articulated after the Second World War and during the educational reform campaigns in New Brunswick during the 1960s) were crushed. The consequences were devastating for those who tried to leave nowhere for someplace and failed. This is a different, though related, form of "cruel optimism" than that explored by Berlant (2011). The most vulnerable are perhaps the first to give up on their dreams, as hard realities quickly dash hopes for anything better. Suicide, or talk of suicide, is another thread that weaves its way through many ethnographies of nowhere places (Garcia 2010; Stevenson 2014). Even if the suicides are grounded in cultural and historical specificity, read together they amount to heart-wrenching reality in nowhere places. This ethnography chronicles a suicide that is both tragic and troubling – an open wound I adamantly refuse to close.

But equally noteworthy are those others, both on the railroad gang and in the settlements, unwilling to sacrifice the precarious freedoms they enjoy by virtue of refusing what they referred to as the "rat race," invariably associated with life in an urban environment, chasing careers and a lifestyle that they could neither imagine nor manage, and that they did not especially envy. I recall Babette, the woman who initially introduced me to people living in the settlements; she was given to unending antics, theatrics, and screw-ups, once failing to get up in time to make an interview for a job in a call centre that she desperately needed. When she phoned to reschedule, she was told the job was already filled. She turned to me and said, "Who cares? Who wants a job that demands you be on time?" Babette had a wicked sense of humour; but beneath it is a stunning rebuke of those who easily bend to the dictates of a job market that delivers neither a living wage nor any form of security. Admittedly, that left her caught between a rock and a hard place.

Maintenance-of-way workers and people from the settlement – even those who had already moved on to urban centres – struggled to retain vestiges of independence; even an inkling of condescension from others could get under their skin and fester, provoking depression, rancour, or sudden bouts of violence. They were unwilling to leave their nowhere for a someplace that insulted their intelligence and limited their independence. Instead, they made do in the moment. And in peculiar ways they were better positioned to survive the disappointments of modernity's failures because they never bought into it in the first place. Such are the freedoms of being off the grid, even if you live next to a key resource, such as the forests on New Brunswick's Crown lands, or, like the railway workers, tarry on the track that was intended to unite a nation.

This way of being-in-time, what Day et al. (1999) have called a "common commitment to the present," is critical to my understanding of freedom on the rail gangs, a topic I discuss in the first chapter, "The Evanescent Freedoms of Life on a CPR Rail Gang." But it is also found in the last chapter, "Unravelling," as we see unemployed friends and relatives from both the rural settlement and urban centres in the Maritimes expend hours and hours creating an all-night murder mystery party that devolves into moments of debauchery and melodrama. In both chapters, the focus is on the unfolding of events that quickly follow the cashing of paycheques or unemployment benefits, events capable of lifting one out of the monotony of work on the track, or the boredom of rural and urban social isolation. These itinerant railroaders, lumberjacks, tree-planters, and intermittently employed urbanites work hard and play hard, all the while eschewing dominant Canadian social expectations in favour of moments of risk-taking revelry and defiance. But, as Day et al. note, the costs of not planning for the day when one is unable to bend one's back to the work are great. People from nowhere risk growing old alone, with their broken bodies, addictions, and troubles, no matter where they end up.

*Being Oriented to the Past: Maritime Gothic*

A deep sense of nostalgia and melancholy endures in Atlantic Canada, not because people want to return to the past, but because the past haunts and troubles the present. For instance, some of my readers stumble over the term "settlement" in my work, which carries with it the ghost of settler colonialism. When I first arrived "up north" in New Brunswick, and tried to explain to people what anthropologists do, I was often told about a phantom ship that is sometimes seen burning on the Bay of Chaleur. I initially paid little heed to this well-known Maritimes ghost story, often trotted out for airtime around Halloween. Familiarity had caused me to be dismissive of a spectral ship whose burning is linked to our brutal colonial past. In some accounts, Mi'kmaq warriors seek revenge for the enslavement of their people by ambushing sixteenth-century Portuguese traders, traders who set their ship afire rather than surrender to savages. In another version, members of the Acadian and Mi'kmaq alliance defeated at the Battle of Restigouche in 1760 (which ended the Seven Year War between Britain and France, a colonial war that began with the mass expulsion of Acadians[19] and ended with the British conquest of North America) still haunt the bay. Still others speak of settlers avenging the kidnapping and rape of a young settler bride by setting afire the ship of a group of picaroons.[20] Some of the people who lived in the settlement where I collected life histories told me the ship carried victims of the Irish potato famine, although that telling is not reported in any of the folklore I have read. It is perhaps not surprising that victims of that famine haunt the memories of these people, some of whom still use the nineteenth-century pejorative "streel" for women with loose morals, a word used historically to describe the famished wisp of an Irish vagabond.[21] Under the sign of a phantom ship the history of colonial settlement in New Brunswick is condensed and kept alive in the present.

Edward Casey began his treatise on remembering by noting that "in the case of memory, we are always already in the thick of things" (2000: xix). The chapters in my book dealing with notions of time and place in New Brunswick are informed by extended conversations about the past. I am particularly drawn to Casey's notion of "ruminescence," which combines the words reminiscence and rumination (1987, 2000: 46–7). He coined the term to capture the ways in which "remembering may give rise to a whole spectrum of emotions, ranging from exhilarating joy to despondent remorse" (46). I focus in particular on the memories of three women in a single family; they are a daughter, a mother, and a grandmother, although in truth the three are composites cobbled from extended interviews carried out with various women who represent the three generations. Each generation has a particular take on the past, which at first glance might appear too personal and too peculiar to be of anthropological interest.[22] But their stories embody and resonate with a past full of enigmatic events, unresolved conflicts, uncertainties, and material things that are sometimes vivid, at other times ephemeral, things associated with scorn, desire, or envy. It is hard to shake off these stories.

My wading through the tides of memory is aided by the work of others who have critically tackled their own memories to achieve a broader understanding of the historical, social, and cultural terrain that shapes their relationships with those who belong to their past, present, and future. Carolyn Steedman's analysis of her troubled relationship with her mother in *Landscape for a Good Woman* (1986) brilliantly draws attention to the way memory can focus on the materiality of day-to-day life, the gritty objects that stick in one's mind. Such items often focus the mind, and the eye. Realism remains the dominant narrative and artistic form in the region, but such objects can return as spectral, gothic forms. Steedman's ability to situate her troubled relationship with her mother in history, and to tease out all the emotional baggage that it entails, informs my analysis of memory. Her work is remarkable in its attention to both documented historical realities and the residual affect attached to those realities. People from the settlements could vividly recall things and events from the past. Indeed, people from the settlements were haunted by their past.

Avery Gordon argues that haunting is "a constituent part of modern social life" and an investigation of haunting "can lead to that dense site where history and subjectivity make social life" (1997: 7–8). Gordon draws upon Raymond Williams' concept of a structure of feeling, that provocative tying together of "feeling and activity; region and time" (Williams 1973: 4) that comes to animate idiomatic and commonsensical ways of viewing the world, but also of concealing historical and social-structural arrangements and realities that shape social encounters and relationships.[23] As Gordon notes, particular images – like a spectral ship – can be read as signs of the social. Justin Edwards (2005) writes: "The effects of marginalization, segregation, ostracization and oppression haunt Canada's history with violent acts that refuse to be hidden. The nation's unjust acts force us to view the country as a fragile entity that is pieced together out of the ideological abominations of a disturbing past" (110). When I was in the field in the 1990s, the legacy of the Roman Catholic Church was especially haunting. The women of whom I write are not often the subjects of Maritime history,[24] but in the literary fiction of Atlantic Canada one can glimpse their presence, if only in fleeting, pathetic, or dangerous imagery, as threatening the social fabric of Maritime rural life. Few readers are likely to recall the opening passages in L.M. Montgomery's *Anne of Green Gables*, when Marilla Cuthbert and Mrs. Rachel Lynde gossip about "those stupid half-grown little French boys," "London Street-Arabs," and demonic orphans who either burn down the house or poison the wells of good English-Canadian benefactors (1908: 5–7). The 1990s CBC television series *Road to Avonlea*, based on Montgomery's turn-of-the- twentieth-century novels, pretty much erases Anne's grim tales of exploitation and poverty, which were her fate prior to Avonlea, and which are the source of her overactive imagination. Rob Shields (2017) argues Anne's overly romantic imagination is linked to the orphan's need and desire to find a home within settler society. It expresses a deep and powerful longing to belong. In contrast, the 1990s series evokes nostalgia for a vanishing rural life, as do various national theme parks in New Brunswick, such as King's Landing in the Saint John River Valley, and the Acadian Village in Bouctouche. As a child, I was taught history from the vantage of such gentle vistas.

But as a child I also read the "Anne-with-an-e" novels and absorbed some of their darkness, a darkness that makes sense if you live in Atlantic Canada. The 2017 production and retelling of the *Anne* series created by Moira Walby-Beckett (2017) is attentive to these darker threads in the novels, and Anne's flashbacks to her life before Green Gables takes a decidedly gothic turn. The move from nostalgic to gothic forms of rendering the Montgomery novels speaks to the social and political turmoil of the present. The women of whom I write were already embracing the gothic in the 1990s. The lives of impoverished Maritime women were always at the margins of my world, their poverty, their despair, and their impudence tugging at my consciousness, at my sense of well-being.

This book is partly about those kinds of memory, both particular memories and forms of remembering that create particular literary genres, which worked in me as much as in the people of whom I write, and which I call Maritime gothic, a form of remembering haunted by ghostly presences that will not go away, despite various forms of, and institutions for, whitewashing the past in a fog of nostalgia. These ghostly presences point to the failures of our social institutions to meet the needs of the most vulnerable, to cruel class and ethnic relations, and to tensions between the city and the country; but they also capture the remarkable resilience of the imagination, which works to refashion the world according to one's needs and desires. Maritime gothic draws attention to a local sensibility, in which knowledge of the world is *felt* viscerally through the senses and the emotions. It is a form of knowing that is attentive to sensitivities, rather than to facts, and takes seriously the sorts of things science, even the social sciences, might dismiss.

**Colonial Formations and Rancour as a Structure of Feeling**

The settlements I refer to represent a late pattern of settlement on the periphery of New Brunswick's forested Crown lands, but the very words *settlement* and *Crown lands* recall a deeper colonial past, one never fully severed from the present after Confederation. In part, this is because many Maritime families can trace their own family history and attachment to the landscape over generations that predate Confederation, as does my own family.[25] But the settlements referred to in this book are of a later vintage, when grants were made available in the late nineteenth and early twentieth centuries to largely indigent members of the local population in Restigouche County, including members of the Mi'kmaq nation who chose to live off-reserve, and the descendants of earlier waves of colonial settlement, including Acadians, French Canadians, British merchants, and lastly the Irish, who arrived in the region just prior to Confederation (Power 1991). Other than a few prosperous English and Scottish merchants, most of these people were employed as lumberjacks at one time or another, in an industry which has always been vulnerable to the vagaries of the market. The land grants were intended to offer some relief to the small villages and towns bankrupted by the reduction of their tax base owing to out-migration and jobless-ness among its residents, many of whom required public assistance. The province issued these land grants reluctantly, especially once intensive management of the timber reserves on Crow lands was underway. As William Wicken explains:

> By the 1920s plans to reorganize the management of provincial forested lands reflected changes in the region's political economy and was a result of a compendium of factors, including the aftershocks of a globalized war ... The 1920s therefore represented a new conjuncture in contestation between those, such as Mi'kmaw families and other poor rural residents, who had historically used common forested lands to supplement their income and those who owned forested lands, such as lumber companies, woodlot owners and farmers. (2012: 58)

My father claimed that the representatives of large international forestry companies never lost an election in the province, and the recorded history of the region tends to concur.[26] By 1930, two companies controlled the vast forest reserves of northern New Brunswick: the Fraser Companies of Plaster Rock, New Brunswick and International Paper of New York. As they established large pulp mills in the region, governments at the provincial and civic levels cut them sweetheart deals, granting them major tax concessions and even exempting the mills from paying any taxes at all for extended periods. The companies were also given special rates for the hydroelectricity required to run their mills (Wilbur 1989: 117–33; Parenteau 1994a). Following the Second World War, the Irving family would expand its forestry operations into the region, forming a powerful trinity of pulp and paper companies. The citizens of northern New Brunswick were given no such deals and along the north shore the social costs were enormous, as communities lacked the resources to build schools and hospitals. Increasingly this work fell to religious orders, especially those closely affiliated with the Acadian clergy of the Roman Catholic Church (Andrews 1996; Theriault 1982; MacDonald 2000, 2003a, 2003b; A. Young 1982). These institutions remained in place until the 1960s, when widespread reform and secularization transformed the province and brought some redress to the inequities that divided the largely English-speaking south from the French-speaking north. Nevertheless, this past still disturbs memories of many who grew up along the north shore and signs of neglect and poverty still cling to the landscape.

When I was in the field in the 1990s, Mi'kmaq and Maliseet First Nations across the Maritimes and in the Gaspé region of Quebec were challenging provincial restrictions to hunting, fishing, and logging on Crown lands by Indigenous peoples, which violated the Peace and Friendship Treaty Rights of 1760–1. The Sparrow Decision of 1990 upheld those rights, but provincial governments, fearing the loss of total control over resources on Crown lands, were interpreting the law in the narrowest of terms.[27] Newly recognized Indigenous rights to resources on Crown lands fuelled a politics of resentment for some of the rural poor with whom I worked; they wanted equal access to the timber, to hunting and fishing.[28] Some in the region even tried to claim Indigenous ancestry that they had not acknowledged in the past. Indeed, many who live in these settlements and communities along the north shore (and elsewhere) are of mixed ancestry. But none I knew identified as Métis, although claims to Métissage have evolved in parts of the Gaspé and Nova Scotia.[29] Even at the height of the Acadian movement in the 1960s and 1970s, people from the inland settlements of the North Shore did not identify as such, although the clergy who worked in the region often did. The people of the settlements traced their ancestry to multiple nations, and historically their social and kinship relations are deeply entangled, as are the forms of livelihood they pursue.

Some rural white people in northern New Brunswick failed to understand why one set of laws should apply to the Mi'kmaq in the region, and not to them. They angrily pointed to their own poverty and historical dependence on resources found on Crown lands. They could not understand why their own hunting and fishing practices were not treated equally under the law.[30] The tendency to undertand the livelihood practices of local Indigenous and settler populations as distinct became very clear to me early on when I would present papers in the Atlantic region and someone in the audience would approach me afterwards to ask on which "Native reserve" I had worked. When I explained that I had not worked with a Native community, the look of confusion that so quickly replaced what had been a moment of recognition deeply troubled me, and it continues to do so. For instance, a story about being caught illegally fishing, hunting, or taking timber from Crown lands by people from the settlement did not garner the same sympathy shown to the Mi'kmaq or Maliseet who did so. The forms of livelihood and dispossession that cut across historically entangled rural communities is concealed by restricting your analysis to either settler of Indigenous communities, which is not to disparage or disallow distinctions rooted in racist, legal, and colonial historical processes established in the Indian Act, let alone those upheld by treaty rights. Rather, it is intended to draw attention to ways in which the flows of capital, globalization, modern forms of management on Crown lands, and subsequent forms of economic restructuring and neoliberal ideologies disinherited large swaths of people living close to New Brunswick's forested interior.

That rancour should develop between and among those most adversely affected only obscures what they share (or lack) in common.[31]

## Ethnography as a Bridge to Nowhere

The "Bridge to Nowhere" is a reference to a covered bridge that once spanned the Tay River in New Brunswick and abutted property that my father's family owned. It was built years ago, in a time of optimistic settlement that ended abruptly; the road on the other side of the bridge was never begun, let alone completed. When I was a young child, my extended family would gather there to swim and have family picnics, and it remains for me a place of idyllic childhood memories. The bridge was washed away in the floods of 1973, and now only exists in the memories of those old enough to have spent time there.

For me, the "Bridge to Nowhere" has become a central motif and trope on many levels. The actual bridge concretely captures the vicissitudes of the Maritime economy as it historically chased vanishing notions of progress and prosperity. The "Bridge to Nowhere" that now exists only in memory is haunting, as it retains elements of a receding historical *durée* rarely recalled. It is a history I have tried to unpack in this ethnography, not by searching the archive (although I did some of that too), but by being attentive to the actions, stories, and sensibilities of people I have known. And lately, I have found myself thinking about a "Bridge to Nowhere" as a metaphor for examining the responsibilities and betrayals that haunt ethnographic research and anthropological writing. Ethnography produces its own "lonely nature," for our relationships and sense of belonging with the people who live in nowhere places can be so fleeting. But I hold on to the hope that ethnography can provide a bridge to nowhere, by complicating and enriching our understanding of the lives of others we have spent time with and cherished, even if we have at times unwittingly hurt them, or, for that matter, been hurt by them.

The chapters of this book are written as essays, each grappling with a different set of theoretical problems provoked by unsettling or compelling events, and divergent points of view as to the significance of those events, events which I continue to revisit and churn over. The chapters are linked through this recursive gesture, but they unfold historically, beginning in the 1980s, as I retrace ethnographic moments that have shaped my understanding of Canadian nowhere places. While relistening to recordings of stories from northern New Brunswick, I am always taken by the way the word *so* punctuates the conversation. At the beginning of a particular segment in a story, it is used to indicate a response to what went before, to explain why certain events follow other events; but it is also sometimes used to end a story, as if to say, "so, make of that what you will." *So* is a little word that works recursively, nodding to the past and to the future, but pointing to the indeterminacy of human action, because, of course, it could have indeed been otherwise.[32]

In another sense, *so* is offered as a challenge, as in "so, what's it to you?" In all utterances of the word, we capture the explicable and inexplicable, the beliefs and uncertainties that contour human interactions and understanding. In some ways, these essays might be said to do the same: first recalling the unfolding of events as I witnessed them and tracked them in fieldnotes, then testing or playing with them for a moment against theoretical debates, but in the end never exactly closing the loop. Then I plunge headlong into another essay, only to repeat the same impossible exercise of trying to make sense of the dense complexity that is real life in troubled times. That my own memories and emotional baggage are wrapped around these essays only complicates the matter. *So.*

*So, where to begin ...*

We are the navvies who work upon the railway
Swingin' our hammers in the bright blazin' sun
Livin' on stew and drinkin' bad whiskey
Bendin' our backs 'til the railroad is done.

Gordon Lightfoot, "The Canadian Railroad Trilogy"[33]

Four decades ago, in the early 1980s, I spent two years labouring in Western Canada, cooking for men who worked seasonally fixing railroad tracks. The impetus to revisit those days happened when my colleague Bianca Dahl convened a workshop called "The Ethnographic Pact," which was inspired by the literary scholar Philippe Lejeune and his concept of the "autobiographical pact." According to Paul Archambault, Lejeune was concerned primarily with what distinguished autobiographical texts from other personal narratives and "arrived at the notion that only the autobiographical pact can assure the reader of the identity between the I-you-, or he-narrator and the author on the cover" (1998: 240). Ethnography similarly rests on the assumption that the author is a credible witness to the events and customs discussed in the texts they produce.

Both memoir and ethnography are dependent on first-hand accounts, of having been there. Without question my personal history and those of the men about whom I write are enmeshed in the events that follow. I have long accepted Clifford Geertz' (1980) understanding of ethnography as a blurred genre, and in my work the ethnographic and autobiographical are sometimes tightly, if uncomfortably, woven together. But surely the ethnographic pact involves additional obligations concerning the representations anthropologists create about others. The strength and fragility of such an ethnographic pact is the subject of the following chapter, "The Evanescent Freedoms of Life on a CPR Rail Gang."

The events I describe in the chapter fall outside of the sanctioned ethnographic encounters that punctuate my academic career and are drawn from memory. This fact alone disrupts any pretence of being based on rigorous ethnographic fieldwork, although that did follow when I returned to university to complete a master's thesis on the subject several years later. Nevertheless, when fellow anthropologists share memories of their earliest ethnographic encounters – occasions when previously held notions and values get seriously challenged – I return to the early 1980s when I lived in a boxcar that was shunted from siding to siding along the CPR track that criss-crosses Western Canada from the Prairies into the Rocky Mountains. Thus, this essay privileges knowledge that comes from immersing oneself fully in another way of life. At the time, I was cut off from all forms of regular correspondence with family and friends. I wrote letters, but it was a one-way form of correspondence because I lacked a return address. The time of continual connectivity, one which allows my students to correspond with me instantaneously from half-way around the world, had not yet arrived.

The crew with which I worked had a number of men from the East Coast, men fleeing the collapsing cod fishery in Newfoundland, the closing of mines in Cape Breton, and the loss of jobs that attended the increasing mechanization of work in the region's forests. Rural communities in Atlantic Canada had long been dependent on wages from seasonal labour, and the economies of the Maritimes rested almost entirely on extractive industries. As jobs in the Maritimes gradually dried up, many young people left home in search of work elsewhere. Of course, such out-migration from the Atlantic region started long before the 1980s and continues to this day. The iconic film *Goin' Down the Road*[34] captures a moment in the 1960s of that out-migration, when two men from Cape Breton leave home to seek work in prosperous central Canada. The portrayal of the feckless characters Pete and Joey, who find factory work in Toronto, resonates strongly with the antics and cavalier attitude toward work I found on the railway in the 1980s. This chapter offers a glimpse of the out-migration from Atlantic Canada twenty years later, when the centripetal forces shifted to Alberta's oil patch.

However, it was not only labourers picking up stakes and moving out of Atlantic Canada. I joined a steady stream of young university graduates heading west to find employment. Many resettled across the country. Several factors led me to the isolated world I describe in the following chapter, but what I experienced as pure chance and circumstance – the subject of autobiography – fits into that longer history of Atlantic Canadians moving westward, an aspect of ongoing Canadian settler migration. Kate Beaton's graphic memoir *Ducks: Two Years in the Oil Sands* (2022) captures a more recent moment in that long exodus from the Maritimes. Beaton bravely documents the forms of gender violence she encountered. I lacked the courage to do so, but perhaps my silence on such things marks one of the distinctions between the autobiographical and the ethnographic pact. Nevertheless, I wept when I read her account, which was all too familiar. Recently, I have wondered how many of the angry yellow-vest labourers from Western Canada who drove to Ottawa in 2019 belong to this long migration? Is their fear of losing employment in industries that have become environmentally unsustainable steeped in memories of earlier dislocations? The repulsion I feel toward a kind of anger that can veer into racist rants and white-settler pugnacity is tempered by my concern for labourers trying to make a living in what will inevitably become another nowhere place. I read the phenomenon of the yellow-vest movement as a class issue that lies at the heart of the Canadian economy, an economy built upon the plundering of natural resources.[35]

So, what follows in this chapter is an account of what I consider to be my very first ethnographic pact, which I made long before I became a professional anthropologist. Honouring that pact has meant different things at different times, and influenced what I felt I could, or could not, reveal at different moments in my life. For instance, I was careful not to write so frankly of events explored in this chapter when I wrote my MA thesis[36] about work on rail gangs, for fear of putting men I knew at risk of losing their jobs. Although the prospects of anyone in CPR management actually reading an MA thesis in anthropology are slim to non-existent, I had carried out my MA research with their permission and knowledge. That fact alone made me wary. Such consequences are no longer an issue, as all concerned are well past the age for such arduous work. Nevertheless, following ethnographic practice, I have used pseudonyms throughout.

The men I knew typically found work on rail gangs by chance, often after an evening of drinking in a local bar, where they met a group of railway men just passing through. Word that labourers were needed would lead them to pack up their few possessions and make their way to the track. If they were lucky, they joined the gang and soon left town, leaving their problems behind. In many regards, the men I knew resemble those Edmund Bradwin met when he went to work in hinterland labour camps as an instructor for Frontier College prior to the First World War.[37] Indeed, the two gangs I worked on still employed a university student from Frontier College for the summer, but the work they did was less focused on literacy and more geared to meeting what they saw as the psychosocial needs of the men. That shift in focus is noteworthy, and not entirely misguided, although wholly inadequate for addressing the broader realities of seeking work as labourers at the close of the twentieth century. In retrospect, we were all teetering on the precipice of a new neoliberal era, when the organization of work and prospects for employment in the hinterland would be radically altered.

# Chapter One

# The Evanescent Freedoms of Life on a CPR Rail Gang

The Maritimes, where I grew up, were hit hard by the economic recession of the early 1980s, and employment prospects for a young woman with an honours undergraduate degree in social and cultural anthropology were at least as limited then as they are today. Like many undergraduate anthropology students, I discovered anthropology quite by accident, but it immediately captured my imagination and introduced me to possibilities of life beyond my somewhat privileged, if deeply provincial, understanding of the world. It profoundly reshaped the way I looked at things and, what is worse, ruined me for most types of steady employment, which I thought boring or dull. Not that there was a surfeit of secure jobs to be had, but many of my friends had followed more practical career paths when in university. So, after a short stint working in a cooperative natural food store (at that time the coolest and most ethical form of retail I could find), I followed the path taken by many young Maritimers of my generation and headed west to seek good-paying seasonal work that would satisfy my quest for adventure and fund my travels abroad in the winter months. I went with a slightly older hippie friend, who had a few years prior grown bored with living off the land and returned to university, where she completed an honours degree in English literature. We were both proud of acquiring what our parents feared were useless degrees.

We flew from Fredericton, New Brunswick, to Calgary, Alberta, and landed jobs as cooks on a CPR extra-maintenance-of-way railway gang before the week was out, proof to us that there was an employment boom in Western Canada, although many there were complaining of a slump in the oil sector. The roadmaster met us at the railway station in Red Deer and we drove a ways out of town to a dusty siding, alongside track that sliced through a patchwork of vibrant yellow fields planted with rapeseed. We were introduced to the bull cook, Bob, an older (although certainly younger than I am now) recovered street rummy, whose job was to clean the men's bunkrooms and care for the "outfits," the term used by railroaders to refer to their portable home on the track. Bob took us to the three cars at one end of the track that would become our domain: the dining car, the kitchen car, and the car that was partly for food storage and partly our sleeping quarters. Our end of the train was separated from the labourers' bunk cars by a loud generator mounted on a flatbed, which provided a noisy and very effective partition between the male labourers and female cooks. There was a shower in our room, but no toilet. An outhouse was erected beside the track when we were in the middle of nowhere. In small towns, we were advised to use the public washrooms located inside the rail station, which afforded neither privacy nor cleanliness. Having arrived in Red Deer just after lunch, we were told that we should prepare supper for 6:00 pm, as forty men would be returning to the outfits by 5:00 pm. We set to work in a state of apprehension and fluster, hauling things from freezers, taking inventory, scouring and swabbing down everything in sight, because the two previous cooks, who had just recently been "run off," left everything in filthy chaos, and a large extended family of mice had moved in.

I learned later that we only survived those first few weeks on the gang because Bob, the bull cook, alarmed by our innocence, or, as he put it, the fact that we were as green as the grass, took pity and quickly spread a rumour, telling the men that we were young missionaries in training from a Christian Bible school in Red Deer. His little lie bought us precious time, time to learn the rhythm of work – which in midsummer started at 3:30 am – for the cooks had to have breakfast ready for the men early so they could be out on the tracks in the cool of the dawn before the steel rails expanded in the heat. As soon as the men departed, we started lunch, which was picked up by the foreman and delivered to the men at noon. Then we grabbed a one-hour nap, or took a walk, before beginning preparations for supper. After supper, we scrubbed the dining and kitchen cars down in a futile attempt to keep creosote at bay and planned for the following day. We were done by 8:00 pm on a good day, and we worked seven days a week, as most of the men were homeless, or, perhaps I should say, most of the men had made their homes on the gang, at least until the snow would begin to fall and the outfits shut down for the winter months.

I experienced in those early days on the railroad the most profound solitude, for there were no telephones, let alone cellphones and/or Internet connections, and the men kept a very respectful distance. I did have a shortwave radio (which mostly did not work), in which I could also play cassette tapes. Before leaving home, my brother had recorded three albums for me: Joni Mitchell's *Shadows and Light*, a haunting solo recording by the Sicilian guitarist Joe Pass, and a recording of Arthur Rubinstein playing Chopin's Nocturnes. The latter I especially liked to play in the pre-dawn, as I was serving breakfast, and at dusk, as I was serving dinner. It helped to calm my nervousness as I worked under the gaze of forty-some rugged workingmen. Occasionally, some of the men would nod at each other and smile, and then say something like, "it's different, I kind of like it," or "interesting music." This lasted for about a month, maybe longer, until Corinne, my ex-hippie friend, blew our cover.

One evening I saw her pull a young man to the side, and quietly ask him a question. I noted the shock on his face, and then he nodded his head. After he left, I asked Corinne what that was all about? "I asked him where we could get some hash" she said. I had never smoked hashish in my life, although I had once accidently ingested a brownie that gave me supernatural abilities to hear conversations continents apart; but, as I said, Corinne was an ex-hippie. More than that, she was bored, and increasingly found me irritating. Living and working together in such close quarters bred contempt. She told me she hated the sound of the brush through my unruly hair in the early morning. It made her want to scream. So, Corinne was desperate and determined to extend our engagement with the railroaders beyond the kitchen. From that time on, it was open season on the cooks, and negotiating our place on the gangs required considerable skill.

One of the consequences of Corinne's request for so-called recreational drugs – a bit of a misnomer on the gangs, as many of the men used pot to help combat the dangerous boredom of repetitive work – was that we entered a season of exhausting sociality with the gang, dashing off after supper to join the men at one of the local bars, or – I shudder to recall – seedy strip clubs, that had over the years sprung up beside the grain elevators located along the tracks in southern Saskatchewan and Alberta. We would feed coins into the jukebox and dance, or shoot a couple of games of pool, before eventually wandering back to the outfits to catch a few winks before returning to work.

One evening, while sitting in an out-of-the-way Prairie honky-tonk with a group of railroaders, one of the men, Francis from Newfoundland, came swaggering into the joint with a brazen smile on his face, which was framed by a lion's mane of blond curls. I could see several of the men sit up and take note, in anticipation of either a hearty laugh or a knockout brawl: a good time, either way. Troy, a compact, elfin Prairie lad, who had been sitting with his back to the door, turned around to face Francis and burst into laughter. He then complimented Francis, admiring his spanking new leather jacket. "Thanks," said Francis, as he pirouetted to show off his new duds, "just when I thought no one cared, I got this terrific *Christmy* present." The men howled with laughter, banging their fists on the table, and Troy threw his arm around Francis, telling him he was the best and was pleased that he liked his present. Troy then made a place at the table for Francis and ordered another round of draft beer to celebrate.

It turns out Troy had bought the leather jacket for himself about a month before when he was in Calgary, but it had been stolen from his locker shortly thereafter. From that evening on, Francis and Troy were pretty much inseparable, and within a few weeks the roadmaster placed the audacious Francis on Troy's machine as an apprentice and second operator, a promotion accompanied by higher wages, and relief from the gruelling labour of swinging a pickaxe and pounding spikes or tapping plates all day long.

Mind you, theft as a form of flamboyant "gifting" carries with it considerable risk. But then, as anthropologists know, all gifts do. When Lester, Troy's older brother, a prison-hardened bully who could be disarmingly charming, stole a high school ring from Charlie, an annoying self-serving and self-satisfied brute who put a little too much store in that ring, a status symbol that showed he had actually finished high school, the outcome was very different. An unwillingness to graciously accept the terms of *Christmy* present exchanges caused Charlie to have a temper tantrum, and Lester decided to teach him a lesson. That night Charlie hobbled into supper with a black eye and bruised ribs. A less stubborn man would have departed from the gang.

So, on the morning I went to put my Chopin tape in the machine, and found it missing, I feared trouble was brewing. It took weeks before someone finally asked me why I no longer played that "chop'in" music. The kitchen suddenly fell silent, and all the men, who were lined up for supper, tensed as they turned to look at me. I shrugged my shoulders, smiled and said something like "It's gone … I've lost it. I hope it found a good home." There was a collective sigh, followed by laughter, and much talk about somebody's *Christmy* present being played on a ghetto blaster out on the track. That evening the ex-heroin junkie Richard knocked on my boxcar door seeking an invitation in, which I politely refused. The person to whom I had bestowed a "gift" thus revealed himself, and I was careful to respect the honour among thieves while deftly refusing his solicitations.

For a while, my reputation as a goody two-shoes from the right side of the tracks served me well. And in this way, I made my first ethnographic pact, the one that would, for a short time, protect me while I kept dangerous company on a CPR extra-maintenance-of-way railway gang in Western Canada. To this day, I have only to hear the opening chords of Chopin's Nocturne in E Minor and I am transported to that world.

## Making Sense, Anthropologically

How are we to understand the significance of objects stolen, only to be provocatively and publicly flaunted as *gifts* from the victim to the thief at a later date? In what sort of community would such a gesture be understood, let alone tolerated, even celebrated?[1] The *Christmy* present was not a gift within a proper gift economy, in which the moral values of a community encompass demonstrations of wealth that create chains of reciprocity and social obligation involving kin and other social groups in a "total social fact";[2] it was not a pure gift involving some form of sacrifice, in which nothing is expected in return;[3] and it was too personal in nature to be considered a classic instance of negative reciprocity, although the potential to threaten sociality was likewise present.[4] The *Christmy* present does not properly fit with any of these classic forms of gift exchange, yet its significance was tacitly understood by all involved and captured brilliantly the ethos of the gang. *Christmy* presents were used to forge or destroy relationships that were at best fleeting, but were all the more intense for their evanescence. The men were involved in an escalating form of agonistic gift exchange that always had the potential to end badly, to crash and burn, but could also create momen of transcendent *communitas* that belied the otherwise rigid conditions of an all-pervasive workplace.

Many scholars (including, most notably, Beidelman 1989, Gilsenan 1976, Handelman 1998, and Mauss 1990) have highlighted the key features of agonistic gift exchange, in which bravado and cunning, the thrust and counter-thrust of challenge and riposte, might simultaneously threaten or enhance a vulnerable sociality, especially when and where an egalitarian ethos is valued. As Laidlaw notes, "Gifts evoke obligation and create reciprocity, but they can do this because they might not: what creates the obligation is the gesture or moment which alienates the given thing and asks for no reciprocation" (2000: 186). Both the compulsion to accept and the refusal to recognize the stolen item as a genuine gift were present in this game of honour that pulled all members of the gang into its risky orbit. Reputations were at stake.

In his discussion of Homeric values in ancient Greece, Tom Beidelman notes, "Goods taken by force, theft, or trickery, especially if it went unchallenged, won the respect of others" (1989: 231). On the rail gang, the exchange of *Christmy* presents became a highly idio-syncratic, ritual-like experience that Don Handelman (1998) calls a "proto-event," a term he coined to capture those playful, but poten-tially disruptive, forms of sociality that can develop in workplaces, orienting "players to certain forms of performance and experience that played with particular ambiguities safely hidden from view in the usual order of things, but ... acutely felt by the players" (1998: 98). Seemingly created spontaneously, the *Christmy* present's "cachet was restricted to these men, to their relationships, to their predicaments" (ibid.). I returned five years later – with a proper research project in hand – to a different rail gang that had an identical workplace struc-ture and similar social tensions, and discovered that their exchanges indeed played out differently.

In these instances of stolen objects reinterpreted as gifts, it is the qual-ity of the things stolen/given – and not some abstract monetary value – that matters. As Jonathan Parry and Maurice Bloch argue, "The gift of specific objects always retains an element of the person who gave it" (1989: 5). The objects were chosen deliberately; they captured something of the essence of the individual to whom they had belonged, through the sizing and cut, even the smell of the leather jacket, the worn contour and insignia of the ring, the handwritten label on the flimsy cassette. The leather jacket, the graduation ring, and the Chopin recording car-ried the mark of the individual from whom the object had been stolen. As such, the objects were "animated by the personality of the donor" (Taussig 1980: 36–7; cited in Parry and Bloch 1989: 11). While a person whose home has been broken into by thieves may claim to feel person-ally violated by the act, this may, or may not, have been the intention of the thief. A theft of hard cash means one thing, a theft of one's under-wear another, but the intentions of an unknown thief are to a certain extent inscrutable. This is not so when the railroader claims a *Christmy* present: His intentions are made explicit. In a flamboyant, almost cer-emonial, display, an invitation to establish or destroy a form of personal relationship was proffered in a workplace otherwise strictly governed by the company rulebook and labour agreements negotiated with the Brotherhood of Maintenance of Way Railway Employees. Not only did the *Christmy* present acknowledge the risk inherent in such personal relationships, it also points to the fragility of labour processes that could chew you up and spit you out in a flash. These highly personal chal-lenges and reactions only make sense if you consider a particular ethos of the gang, one in which the rugged equality between men who lived on the very margins of society was deeply valued, despite a working environment that denied them their freedom.

**Working on the Railroad,** *all the live long day ...*

For all intents and purposes, to work on a rail gang is to be under the thumb of the company day in and day out, since one both works and resides on company property, property that is closely regulated by both the industry and federal law. The company tells you where to sleep and what to eat, deducting the costs from your wages. The company determines when you rise in the morning and what sort of work you will do, and it sets rigid rules for behaviour. Failure to abide by the rules can lead to, at the roadmaster's pleasure, immediate dismissal. A roadmaster's penchant to turn a blind eye to all manner of infractions, such as drug dealing, drinking or toking, or bringing women back to the outfits, is no protection against dismissal should he suddenly find you an unreliable worker. Such discretionary power can lead the roadmaster to exert absolute control over the men and their work. And yet, those of us who worked on the gangs often felt we were leading a wildly free existence. The agonistic *Christmy* gift exchange found on this rail gang, I would argue, illuminates and addresses this key contradiction in much the same way as agonistic gift exchange addressed "tensions between egalitarianism and ranking (domination)" in Homeric Greece (Beidelman 1989: 229).

In theory, work assignments are strictly controlled by seniority and time spent moving through the ranks, a system which extends across a network of extra-maintenance-of-way gangs in particular geographic regions. When a worker first arrives at the "outfits" he is issued three pocket-sized books which outline the responsibilities and codes that govern railroad procedures: 1) *CP Rail: Maintenance of Way Rules and Instructions*; 2) *Uniform Code of Operating Rules*; and 3) *Wage Agreement No's 41 and 42 between Canadian Pacific Limited and the Brotherhood of Maintenance of Way Employees*. But on the track, this system of codes bends and shifts according to the judgment of the roadmaster and the ability of individual railroaders to gain experience on the machines. The workers under the supervision of a single foreman can cover long distances, but foremen tend to hover over the track labourers doing the most physical labour, like swinging hammers to tap plates or shovelling ballast. These men have the least seniority and, in order to move through the ranks, they must find a way to gain experience on the machines, so that when an opening presents itself the foreman will recommend one of them for promotion. Jockeying for a better position involves backbreaking work and a certain amount of chutzpah, since jumping on a machine to figure out how it works means you have abandoned your assigned post, something best done when the foreman is distracted elsewhere. Cunning and gumption go hand in hand on the gangs, and an action that might be grounds for reproach in one instance is rewarded as initiative in another.

However, it would be wrong to conclude that the theft of the leather jacket was an opportunistic ploy on Francis' part to gain a new position as an apprentice machinist. Such a ploy would have failed abysmally had he not already proven his mechanical abilities and willingness to help and take instruction from Troy. Both men shared a work ethic that involved getting the job done, despite stupid rules that might get in the way. As the men used to say to me, "There is a right way, a wrong way, and a railway." Indeed, in its ironic playfulness, the *Christmy* present episode re-established Francis and Troy as equals on the gang, despite a rigid seniority system that placed Francis in a position beneath Troy. Both men were supremely confident and recognized in each other a form of manliness that framed attachments to things and positions as acquisitiveness and pettiness, qualities that could get in the way of getting the job done, and could also get in the way of having a good time. Together, Francis and Troy confounded the rules by asserting another set of values in which doing physical work under harsh conditions mirrored a spirit of independence, toughness, and machismo. They were like the gandy dancers[5] in Allan Donaldson's short story *Paradise Siding*, who "could eat steel washers for cornflakes ... and dance ... through hell in an overcoat" (1984: 106).

But when Lester stole Charlie's high school ring an entirely different sort of game was at play, although equally attuned to workplace structures and tensions. As the hot summer came to an end that first year I spent on the track, and the morning air grew chilly, some maintenance-of-way gangs in the region were scheduled to shut down earlier than others. We began to hear rumours about men from other gangs threatening to "bump." That is, a qualified railroader with more seniority on any machine in the region could bump a person on another gang off his machine, and then that person could attempt to bump another. This system of bumping across gangs threatened the social solidarity of gang membership in a very real sense, and often led to a demotion for the person who was bumped.

Shortly before I arrived on the gangs, Charlie-with-the-high-school-ring had bumped his way on to our gang, and, I was told, one of the more popular men had been forced to take a position elsewhere. Charlie's manoeuvring across the gangs was resented, and was especially anathema to Lester, who had recently returned to the gangs after serving time in prison. I got the impression that Lester and his bumped buddy had once held considerable sway over the gang, but while Lester was in prison the lay of the land had shifted. Was he jealous of the popularity his younger brother Troy now enjoyed? Was the revulsion Lester felt for Charlie rooted in his recognition of someone who, like himself, would stop at nothing to get ahead? All I know for sure is that when Lester stole Charlie's ring and called it a *Christmy* present, it was a direct challenge to all, intended to reassert and solidify his reputation.

There is a qualitative difference between the respect of others won by Francis and Troy, and the type demanded by Lester and Charlie. Entangled in these instances of stealing and gifting are meditations on values and judgment that speak to character and reputation. As F.G. Bailey notes, "To have a reputation allows one to be a member of the community, even if the reputation is bad" (1971: 7). Furthermore, "it is not that some exchanges are co-operative and others are competitive: *all* exchanges have the seeds of both these opposed things within them" (ibid.: 24). If I found the antics of Francis and Troy downright seductive, the sort of power Lester wielded on the gangs frightened me. Whereas the theft/gift of the leather jacket seemed to me to challenge the very competitive forms of acquisition and getting ahead from which I felt I had so recently escaped, the theft of the high school ring seemed mean-spirited and nasty. The spirit of the gift[6] found in the first iteration of the *Christmy* present was later poisoned[7] by Lester, who enjoyed power over others.

Lester had tons of seniority and was pretty much untouchable as one of the few men in the region with the expertise to run the complicated Torsion Beam, which required mathematical and computer skills few managed to acquire on the gangs.[8] Indeed, he worked the most sophisticated machine on the track and spent the winters in the central machine shop as a mechanic, a coveted position, as it afforded full-time, rather than seasonal employment, which even the roadmaster did not enjoy. That he was even able to rejoin the gang after serving his prison sentence speaks volumes about his seniority and exceptional abilities as a machinist.[9] The other men respected his skills, but they also knew he was a bully, to be ignored at one's peril; a lesson I would later learn the hard way, when Lester organized a protest to assert power over the cooks. We were not required to provide lunches over long weekends, but Lester convinced the men that they should show up and demand lunches be provided. He did so on a day I was alone in the kitchen, prepping for dinner. But that first season on the gang I was still protected by the chains of reciprocity that began with a *Christmy* present. As such, I descended ever more fully into bouts of debauchery and anarchy in which chaos tempted the fates. We called it freedom.

## Evanescent Freedoms

All railroad men, no matter how much they grumble in the heat of the day, want a season of work to last as long as possible. Shockingly to me, many approached shutdown in late November without having saved a penny, despite the fact they made relatively good wages, certainly better than the cooks, who worked for a catering company under contract. (Still, I was able to save enough money to forgo collecting what was then called unemployment insurance so that I could backpack through Europe in the winter months with Corinne.) On paydays, the foreman would collect our signed cheques and drive to the nearest town to cash them, as banks were unwilling to serve transient workers who lacked a proper home address. Indeed, being turned away from a bank produced one of those early moments when my fall from the middle class was made crystal clear. Consequently, we – cooks and railroaders – stashed unseemly amounts of hard cash into our wallets and pockets.[10] Only a very few married men (four, in total: the roadmaster, the foreman, and two machinists) thought to put any money aside. They held on to their paycheques until they could visit their wives, good women[11] who looked after banking and expenses and gave their husbands an allowance.[12] These were the only men who had a clue about where they would spend the off-season winter months.

I could never quite figure out where all the money went, though in the evenings, and on those rare weekends off, orgies of consumption were the order of the day. Pints of beer would accumulate in front of me at the local tavern as the men bought round after round to be shared by all. I would wait until they were too drunk to notice and then surreptitiously slide glasses across the table to others, for they refused to take "no thanks" as an answer. Their generosity knew no bounds, and they often urged me to keep up, which I knew would be foolish on many levels. On the very occasional long weekend off, the men could blow an entire paycheque at the bar, up their nose in a seedy hotel room, or on the lot of a used car dealership, anything that would provide an immediate escape from the monotony of work and life on the track.

Sophie Day et al. (1999) note a particular orientation toward the present in far-flung communities that include hunters and gatherers, peasants, day workers and prostitutes, for whom this easy-come-easy-go attitude toward cash would make perfect sense. They argue that such people fail to adopt "mainstream notions of work, productivity, and long-term economic planning" in favour of an "'anti-economic' stance ... part and parcel of a specific set of attitudes towards time, person, and community" (ibid.: 1). The authors go on to suggest such attitudes reflect an innate faith in the "idea of plenty." However, the men I knew were too well acquainted with periods of want to harbour such deluded optimism.[13] Want and a lack of opportunities elsewhere, or a need to get out of town fast, had landed them on the track in the first place. If they had faith in anything, it was in the strength of their bodies to bend to the task at hand. The arrogance of youth is not particularly class-specific. But such forces did create a disconcerting impression of having escaped through a wormhole to a life on the gangs, where an orientation to time, person, and community was strangely altered.

Wolfgang Schivelbusch (1986) writes of the time-space compression created by railroads in the nineteenth century that turned the space between destinations into dead space.[14] It is into that dead time and space that gang members escape and thrive, finding a particular form of freedom, where "freedom's just another word for nothing left to lose."[15] But more than that too: When the protagonist of *Paradise Siding* recalls spending a season of work on a maintenance-of-way gang in his youth, he tells us "Paradise Siding was the beginning and the end of the god dammed world" (Donaldson 1984: 103). The men on extra gangs live in the in-between zones, lost on sidings in the middle of nowhere – that is, a *nowhere* created by the railroad in the first place. On the other hand, time spent in an actual destination, especially an iconic tourist destination like Chateau Lake Louise, a resort built by the CPR at the turn of the twentieth century to attract the wealthy to visit what would become Banff National Park, could be especially dangerous for gang members, those interlopers from the dead zone.

After months of sweltering over propane stoves during the dog days of a Prairie summer, I was delighted to learn that we would soon head into the Rockies to work the stretch of track running between Lake Louise and the Kicking Horse Pass. All of us happily anticipated relief from the Prairie sun. The machines were loaded onto flatbeds, and the outfits hooked up to the train that would slowly move us to the region. I recall opening the door of our sleeping car and sitting half-in and half-out like a hobo, breathing in the mountain air, as we were somewhat violently dragged by a large freight train with multiple engines into the mountains. It was exhilarating; even if we did arrive to find the kitchen, which we had carefully packed and tied down, reduced to shambles. For a while that summer our outfits straddled the Great Divide in the Rockies.

It must have been Labour Day weekend, one of those unusual times when the men were given three days off in a row, although not the cooks, who worked every day (but we only had to prepare two meals, breakfast and supper, and breakfast was later than usual, so it seemed like a holiday). Lake Louise was the nearest destination and watering hole to the siding we were working from, and Corinne and I were excited to join a carload of men heading to the resort for a night out on the town. We arrived early enough to do a bit of sightseeing because I was eager to feast my eyes upon the turquoise water of the glacial lake pictured on the covers of my Grade 5 Canadian history and geography textbook. The image had left a lasting impression. The men indulged me, and then we went looking for a friendly place to drink and hang out. That was much more difficult, for the average joint was crawling with tourists – local and international – sporting mammoth cameras and that look of insouciance only the wealthy can pull off. Nothing appealed. Finally, a doorman suggested a dance pub on the premises of the Chateau Lake Louise hotel frequented by ski bums and college students who worked at the resort. Corinne and I thought that sounded terrific. We were wrong.

We managed to commandeer a couple of large round tables, and the men began to survey the room as they ordered rounds of drinks. Okay, we probably stood out, but I felt at home, which is why I failed to notice the extreme discomfort some of the men were experiencing, even though Shane, one of the railroaders, had tried to warn me. A sweet, gentle, Prairie farm boy with the bluest of eyes, Shane kept smiling shyly and telling me his trigger finger was getting really, really itchy. I had no idea what he was talking about, just giggled repeatedly, and encouraged him to relax, to dance. Not a chance: None of the men were dancing, which was odd because they could sweep Prairie honkytonk girls off their feet.

As the place got busier and busier, the men got drunker and drunker, and the dance floor was pulsing to "Echo Beach."[16] Corinne and I were manically dancing away with the resort workers, when suddenly Ed, an always kind and caring person, grabbed our elbows and began to shepherd us away, whispering in our ear, "We need to leave now." He had already collected our purses and other paraphernalia, and when we got to the door, he said: "Run." I was vaguely aware of railroaders spilling out of the pub like ants from a disturbed anthill. We jumped into the front of Ed's truck and took off, picking up stragglers along the way, who hurled themselves onto the flatbed as we slowed down for them. The ability of railroaders to jump a truck or train on the fly always impressed me: their strength and athleticism were beautiful to behold.

Ed explained that shy Shane, convinced people were giving him dirty looks, had smashed his fist through a window in an explosive bout of anger. We spent the next hour or so driving around the mountains carefully avoiding passing Mounties, who were speedily making their way to Chateau Lake Louise, until we found, somewhere on that mountain, a phone booth. Ed spent some time on the phone with the local RCMP detachment until it was determined that our missing men were being held in the bowels of Chateau Lake Louise, where the RCMP kept temporary holding cells, as needed. We drove back to Lake Louise and held congress in the parking lot. It was determined by consensus that I should go in and find out what was happening, because I was the only company present who did not have "priors," that is, I did not possess a criminal record. News to me.

Never underestimate the tug of reciprocity. Nothing else can possibly explain why I felt compelled to enter the Chateau Lake Louise in search of brawling railroaders. Just inside the imposing doors of the Chateau I found the night clerk, who fixed me with a withering look and led me into the deepest chambers of the basement. He refused to dignify my presence with a single word. A momentary look of surprise crossed the hangdog faces of the six railroaders sitting there, like a group of delinquent schoolboys lined up outside the principal's office. How the mighty had fallen. I trailed behind the clerk, who alerted two RCMP officers, sitting in a glass-enclosed cubicle, of my presence. They beckoned me to enter and the clerk left, shaking his head.

An officer asked, "How do you know these men?"

I replied something like, "I'm a cook on a CPR extra-maintenance-of way gang, where the men work. We are parked just outside of town. The men will lose their jobs if they don't return to the outfits immediately. We will be moving down the track in a day or so."

Tap, tap, tap of the officer's pencil: Then belligerent grins began to spread across the faces of the Mounties. "How did you come to be working on this gang?"

Shrug of shoulders. "And you are willing to vouch for these men?"

"Yes, I am."

"Can you promise they will never set foot in this town again?"

"Um, yes, I will."

"Well, I never ..." they said, as they shook their heads in ... what? Dismay? Bewilderment? Relief? Amusement? Yes, probably amusement. Their smiles suddenly seemed genuine.

I smiled back.

"Okay, but you will have to sign these forms, and we will hold you personally responsible for these men."

"Yes, okay."

The Mounties told the men they could go; they also told them I would get into a lot of trouble if they ever showed their faces again in Lake Louise, or in any other town in the national park. We left in subdued silence, walked to the truck, and crawled onto the flatbed, where we lay on our backs in relief and looked at the stars. When Ed's foot hit the metal, we began to laugh so hard we were gasping for air. We had escaped yet again, back to the dead zone. Freedom never felt better.

## Reaching the End of the Line

Forms of reciprocity and gift exchange, especially in its most agonistic forms, require constant tending. When Corinne and I returned from our winter travels to begin our second season on the track, we found that the men who had previously been so central to our social lives had found other women, in the communities where they had wintered, to charm with their ongoing rounds of competitive jousting. I came to realize *Christmy* presents primarily solidified homo-social relationships on the gangs, and only an incredibly naïve young woman would think she could enter the fray on equal footing.[17] Lesson learned. Eventually, the manic sociality that followed the theft of my cassette of Chopin gave way to nothing but the unending tedium of the work day. Periods of solitude I had once enjoyed began to weigh heavily on me, and unbearable loneliness entered my being.

During the second season, I paid more attention to the lives of men who had worked the gangs for some time, and I could see that the days also weighed heavily on them. They tended to withdraw into themselves and appeared trapped, angry, or depressed. Years of substance abuse ravaged others. A few men in their mid-thirties, looking much older, were dismissed when they failed to make the early morning shift. Jobs in the dead zone tend to lead nowhere. I have often tried to imagine where the men I knew ended up later in life. I imagine a few found good women to shelter them while they sought new forms of employment, but the more decrepit and vulnerable among them must surely have suffered.

As with other women who develop "lonely natures" as a consequence of having experienced periods of extreme social isolation in nowhere places, the lessons learned can be powerful. All of the things I learned about life on railroad gangs were merely confirmed when I returned to another gang as a graduate student with a bona fide research project, and while the interviews and careful documentation of age, education, family and work history provided proof of some sort, the earlier participation in the daily grind and rabble-rousing revelry, occasional mayhem, and all manner of events that ritually bound us together as a collective belonged to the pre-research years. I still believe that is when I did my best ethnographic work, by which I mean I let the railroaders set the agenda, my hands were off the wheel, and I was most definitely not in control. To be frank, the men on the gang betrayed the pact they had sealed with a *Christmy* present of Chopin tunes long before I left the gangs, but I have remained steadfast, which is how I know that the pact I made with the men was an "ethnographic pact." Betrayed or not, the gang members taught me about vulnerability, reckless abandon, the fleeting nature of our privileges and relationships, and the precarity of our lives. And that is a gift beyond compare.

*So, a journey to northern New Brunswick with Babette ...*

In the following chapter, "The Family Gothic," I jump to the ethnographic beginnings of my doctoral research in Eastern Canada, which I began about a decade after my sojourn on the railway gangs in Western Canada. Originally, the thread that connected my interest in the two regions was railroads and railroaders, especially maintenance-of-way workers. So, I did a bit of preliminary fieldwork in Campbellton, New Brunswick, early in my doctoral program, which had once been the location of an important maintenance yard for the Canadian National Railway. However, deregulation of the railway industry in the 1970s led to the steady abandonment of unprofitable railway routes in Eastern Canada and elsewhere throughout the 1980s. By the time I arrived there in the early 1990s the maintenance yard was a mere shell of its former heyday, as deindustrialization continued apace in the region. Most of the men who had once worked in the yard had moved on to look for work elsewhere, or retired, and a research project about railroaders in Atlantic Canada was one better suited to a historian than an anthropologist.

But more than that, I came to realize the thread that loosely tied my research interests together was not really railroads, after all. Rather, I was intrigued by ways of *being* – however they may manifest – of people who live, and try to make a living, in places in the middle of nowhere. People negotiating the unpredictableness of circumstances largely beyond their control also drew my attention. The elaborate game of theft reinterpreted as a gift that could create or dissolve social relations among men living in an isolated work camp disturbed my thoughts for decades. Mulling over the tension between the rigidity of that workplace and the utter audacity of workers responding to each other and to the world they inhabited points to the "ethical entailments" that are present in all social action (Lambek 2015: x), as complex social relationships, imagination, and judgment are continually at play. The very ordinariness of the ethical (Das 2007; Lambek 2010; Mattingly 2010, 2012) is a thread that runs through the chapters of this book. Historical residues and resonances shape but do not limit character and judgment. The possibility of acting otherwise is always present.

So, I switched my attention to the small settlements skirting the edges of New Brunswick's vast Crown lands and timber reserves and I did so largely because of a friendship I had formed with a highly unpredictable and fascinating woman whom I had met some years earlier while working in the port city of Saint John. Through the woman I call Babette, I came to understand the history and some of the hard realities of life in New Brunswick in unfamiliar ways. In "The Family Gothic," my attention turns to narrative, to ways of telling stories. Babette's is the first of three life stories that act as touchstones for the three historical periods discussed in the following chapters. The life stories of Babette, her mother Rita, and her grandmother Ernestine trace the crippling effects of poverty and neglect over three generations, while bearing witness to the social and cultural changes that contribute, over time, to what I call "gothic sensibility" and "rancour," as structures of feeling in the present.[18]

In the following chapter, every aperture in the landscape opens onto the uncanny, enmeshing its inhabitants in a history that fixes one in place. The attachments to *home* are as deep as they are troubled, and Babette's "going up home" triggers a surge of disturbing memories, including those which psychoanalysts call "repressed memories." At the core of Babette's recovered memory is abuse, and in the early 1990s the idea of recovering and exploring memories of abuse, often in a therapeutic context, had reached a fever pitch in North America. When I began this work, important contributions to the anthropology of memory were considering this phenomenon from a social and cultural perspective, and I was deeply influenced by this literature.[19] It opened avenues for broader historical, cultural, and psychological ways of making sense of troubled times. Over time, this way of reading the social would sorely test my friendship with Babette, and eventually she would sever our relationship. I will say right from the outset that the bond I forged with Babette continues to haunt me and this entire project.

# Chapter Two

# The Family Gothic

The "double" has become a thing of terror, just as, after the collapse of their religion, the gods turned into demons.

Sigmund Freud, "The Uncanny"

Months before I returned to the Maritimes in 1992 to begin my doctoral research, I re-established contact with my friend Babette. She was excited when I told her I was thinking of doing ethnographic fieldwork in the place where she had grown up. She was already living in Halifax, Nova Scotia, by then, but I asked if she would be willing to travel to northern New Brunswick to introduce me to some people and to help me learn the lay of the land. I knew she was not working at that time and offered to pay her fare. She readily accepted and laughed that she would become my "Deep Throat" informant. She caught a bus and met me at my parents' home in the southern part of the province. From there we drove north, as she regaled me with stories of people from her community who, over the years, set the woods on fire to create employment for fire crews. As firefighters, they were known to sometimes cut the water hoses to prolong the work of putting the fires out in order to collect enough "stamps"[1] for employment benefits. I had heard these stories before. Indeed, it was because of such stories I was heading north to study the "weapons of the weak." Others had attributed nascent political intentions to such activities, something of which I was sceptical.[2]

Just a year before, Babette's community had become the focus of a documentary, which she had recorded and mailed to me the previous winter.[3] According to the documentary, the incidence of arson had reached new heights in recent years, as people had gone from burning down forests to burning down their own homes to make insurance claims. Consequently, insurance companies would no longer sell policies to people in the settlement, which was very upsetting to the local parish priest, who, in the past, had worked hard to help local impoverished people secure mortgages, and then taught them how to build new homes. Throughout the region, he was fondly referred to as the carpenter priest.

Such initiatives had transformed the rural landscape of my own childhood in the 1960s, as stretches of the tarpapered shacks that hugged rural roads and railway lines throughout New Brunswick were replaced with houses with foundations, aluminum siding, proper windows, and indoor plumbing, although often without steps to the front door, so that the new home would be considered still under construction and thus be assessed lower property taxes. Whether that strategy actually worked or not, I can't say, but it was a common enough sight on many rural roads. I can recall the excitement of visiting my own relatives who had just recently equipped their far more substantial century farm homes with indoor plumbing. Previously, their comfortable homes had been fitted with indoor hand-pumps; I loved to work these pumps so that I could drink from the dipper, which always hung by the sink. In the winter, when my family would return from visits to my grandparents' farm at dusk, we would shorten the trip by cutting through the Killarney Road, which lies on the northern outskirts of Fredericton, the provincial capital. Passing by some hunched old man lugging buckets of water from the roadside spring to his home, my parents would remark sympathetically. Over the course of a decade, that stretch of road was visibly transformed. Even the bumps and kinks in the road disappeared, as if someone had lifted the corner of a carpet and given it a good shake. Such progress throughout the 1960s was a wondrous thing to behold.[4] Setting out along this same stretch of road some thirty years later with Babette, I found it hard to reconcile my childhood memories with the tedium of strip malls and suburban development that was altering the landscape yet again. It was no longer the desperately impoverished Killarney Road of my early childhood memories.

The trip from Fredericton to the north shore of New Brunswick takes a good four to five hours. Babette and I passed through the dense woods and small villages in the interior until we caught the pungent odours emanating from the town, which is situated near the mouth of the Miramichi River. As I have already noted, I was taught that sulphur had the "smell of money," so central was the forest economy and its pulp and paper mills to the prosperity of New Brunswick. From there we joined the main highway that skirts the windswept coast of the North Shore. The entire North Shore lies between the estuaries of the

Miramichi River to the south and the Restigouche River, which separates New Brunswick from Quebec's Gaspésie, to the north. Situated at the mouths of both rivers lie pulp and paper mills, the small cities and towns that are the administrative and service centres for the region, and Mi'kmaq First Nations communities. Most of the people who live in the region are descended from the Mi'kmaq, the English and Scottish merchants of the seventeenth and eighteenth centuries, the Acadians who fled to the region during and after the great deportation in the eighteenth century, and the Irish refugees who settled there in the nineteenth century to work in the timber trade.[5] The powerful and the "filthy rich" have also travelled to these rivers, to escape the clamour of the worlds they govern and cast their rods for the Atlantic salmon that swim in the still pools that lie upriver, well beyond the rotten-egg stench of the mills.[6]

As a small child, I would sometimes travel "over north" with my father, who worked as a surveyor for what was then called the Department of Lands and Mines. My younger sister and I would sit in the back seat of his red Pontiac and watch as the landscape changed from the rolling hills of the forested interior to the scrubby and denuded coastal lands. The small Protestant and Roman Catholic churches found in the little villages of the interior forests were replaced by grander Roman Catholic churches in the coastal towns and villages. As we went north, people's homes seemed to shrink, and we noted small differences in decorative details, such as a slightly different way of shaping a porch railing, or flamboyantly painted exteriors.[7] In these seemingly insignificant details we detected a difference, as we passed from the predominantly English-speaking and Protestant south into the mostly French-speaking and Roman Catholic north.

My father seemed to know every back road in the province, and we would be told to roll up our windows as he headed down a dirt road until he found the small rural home he was seeking. My sister and I remained quietly in the backseat while my dad went out to greet the large dog that would inevitably announce our arrival. Then he would turn and open the trunk, producing the survey maps and deeds for the property and surrounding lands. Eventually, a woodsman would walk down the lane to meet us, while his wife and small children gathered in the doorway or sat on the steps to watch. Although my father spoke no French, language never seemed to be a barrier and soon looks of suspicion evaporated.[8] My father was a natural fieldworker, something I would only come to appreciate much later, as I found approaching isolated homes in the backwoods daunting, the yapping mongrel the least of my concerns.

I mention all of this because it marked an initial awareness of otherness, experienced from the backseat of my father's car. I suspect that the children, who sat on those doorsteps silently returning our gaze, were coming to the their own awareness of otherness, in their case inflected by a sense of wariness concerning interlopers who carried maps. Was our presence cause for resentment? Did they wonder why my father was there? Why was my father there? Our curiosity was piqued, but so too was our sense of our own identity, our social position, our prospects, and our uncomfortable sense that others were able to place us in a larger order of things, of which we had little or no control. In this most innocent of encounters, as children cast sideways glances at each other, our sense of who we were took shape. And when I met Babette, so many years later, I had this uncanny sense of having met her before, as a small, pasty-faced child in tattered clothing, on the back step of a weathered house that looked too small for the brood of children living there. From the very beginning, Babette and I seemed to recognize each other.

What is one to make of such recognition, in which an understanding of sameness and difference is so deeply entrenched? What is involved in an ethnographic project that explores the vaguely familiar and the deeply provincial? Researchers and subjects negotiate what they think they already know about each other. And then researchers must also contend with their own pasts, which are both entwined with and separate from those of the people they come to know in the field. Often the things people told me about their lives and pasts seemed so familiar I thought their disclosures unnoteworthy. The details of their lives clicked easily into a preconceived and commonsensical place. Yet there were times when I felt stunned by what I heard, unable to make sense of it in terms of a history I assumed we held in common. For instance, I once had a long leisurely chat with a man my age and we found ourselves recollecting our first day at school, which we had both found frightening. We recalled sitting silently in our respective classrooms, too shy to speak to other children or to respond to our teachers' questions. This exchange was not the least bit odd to me as we both grew up in an era when few children went to daycare and the first day at school at the age of five or six represented the first time most children in New Brunswick were no longer in the care of their stay-at-home mothers. I imagined us, one in the south, the other in the north of the province, sitting in our classrooms doing and feeling pretty much the same things in September of 1963. But then he told me something that I initially found incomprehensible. One day, after his mother packed his lunch and sent him on his way to school, he ran off and hid in the woods. The nuns[9] who ran the school sent for his mother and she went and found him and dragged him back to school. The following day, and the day after that, the same thing happened. Finally, his mother got fed up and told him he didn't have to go to school anymore. This gentle, shy man, with whom I had just moments ago felt so connected as a fellow child of the 1960s, had received absolutely no schooling.

While I was used to speaking to the elderly in the community who had very low levels of education, or those my own age and younger who dropped out of school early, typically at the age of sixteen, this story unsettled me, for it did not fit in with my preconceived understanding of social history and family attitudes in the 1960s, a time when the importance of children's education was widely acknowledged.[10] When I later asked his mother about this, she explained that he lacked the will to go to school and she did not have the time or energy to chase him down. That a parent might concede to a child's will on such a point had never occurred to me. I'm told I was a rather wilful child myself, but I believed truancy officers would track down children who refused to go to school. Parental authority and the letter of the law went hand in hand in my neck of the woods. All the children I knew were told if they got into trouble at school, they could expect worse when they got home. I wondered how this man and his parents had escaped the letter of the law, for apparently the truancy officers never appeared and the monthly "baby bonus" continued to arrive.[11]

This represents just one of the many moments when I was forced to reconsider a social and political history I thought I knew by virtue of having lived it. It rather aptly points to the limitations of taking one's own lived experience as an unmitigated source of knowledge. The niggling doubts that emerge at such times can be humbling, but also instructive. Indeed, it is a common narrative strategy in ethnographic writing to begin with an event in which one's preconceptions unravel. Whether the anthropologist fully understands the significance of that jarring moment while in the field, or later while writing, is never made entirely clear. But here I want to draw attention to the very peculiar way in which this exchange involving memories of going to school unsettled me. In this instance, my initial incomprehension did not give way to a novel way of thinking about the world, but instead gave me nightmares in which I was again travelling along the dirt roads of my early childhood. It returned me to a world I once knew but had forgotten.

My nightmares often ended in a place I know very well. I would be swimming under the "Bridge to Nowhere," fearful of lamprey eels lurking at the bottom of the deeper pools of the Tay River. As a child, I was told to play near the banks of the river, where little minnows gathered.

But in this dream, I had floated out into the middle of the river. I awoke from my nightmare in a sweat, recalling an oppressively hot and humid day when my father came home early from work to drive my family out to the "Tomb Place" to cool off in the river. We were astonished to find a young family living in the derelict farmhouse that still stood there. A man my father had hired from "over north" to work on his wood-lot had brought his family "down south" to live with him. His very young, pregnant wife stood in the doorway with two toddlers hanging onto her skirts. They were relieved when my father allowed them to stay, although I could not imagine how they would ever manage, as the house had been vandalized and stripped of its wood stove and all amenities. Halloween pranksters had smashed the windows long ago.

The covered "Bridge to Nowhere" crossed the river by the Toon Place, an abandoned farm that my father and uncle owned. It was named after immigrants from England who had tried to turn woodland into farmland in the Depression and war years, only to abandon it when the dreams of making a living off the land died. My younger sister and I were adults before we realized our relatives were saying "Toon," and not "Tomb," when referring to the place. "Tomb" captured a childhood imaginary, which returned and seeped into my nightmare. The covered bridge had been built in an optimistic era of settlement, but the road on the other side of the bridge that was to connect the settlement to other places never materialized. The bridge was washed out in the floods of 1973, erasing the memory of hopes long gone. I had not thought of such things in years, but vexing memories began to emerge during field-work, as I began to see links between my past and the past of those whose stories I was collecting. Thus, stories I found initially shocking became uncannily familiar.[12] I was reminded of things I once knew, as a child knows without fully understanding. Perhaps I had simply repressed the knowledge of those other children living nearby in utterly dire circumstances. If so, it had more to do with the passage of time and ideology than personal trauma. That fact alone makes my revisiting of the past different from Babette's, as she was deeply traumatized in her youth by poverty and neglect. Still, the "Bridge to Nowhere," the dusty roads to settlements that long ago abandoned farming, the ragtag children and their careworn parents, also haunt my memories.

My goal in this chapter is to explore the uncanny for its historical and cultural resonances.[13] As Steedman notes, in Freud's essay on the uncanny, "the strange and the inexplicable, the most unhomely and weird of things or places, will turn out in the end to be not strange at all, but that which is familiar and well known, though subjected to suppression, usually in early childhood" (1995: 149). According to Steedman, this entire interpretive strategy, or method of disclosure, developed when "a new kind of time came into being at the end of the nineteenth century, which was born both of recastings and rewritings of the historical past, and also of a long development, of an interior space or place within human beings, expressed most clearly in the shape of the child" (1995: 158). In the 1990s in New Brunswick, and in other parts of Canada, this way of interpreting the past took a decidedly literal turn, as people's recovered memories and accusations of abuse began to run rampant in the press and in the popular imagination. As others were quick to note, people's troubled histories and relationships resurfaced within a new register, in which the "return of the repressed" spawned accusations of past abuse. In what follows, I explore the ways in which recovered memories came to dominate Babette's probing of the past.

## Babette's Return to the Settlement

On the final leg of our journey, Babette's stories strayed from familiar terrain to new subjects, and her voice adopted a faraway and oddly detached timbre. She spoke of disturbing and brutal things, unimaginable horrors. She told me that as a child, her father had watched his mother die in childbirth, on a bitter winter's day in a cabin deep in the woods. A neighbour eventually trudged through the snow-clogged path to find the small children huddled together for warmth, the fire having long gone cold. Babette's kin also claimed two travelling salesmen had long ago ventured into the settlement and were brutally murdered.[14] They are apparently buried in the woods to this day, long forgotten. Babette's first boyfriend, who lived across the road, murdered his grandmother with an axe. The friendless boy wrote her love letters from prison. Babette grew more and more agitated as we finally left the highway to travel inland ten kilometres to the small community she still calls home. I grew more apprehensive, although I was fully aware of Babette's penchant for melodrama and was inclined to consider her portrayal of life in the settlement somewhat warped.

Babette was taking me to meet her grandmother, Ernestine, with whom we intended to stay for the weekend. She was confident that her grandmother would be only too happy to take me in as a paying boarder, but when we arrived at her small and spotless house it was obvious to me that this was more Babette's idea than her grandmother's. The first floor of her small A-frame had a comfortable kitchen with a wood stove to heat the house and a small living room with a television set. Off the kitchen was a bathroom that had been added on in the late 1960s when Ernestine found work with a subcontractor assembling telephones for the US Department of Defense. At that time, a bus would collect poor women from the surrounding area and take them to a makeshift factory. It was her only experience as a wage labourer and she used the money earned to install a bathroom and buy a washing machine, much to her husband's dismay. Babette led me upstairs to show me two small bedrooms separated by a curtain, and you had to pass through the first to get to the second. Although I often visited Ernestine over the next few years, I never again went beyond the kitchen, which I always entered through the back shed. Historically, front doors were rarely used in country homes in the Maritimes, unless a coffin was being carried out.

It was evident to me that living with Ernestine in her tiny home would have greatly compromised her privacy, let alone my own, but I could also quickly see this was a moot point. Babette had failed to mention that her grandmother had a boyfriend. Jimmy, a bulky slow-witted man in his fifties, had been living there for some time, although Ernestine, who was in her eighties, periodically threw him out when he stole from her pension to go on a bender. Babette had this bright idea that her grandmother would throw Jimmy out for good if offered a viable alternative of a paying boarder. It was obvious to me she had no intention of doing any such thing and I was appalled to think Babette could be so presumptuous. Jimmy was agreeable enough when sober and he chopped Ernestine's wood and carried it into the house for her, which she could no longer do for herself. He was company of sorts, sitting at the kitchen table for hours on end with a deck of cards, watching the road for signs of activity. Yet Babette's every move during our visit conveyed her annoyance with his very presence. It didn't take us long to wear out our welcome and I realized we would have to find another place to spend the night.

Babette then suggested we go to meet the local parish priest, so we drove down the road, the only road in this settlement, to the manse. When Father Henri came to the door she nervously asked if he remembered her. He did not, but it did not take long for him to determine to whom she was related. We were invited into his study, which was decorated with an assortment of religious paraphernalia, including a rustic crucifix made of birch logs covered in furs and sweet grass, which suggested to me that people of nearby First Nations were included in his flock. Indeed, like most priests today, he ministered to several rural communities in the parish. Within moments of our arrival, Babette asked him if he remembered a house out on the coast run by a monastic order of brothers for religious retreats. He did remember and told us the house had been destroyed years ago and the property sold. He kindly gave us directions to the site and encouraged us to visit the woman who currently lived there, of whom he thought highly. To my surprise, Babette then thanked the priest for taking the time to talk to us and suggested we should be going. Walking us to the car, Father Henri suggested I would have a difficult time finding a place to stay in the settlement, as people's homes were not large enough, or suitable, for guests. He expressed regret that he could not offer me a room in the manse, which was really too large for one person. Alas, he was afraid the parishioners would gossip. I soon heard gossip that there was something fishy going on between the priest and his housekeeper, who went to the manse to cook his meals and clean, neatly confirming his suspicions about his parishioners' inclination to read comings and goings at the manse under a light of suspicion.[15]

Back in the car, it was only too obvious that Babette was in a distressed state of mind. She said that she had been having nightmares about a house used for religious retreats on the coast, and now Father Henri had just revealed that such a house was not a figment of her imagination. I volunteered to drive her out there to revisit the place, if she thought it would help. As we drove to the coastal property, which was located several kilometres from the settlement, I had the sense that I was travelling away from my research project (at that point still firmly rooted in the prosaic lives of rural workers) to probe the mysteries of the otherworldly, a task I thought was better suited to psychics or therapists than to anthropologists. Still, as we drew close to the apparent scene of her nightmare, Babette began to tremble and cower beside me and I could not ignore the embodiment of her daytime encounter with what she called her "nighttime life."

The road leading into the property was long and narrow and I had to negotiate gullies, boulders, and tree branches to get there. We were just stepping out of the car when three large dogs came tearing down the path to greet us, freezing us to the spot. A woman's voice could be heard in the distance, telling the dogs to stop that nonsense and settle down. As she approached, I guessed that she was about my age, and indeed, she was in her early thirties. She walked toward us to see if we were lost. I explained that my friend had memories of visiting this place as a child and that Father Henri had encouraged us to come visit. She introduced herself as Joan and offered to show us about. It is hard for me to imagine a lovelier spot, as it occupied an entire point reaching out into the sea. Rocky boulders lay to the north, while a beach lined the southern edge. Her log home rested in a sheltered nook with trees to the north and an open meadow to the south. The entire landscape was peaceful, and Joan, who calmly walked along side us, seemed at one with the place. The dogs fell into rank and file, and my own small dog contentedly took her place at the back of the pack. I liked Joan and her dogs instantly.

Babette, on the other hand, was anything but calm. She was agitated and cowering like a small child, reminding me of the desperately troubled young woman portrayed in the TV drama *Sybil*.[16] Joan had the good grace to treat this as perfectly normal behaviour and invited us into her home for tea. Over tea she brought out a few old photographs of the religious retreat that had once stood where her log house now stands. Babette blanched. She asked, "Did it have a chapel on the third floor?" Joan thought that *maybe* it did. While Babette sat there quaking, Joan and I struck up a conversation. When she realized I needed a place to live, she offered me her place. In a month's time, she hoped to go on a short trip to Europe but feared leaving her place unattended and had found no one able to tend to her animals. And so, it was agreed that I would return to her place in October to care for her dogs and cats while she travelled. It would give me a place to stay while I looked for a more suitable location closer to my field site, which I still understood in very circumscribed ways.[17]

Thus began a long-lasting friendship, and Joan's place would become a much-appreciated refuge over the years. Joan's mother was an Acadian whose family was deeply rooted to the soil, while her father had come from Britain as a small boy and had been adopted by a local man who needed help on his farm.[18] Throughout her youth, Joan moved across Canada as an "army brat" until her father retired from the Canadian armed forces. In the interim years, between retirement from the army and becoming an old age pensioner, they lived in urban centres in central Canada; but as soon as they were able, most of the family returned to the North Shore of New Brunswick. Joan, the youngest, was especially eager to return "out east," the place where she had spent most of her summers with her large extended Acadian family. When we first met, Joan worked seasonally as a "foreman" on a tree-planting crew made up of people from the settlements and small villages on the coast. A kind woman, she is well known for her commitment to the welfare of animals and the environment; but she is also known as a person quite capable of standing up to bullies. For instance, when Joan realized Babette knew many of her fellow tree planters, she told us about an encounter with a certain man from the settlement they knew in common. It happened this way: Joan learned some of the women who worked on her crew were being charged a hefty fee to get a lift into the woods by one of the less charming men in the settlement, so she offered to help out by swinging by their homes in the early morning to pick them up. A week later, large spikes were buried in the sandy part of the road leading into her place, and all of the tires on her Jeep were punctured. It did not deter Joan in the least, and she made a point of publicly confronting a man most people feared. Joan continued to collect the women from the settlement unchallenged.

Babette and I left Joan's place at dusk, uncertain of what to do or where to go next. Babette was clearly overwrought, so I suggested we find a hotel somewhere. This took us even further away from my narrowly imagined field site, as the closest hotel lay far up the coast. But I was exhausted and ready to call it a day. As we drove away from Joan's place, Babette relaxed a bit. Safely removed from the scene of her nightmares, she confessed to a sudden and vivid recollection of an event at low tide, on the night of a full moon, when worshippers of Satan met to engage in sexual escapades with children and to sacrifice newborn babies. To my dismay, I spent most of that first weekend in the field aiding Babette's quest to track down dream fragments. In October, she came again to visit me while I was at Joan's place, and together we searched every inch of the rocky northern shore at low tide. Babette was convinced that wedged within the crevices we would find the skulls of sacrificial babes.

As Father Henri had predicted, I was unable to find a place in the settlement to live, so I rented a small bungalow in a nearby coastal village, which I moved into during the first blizzard of the season, on Remembrance Day.[19] My field notes verify that I did indeed spend a good part of most days that winter trying to shovel out, as the snow banks around the house grew deeper and deeper. Most people had hunkered down for the winter, and I felt my research was going nowhere, although Joan and I often got together to snowshoe through the woods or across the frozen bay, our dogs following in the path we cut. We would talk about the landscape, our families, and work or lack of work, along the North Shore. We joined a fitness class that met in the basement of a local church hall. Women from up and down the coast and from the inland settlements would remove their Ski-Doo suits to reveal Jane Fonda-esque fitness clothing from Stedmans department store,[20] and we would work out on painted and carpeted plywood steps that the instructor's husband had copied from an expensive gym model and made in his workshop. The ingenuity of those I knew in doing things on the cheap always impressed me. The spare time to be innovative in such ways is, after all, one of the benefits of seasonal work little appreciated by those wedded to both full-time work and consumption.

Several times that winter, I sent Babette train fare so she could come to help me out with my research. This suited Babette to a tee, as she was always eager to travel "up home," but lacked the means and did

not want to visit for long with her family. She refused to stay over-
night with her grandmother while Jimmy remained in the house, and
she thoroughly detested her father's second wife and family, who she
believed monopolized both his affections and pocketbook. I always
looked forward to Babette's visits, believing she would introduce me
to her extended networks of kin. But with considerable skill she would
sabotage my best-laid research plans. Frequently, she would borrow my
car on the pretence of running a quick errand and return hours later distraught at her numerous encounters with people she had deliberately
sought out in search of clues that would unravel the significance of her
night terrors. Years later, Babette revealed that on one of these occasions
she accidentally drove my car into a ditch. Rather than call me for help,
she found an uncle to haul her out. She explained that she kept such
things a secret from me because she lacked a driver's licence. Stranded,
I spent those days cooling my heels and awaiting her return. But always
my anger would fade at the sight of her distress.

In the evenings, while I prepared supper for Babette and Joan,
she explained that her emotions completely overwhelmed her when
she was "up home," turning her into a completely different person.
I made her laugh by noting that she also spoke in a different lingua
franca when on the North Shore, as she adopted an Irish-lilting Fran-
glais when she got excited.[21] She jokingly gave Joan and me lessons in
appropriate settlement elocution, an ability I have since lost, but which
Joan, who still lives on the North Shore, can easily adopt. Laugh as we
might – and we did – Babette told us that she had never been happy
in the settlement. She felt she "belonged with educated people" like
Joan and me, an inclusive way of speaking which, in retrospect, must
have seemed a bit jarring to Joan, who is self-conscious about having
dropped out of school in Grade 8. Joan's return to the North Shore to
escape the rootlessness of urban life stands in stark contrast to Babette's
flight from what she considered to be the backwardness of settlement
life. At the time, I was acutely aware of the ways both women actively
sought out places in which to lead meaningful lives, according to their
personal histories, temperaments, and values. Still, I must note that
Babette was always eager to visit while I remained up north; indeed,
it was as if she felt compelled to repeatedly return to a world that she
found mostly repulsive, for her abiding attachment to the settlement
and surrounding landscape was haunting and disruptive to her peace
of mind. I soon realized that my living on the North Shore had created
a bridge between the two worlds her life uncomfortably straddled, and
so facilitated these returns in ways that were not helpful to either my
finances or my research.

Prior to her visits, Babette promised that we would sit and record her life history, but once there she refused to make the time. She was always restless and protested that she had already done this work with her therapists. She claimed the journals written for her therapists accomplished the same thing, and insisted I read them in lieu of recording her life history. Not a life history in the conventional sense, the journals, written at different times for various therapists, revealed a great deal about Babette's relationship to what she called her two worlds: the poverty-stricken settlement in rural New Brunswick in which she came of age and the urban Maritime city in which she then lived and sometimes worked. The metaphor of "two worlds" she used to explain the way she understood the relationship between both places has a temporal as well as a spatial aspect, for Babette treated her past as a frightful foreign land. As such, the metaphor captured the therapeutic spirit of the times, in which the idea of repressed childhood trauma was the key to explaining unhappiness in the present.[22] In retrospect, it is probably fitting that my initiation to fieldwork roughly corresponded with Babette's to therapy. We were both trying to account for the present by exploring the past, whether for psychological or historical and cultural reasons.

Babette entered therapy a year before I began fieldwork at the urging of her partner, who felt they were in need of marriage counselling. She told me that initially she sat through those sessions sullen and withdrawn, but on one occasion she became provoked and flew into a fit of rage. Within a week the counsellor phoned her, encouraging her to seek individual therapy. The therapist later told her that she had never in her life witnessed such a radical switch from passive to aggressive behaviour. I too had witnessed these lulls and eruptions of temperament, and no longer knew what to make of Babette's behaviour. I began to suspect my appointed key informant to be an unreliable witness. By her own account, she suffered complete memory loss at the age of fifteen, although memory loss seems an inadequate explanation for the state of mind she described in her journal, in which she chronicled intense night terrors and flashbacks that left her seriously depleted and unable to cope with daily life. I thought it was a good thing she had found a therapist with whom to work through her struggles and suffering.

Babette's earliest journal entries tended to focus on daily humiliations and frustrations. I especially recall a description of a cruel professor who set out to thwart her attempt to get an education by publicly humiliating her in front of other students, forcing her to drop out of a qualifying course for admission to university. In discussing it later, I tried to suggest that the professor may have been attempting to draw her attention to alternative aspects of the subject covered, to better prepare her for exams and papers, but Babette was having none of that. The professor, I was told, was as cruel as her mother. In therapy for almost a year, Babette was referred to an expert in the field of post-traumatic memory loss and ritual abuse. According to Babette, her new therapist was convinced that her night terrors and memory loss were the consequence of childhood sexual and ritual abuse. Shortly thereafter, the journal entries shifted radically from recounting the quotidian humiliations of her life, to repressed memories recalled through therapy. Babette's journal became laced with flashes of memory, nightmares, and hastily drawn pictures of gruesome knives dripping with blood, bearded demons, and religious symbols. These detailed eruptions of macabre violence were tucked between her lengthy assessments of countless articles and books about repressed memory written by survivors of abuse, in which Babette disputed earlier theories about split personality as a psychiatric condition. Babette told me she spent a lot of time at the library, and in our conversations, she would not so patiently try to explain exactly what her recovered memories indicated about her past. She also wrote about studies in neuroscience that could, she told me, explain what happens in various lobes of the brain to produce her symptoms. I confess, I did not understand it at all, but Babette was clearly demonstrating her growing competency in the field of traumatic memory theory.[23] Babette appeared to split before my very eyes, as she assumed the voice of a detached and objective medical researcher, offering herself up as a subject or patient. Considering her frustrated ambitions to join what she called an educated class, I couldn't help but think she was trading her ravaged psyche as currency for acceptance into a class to which she aspired.

Especially significant to Babette were grizzly things that her brother, who died as an adolescent in a car accident, began to reveal to her in dreams. She told me the revenant brother was helping her confront the most hideous events of her past. As it so happened, the revenant had visited her shortly before our first trip up north together and led her to the religious retreat out on the coast, where Roman Catholic monks and certain family members performed satanic rituals. I have no way of knowing if the therapist understood such nightmares in the same literalist terms as Babette did, although Babette claimed it was so.[24] For this reason, when we travelled north, she was already intent on tracking down concrete proof that would substantiate her nightmares. Evidence of such abuse would lend support to her many grievances with people from her past who had sorely let her down. She was ready to accuse them of involvement in satanic cults, sexual abuse, and murder.[25]

I want to be very clear here: I have never doubted that the woman I call Babette suffered greatly as a child. I do believe she was a deeply traumatized individual in need of psychological counselling, and, perhaps more importantly, resources to lift her out of poverty. Nevertheless, in what follows I shift my analysis away from the psychiatric discourse of trauma toward local ways of communicating and telling a story, the forms of remembering buried in folklore and sometimes instilled through religious ritual. In doing so, I am drawing attention to the historical and cultural confluences at play in the place where Babette came of age, and not disputing her troubled past or painful present. Together, they afforded especially fertile ground for ideas like trauma and recovered memory to take root. Babette's imagination and language unfurled at a time when radical social change swept through the isolated and impoverished settlements of the North Shore. The movement from repression and dissociation, on the one hand, toward recovered memories and reassociation, on the other, which developed over the couple of years that Babette spent in therapy, takes on even greater significance if we are also attentive to the radical social and cultural transformations afoot when Babette was a child.[26]

## Babette's Childhood

Eventually, I collected several life stories from women living in the settlement, including those from several childhood classmates of Babette. So, when Babette was finally ready to sit down several years later and record her life story, it was already uncannily familiar, for, as it turns out, it is not an uncommon tale. In what follows, I weave together elements from the life stories I collected to produce a singular voice in a composite character. Consequently, I suspect that the women I spoke to, should they read this book, will recognize elements of their lives, and be quick to dispute others. But this remains, largely, Babette's story.

Babette was the second of five children born to Rita and Guy. Rita had her first child at age thirteen, although Guy was in his mid-twenties. Rita was fifteen when Babette was born. They were desperately poor, and Babette remembers playing on the cold dirt floor of their tarpaper shack in the dark of winter, squatting to use a chamber pot in the corner of the room when she was too young to use the outhouse. The stench of those early days lingers in her memories. Babette began school at the age of five in a small convent school operated by the Filles de Jésus. There she received encouragement from the nuns, who recognized her quick intelligence and understood the impoverished and unstable conditions of her life. She loved school and felt deeply conflicted by the care and affection the nuns lavished on her, having been taught to fear and loathe the church at her mother's and grandmother's knee. She often confused me by calling the church "wicked" and most of the nuns "kind."

At school, the other children taunted her. They called her the warlock-whoremaster's bastard. The warlock-whoremaster was the local moniker for her mother's lover, and he bore an uncanny resemblance to a description of Satan an elderly woman once gave me: "Now Satan, he's not what you think. No, no. He doesn't have horns and hooves and all that. No, no. Satan is a very good-looking man, with the black hair and the dark eyes." (Coincidently, all those years later, it was a son of the warlock-whoremaster that left the spikes in the road to Joan's home because she dared to drive his half-sister to work.) Babette grew up in a place where God and Satan, good and evil, battled for turf. While she no longer believes in the devil, she certainly did as a child. Indeed, she once told me: "I spoke to the devil in English. I don't know why that seems so significant to me, but it seems to be. To me, the devil's power was brought up in English."

The Roman Catholic clergy who established schools for the impoverished along the North Shore were predominantly Acadian and French-speaking. While Babette was still in primary school in the latter half of the 1960s, the convent school was converted to a secular public school, and the primary language of instruction switched from French to English. Babette's parents spoke French, but her mother sided with the majority in the community in voting to have the language of instruction changed to English. Women her mother's age claimed to have been humiliated by the Acadian sisters in the convent school, so voting thus was a form of rebuke. But many also claimed to be voting in what they believed was in the best interest of their children. After all, in New Brunswick the powerful had historically spoken English.

When it came time to attend high school Babette was bused with the other children of the settlement to the nearest town. She recalled:

> The emotion I felt most, growing up, was shame. If I stayed late for an activity in high school, the bus would take all the kids from school home at once. Sometimes the other students would ask the bus driver to go to the settlement first so they could see what it looked like. This horrified me. I didn't want people to know I lived in the settlement, especially which house was mine. I'd get off of the bus about a half a mile from home in front of an okay-looking house. After all, we didn't have a bathroom, my bedroom was two pieces of pressed wood nailed to a couple of beams that didn't reach the ceiling, and there were no doors anywhere in the house.

You could see the outside through the cracks. In wintertime, I used to stare at the nails that were in the boards because they were white with frost. I was also ashamed about the things I was never taught that I learned were standard in other homes ... General hygiene,[27] social skills, everything I learned was preceded by the humiliating realization that I was doing something almost barbaric.

Babette was increasingly absent from school and by Grade 10, the year she "lost her memory," she did not attend at all. By then her mother was living with the "warlock- whore-master" and there was constant fighting. Having lost one brother in a tragic car accident, her other brother was forced out of the house when the "warlock-whore-master" accused the boy of sleeping with his mother. At fourteen he had to fend for himself. Babette spent most of her energy avoiding the sexual advances of the "warlock-whore- master." At fifteen, she maintained enough presence of mind to know that her mother's lover was dangerous, even if she could not always remember who he was. Further, she had the wherewithal to realize her memory lapses should be concealed from the strangers in her midst. It seems even the luxury of complete dissociation was one she could not afford.

The following spring, she formed a close friendship with another girl in the settlement. This girl's stepfather had molested her and together she and Babette plotted an escape from the settlement. The girl eventually left for Montreal, but Babette remained behind. Soon after that her mother and younger sister made their own dramatic escape (to quote her mother Rita) from the "warlock-whore-master" and the settlement. Babette moved in with her grandmother so that she could return to finish high school, but the scars of the lost years were too deep, and she soon left to join her mother in the city. There she wrote and passed high school equivalency exams. As she puts it, "I was the first person in my ancestry to finish high school." Still, this remarkable feat meant little in the urban centre to which she had moved, nor was it enough to open the doors to the institutions of higher learning that she soon realized were the only ticket out of a world she despised. A world despised, but one she could not expunge from her life.

Excerpt: Letter to D. Young, 1993.

You know, Donna, I know that I have a lot of determination sometimes, but you know what? I'm really very, very afraid. I don't know if I can do anything anymore. Can I succeed at anything? I'm beginning to think that I can't, which is scary, because without my education, I don't want to live. God Donna. Sometimes I get so depressed. Life just isn't fair. By the way, have you heard about the natives blocking the highways in NB because the provincial government decided to make them pay tax? The government was forced to back down. The way I feel now I'd have sent tanks into the reserves and blown them all away. You don't want to pay your share? BOOM! (Vicious, aren't I) But when you consider the poverty I come from, how hard I struggled, and that *I'm still nowhere* but can't get financial aid to get my education, and that I still owe hundreds of dollars in taxes, I am filled with rage. And they can get their fucking twenty-first century education paid for! Yet natives and the rich don't pay taxes. I am furious. I am disgusted. Okay, I'm sure you disagree with me, but that's how I feel. Extremely disgusted. Fuck them.

Babette knew me well and I did find her remarks about "freeloading natives" deeply offensive. Truthfully, I suspect her intention at that moment was to shock and annoy me, or at least get my attention. On another day, she could as easily dismiss people who said similar things as stupid racists. But the sentiment expressed was all too common when I was in the field; First Nations often bore the brunt of people's rage and their sense of frustration with their own life circumstances.[28] Surprisingly, the very same people who resented what they considered preferential treatment for Indigenous people would ask me if there was any way to trace their ancestry, as they had been told there was "native blood" in their families. They believed such "blood" could make them eligible for forms of federal compensation. Babette's letter expresses her profound frustration, but also the rage and the nastiness that attended the politics of the day, something her therapists apparently showed little interest in, although, admittedly, I have only Babette's word to go on.

As naïve as such literalist interpretations of nightmares and repressed memories now appear, they were pervasive and persuasive in the early 1990s when I did fieldwork. Looking back, I see such literal interpretations of the grotesque as part of a much wider social drama in which broad anxieties about morality, authority, and history were being played out. Novels, plays, television dramas, talk shows, and the evening news were full of frightful revelations of the abuse of children and appalling misuses of authority. All of the institutions that once held responsibility for the care, moral instruction, and discipline of children were regarded suspiciously.

## Maritime Gothic

Although Babette's obsessive hunt for clues to her own past that would explain her ongoing state of mental distress and unhappiness was an extreme instance of this tendency to paint the world in gothic shadows, it was not atypical. Her family and friends considered her quest to unravel her personal story captivating, even if they seemed wary of where it might lead, for fear she would bring family secrets, best kept hidden, out into the open. By the same token, others had openly substantiated aspects of Babette's life that worked their way into her nightmares. Nobody was denying the extreme poverty and neglect, instances of sexual abuse and violence, or the stories of miscegenation that circulated in the community. Within this Canadian context, I use the word "miscegenation" with some hesitation as it implies a false science of race upon which American laws were built to prevent intermarriage between "peoples of different races." Nevertheless, it would be naïve to ignore the ways in which such racist forms of thought also shaped social relations in Canada. Historically, many families along the Northern Shore of New Brunswick (and elsewhere) hid or denied their Native Canadian heritage. The preoccupation in the 1990s with "native blood" in one's family that might be worked to "milk the system" points to the ways in which Canadian racist attitudes and laws, as manifested in the Indian Act, influenced political and social relations at the most intimate levels of family and community life, so that assuming complex ethnic identities became fraught with notions of privilege and rights against those of contamination and shame.

Others along the North Shore openly discussed the suspect behaviour on the part of a few Roman Catholic clergy who had at one time worked in the region. Such disclosures were open secrets, if they were secrets at all, but such disclosures could never comfort or satisfy Babette. Instead, the power of Babette's stories to both enthral and disrupt lay in her insistence on there being something more, of an unspeakable excess, beyond what was widely known. According to Eve Sedgwick (1980), the conventions of the gothic as a literary genre hinge, for the most part, on a past that cannot be known, a past that is by its very nature fated to remain *unspeakable*, an unknown found lurking in the depths of one's psyche, one's nightmares, one's history, one's environment. As Babette's dream state, what she calls her nighttime life, began to bleed into her quotidian life, she encountered a proliferation of doubles – rather than indisputable facts. Doubles represent stories within stories that are highly repetitive, so that parallel plots endlessly "spring up and multiply" to continually reproduce a sense of the "unspeakable" (Sedgwick 1980: 21–2). Doubles have a chiastic structure commonly found in oral traditions, a structure intended to reinforce the message. In the gothic, utter helplessness in the face of insurmountable horrors is the central message. In the gothic, "imagination and emotional effects exceed reason" (Botting 1996: 3).

Babette's stories and diaries are full of conventions commonly found in gothic folk tales and fiction. For instance, revenants who return to reveal secrets, such as the brother who visits Babette in her dreams; live or hidden burials, as in the mother and children whose cabin is buried under snow; or the foreigner who blithely wanders into an unknown place to sell his wares, and is bludgeoned before being buried deep in the woods. There is the continual movement from a dream state into an awakening that repeats or confirms the horror of the nightmare, as in dreaming about a monastery and then finding yourself on the property where it once stood. Another recurring theme is the passivity of childhood, as in, again, the children huddled for warmth beside the corpse of their dead mother, the babies ritually sacrificed and hidden in caves, vulnerable adolescents banished from their homes, or even the innocent student humiliated by a cruel professor. In the gothic, violence is especially pronounced during liminal phases, such as full moons, births, transitions to adulthood, or flights from domestic violence, such as the escape Babette's mother made, although abandoning Babette in the process. As any anthropologist worth their salt knows, crossing thresholds makes one especially vulnerable.[29] In the gothic, the very rituals intended to provide protection through such precarious passages and transitions are perverted, twisted into the macabre double of the original, thus thwarting any possibility of escape.

Especially notable in Babette's stories are evocations of a religious past made mysterious and representative of an irrationality that threatens the present. Margot Northey (1976) notes that in French-Canadian settings the early gothic explored a "voyageur spirit of rebellious freedom" in which their "encounter with unaccountable evil or mystery" of an unknown wilderness and the Indigenous peoples who lived there resulted in "moral confusion or uncertainty" (15). Within French Canada, this was initially tempered by a tendency "to squeeze the tale into a spiritually ordered framework in which conventional Catholic beliefs and practices are brought to the fore" (15). But after the British conquest of French Canada, "Anglo-Saxon liberty, progress, and intellectual vitality" are pitted "against Roman Catholic absolutism and intellectual torpor" (14–15). Catholicism itself becomes the irrational force that threatens the march of progress in the settler nation. One can read within these historical developments of the gothic in Canada two displacements: first, an Indigenous worldview is suppressed and returns only to haunt and undermine the Catholic moral order of early French society; second, Catholicism itself is rendered dangerously archaic by conquest, which meets its apotheosis in the Quiet Revolution in Quebec, or, in New Brunswick, by the comparable Acadian nationalist movements of the 1960s, in which a secular worldview takes hold. In this way, as Freud so brilliantly notes, "the 'double' has become a thing of terror, just as, after the collapse of their religion, the gods turned into demons" ([1919] 1955: 236).

In Babette's stories, I see a family resemblance with other stories told in the region, like those told about a spectral ship found burning off the Bay of Chaleur, as discussed in the introduction to this book. In Babette's story of detachment and rejection, what Kristeva calls "the abject," comes to saturate the landscape of the North Shore. Babette's attempt to place her nightmares within a new frame of psychiatry and science that focuses on the suppression of memories in childhood largely fails, only to be swallowed whole by the "powers of horror" that haunt the landscape and are kept alive in the oral traditions of her community. While Babette picked at her past like a child picks at a scab, I always felt her past was not so much repressed as angrily replaced by a "sublimating elaboration" in which the fantastic and the terrible hold us captive (Kristeva 1997: 234–5). As in the gothic, Babette mines the past for significance, moving from the domestic realm of family secrets and neglect, to broader state and religious institutions, only to end with a tirade against the perceived privileges of close-by *others*, the Mi'kmaq of northeastern New Brunswick. She is always the victim. In "Powers of Horror," Kristeva (1997) argues that the uncanny gathers ominously in states of abjection. In abjection, one casts off the unseemly and unbearable, turning it into an object external to one's self, where it festers and manifests itself as the other. Indigeneity, Catholicism, and even close kin come to represent all that is loathsome and threatening.

As Sedgwick notes, among the more troubling aspects of gothic doubles are "dangerous distortions and interferences" that severely inhibit one's ability to see themselves in others (1980: 45). In other words, in the gothic, everyone is fated to remain isolated in their own private hell. So, while the gothic exposes layers of dispossession and discontent as it dredges up the past, any emancipatory potential flounders. Indeed, in Babette's letter, it is the refusal of the Mi'kmaq to remain spectral, as they rise up in protest, that provokes Babette's virulently racist reaction. As Marlene Goldman notes, in gothic fiction "[Native] peoples have served as what psychoanalysts term 'self-objects' for settler society" in which "the settler's obsessive reliance and bond with the figure of the Native and the latter's enforced displacement and homelessness … perform the psychological function of consolidating and maintaining the settler society's sense of being at home" (2012: 246). But, she asks, "What happens if the dead refuse to stay dead, but maintain a wayward and more or less obtrusive presence within the world of the living?"

(2012: 298). I found a very troubling and close relationship between a broader gothic sensibility in the Maritimes of the 1990s, in which the histories of abjection and dispossession resurfaced, and a growing politics of resentment and rancour, as evidenced in Babette's inability to countenance an ounce of sympathy for either her kin or her neighbours. Goldman finds embedded in Canadian fiction a similar warning "against clinging to ancestral ghosts by showing how the characters who perceive themselves solely as the victims of history efface their own agency and their capacity to victimize others" (2012: 303).

In the 1990s, there was an appreciative audience (in the form of therapists and an anthropologist, no less!) ready to entertain even the most fantastic of Babette's stories. It was as if we had collectively lost our bearings and could no longer distinguish between fact and fiction, reality and fantasy, myth and history. I am not arguing that we should simply dismiss the content of Babette's imagination as a simple by-product of the culture and psychobabble industries. Quite the contrary. I think her machinations are historically significant and bear the weight of the past. Again, I take my lead from the literary criticism of the gothic, which suggests that a "disturbance of psychic states ... does not signal a purely subjective disintegration: The uncanny renders all boundaries uncertain and ... often leaves the readers unsure whether narratives describe psychological disturbance or wider upheavals within formations of reality and normality" (Botting 1996: 11). As literary critics Smith and Hughes argue, "Gothic tales, their contradictions, ambiguities and ambivalences, provide a dense and complex blend of assertion and doubt, acceptance and defiance, and truth and falsity and in this way provide a space in which the key elements of the dominant culture become debated, affirmed and questioned" (2023: 3).

As such, I find within Babette's need to discover some horrible event in her childhood that would explain her nightmares and deep unhappiness, and the poverty and neglect that created a life of intermittent employment and homelessness, the same gesture to the past that contours Maritime settler history, in which "preoccupations with the past are revelatory of an unresolved conflict about the present" (Steedman 1995: 158). What is remarkable to me is the way in which the machinations of Babette's distraught psyche so perfectly melded with the sensibilities of the day, in which a more diffuse Maritime Gothic sensibility sprang up to express a deep attachment to a troubled past.

Throughout the 1990s, under neoliberal globalization, the forest industry was radically altered, leading to massive unemployment (Sandberg 1992). The provincial government pursued "rational" and competitive management practices that served the needs of an industry that was being completely severed from notions of livelihood in the region. As jobs and prospects dried up, staying "up north" became untenable for many. The very notion of "up home," by which Maritimers reference the places from which they come and to which they feel they belong, began to fray, and in its place, grievances were left to fester and mutate. Maritimers know only too well that people in other regions of the nation consider an inability to weather changes wrought by the global economy to be symptomatic of regional backwardness. As a consequence, Maritimers often feel misunderstood and resentful. Some might say we collectively carry a massive chip on our shoulders.

Herb Wyile (2011) suggests Atlantic Canada's relationship to the rest of the nation is even more complex, as others come to fear what the region represents in the national psyche, a place in which, under neoliberal globalization, jobs in the resource economy were lost to mechanization (as happened to jobs in the woods), a place where depletion of resources destroyed communities (as happened in the Newfoundland fishery and in the coal fields of Cape Breton), and a place where the manufacturing sector was dismantled (as happened with the pulp and paper industry of New Brunswick), because "Now Masters Have No Borders."[30] Consequently, Wyile (2011) argues that others read the often bleak fiction of Atlantic Canada – which does not neatly conform to the romantic rural simplicity promoted by the tourism industries of the region – as "speculative fiction," because the realities faced by Maritimers foreshadow the inevitable decline and ruination of other nowhere places built to extract resources. The boom-and-bust cycles of economic life are shown to have an end point; the literature portends a loss of community and frightening prospects for families that make their homes in nowhere places. And then there is the frightening afterlife of resource economies: the poisoned rivers, forest fires, floods, unspecified illnesses. Maritime Gothic explores the closing futures of resource extraction by dwelling on other forms of return. By revealing the ghosts and monsters that return to haunt a region once the industries depart, Maritime Gothic disrupts the Canadian settler worldview of an endless resource-rich wilderness to be tamed and exploited.[31]

*So, elderly Filles de Jésus remember building a convent school ...*

In the following chapter, I examine some of the home truths (the *Heimlich)* that lie beneath the uncanny (the *Unheimlich*) of northern New Brunswick, as discussed in the previous chapter. It was not until I briefly left the North Shore, in the midst of a six-week stint as a substitute teacher in the settlement's elementary school, that I began to get a sense of a past way of life little understood in the present. I travelled south to Moncton to visit the mother house of the Filles de Jésus, a Roman Catholic congregation of women religious. I turn now to aspects of Maritime social history that lie alongside, if not buried beneath, the stories told by Babette, her kin, and neighbours. Here, history is revealed from an entirely different perspective, that of Acadian Roman Catholic teaching sisters who were once ubiquitous on the North Shore, as well as in other Acadian regions of the Maritimes and along the Gaspésie of Quebec. The women religious chronicle the past by referencing the raw materials and the objects that help to distil lived experience and social history, lending their narrative verisimilitude.

The problem has always been to hold these two very distinct ways of chronicling the past in tandem. It would be easy to elevate the realist stories told by the sisters as revealing the social history of the region, and to dismiss the gothic as fantastical, with its reliance on connections between doubles that pile one on top of the other to create a sense of entrapment.[32] Both temporalities – the gothic, endlessly caught in dreadful repetition, and realism, capturing vanishing historical durations by dwelling on the materiality of one's environment – saturate the landscape, literature, and artwork of the Maritime region. The literary critics Marta Dvořák and Coral Ann Howells suggest that in the literature of the Atlantic region, "realistic landscape description begins to falter under the subversive influences of a more fantastic gothic topography" (2006: 8). "Realism teetering on the edge of fantasy" (ibid.) pretty much captures the faltering sensibilities found in the following chapter, as the social history recounted by the Filles de Jésus is quickly ousted by the more troubling memories of Rita, Babette's mother, who attended the convent school built by the sisters in the 1950s. Rita's life history combines elements of the hard realism often found in "poverty narratives by women" (Rimstead 2001) with a sense of gothic entrapment. Again, I am arguing that we need to hold both ways of making sense of the past in balance, as both have something truthful to impart and entail ethical judgments. In other words, the narratives capture the ways in which individuals engage with others, make decisions in difficult situations, and help create – through story and action – the worlds they remember and once inhabited.[33]

The oral histories of the elderly women religious I spoke to reveal a pattern of life and a worldview born of Roman Catholic praxis rooted in traditional Acadian social structures, although the religious congregation originated in France. Acadians of the late nineteenth and early twentieth centuries held ultramontane beliefs, more widely associated with Quebec. Essentially, the church in the Maritimes was concerned with the survival of Acadians as a people, and they espoused a particular view of community grounded in a rural moral economy that was both Roman Catholic and French-speaking. As seen in the previous chapter, that way of life, especially when it takes on a more gothic twist, is so at odds with current times it seems almost unintelligible. In the gothic imagination, Roman Catholic clergy are vilified and associated with the historical abuses of the church, rather than with forms of Acadian survival and resistance in the region. But this chapter pauses to consider the worldview and times that shaped the actions of the women religious who went to the settlement to build a school in a time of economic crisis. The women religious I spoke to hold notions of human solidarity and Roman Catholic subsidiarity that belong to a world that was largely erased during the secularization of education that took place during the 1960s in New Brunswick. It should be noted, however, that the women religious I interviewed welcomed these progressive developments, even if it led, inevitably, to the decline of their own religious order and work in the region. When I visited the elderly sisters in the winter of 1993, they still occupied a sprawling convent in Moncton, but the property has since been sold. The tiny congregation of elderly women moved onto the single floor of a nursing home, enabling the women religious to remain in community until their deaths. The sisters' way of life, and their point of view, has slipped into the past.

Still, one can catch glimpses of that past in the five-volume series *The Way It Was along My Bay*, created by artist and local historian Vetta LaPointe Faulds. For instance, in volume 3, *Six Villages and an Island*, there is a reproduction of a delightful painting, *Disrupted Prayer Walk*, of two Sisters of Charity hopping a fence to avoid a charging ram (2005: 43).[34] According to the accompanying text, the women religious had returned to visit family, and an elder from the region laughs as she recalls the event from her youth, claiming to have deliberately set the ram loose. But the nuns are the object of her gaze, and the nuns' story remains untold. Still, there are several things to note. The Sisters of Charity are an English-speaking congregation active in the region, indicative of the historical division of Roman Catholic dioceses in New Brunswick along linguistic and ethnic lines. The North Shore, as I have already noted, was never a homogeneous Acadian rural community. Further, many of the landscapes focus on other Protestant churches that dot the landscape. This is yet another reminder of waves of settlement creating an ethnically diverse region. The rural and moral economy of the region was never unique to an ethnic enclave, and the lives of descendants of Indigenous and settler communities remain deeply entangled. Despite pockets of French-speaking Acadians, the ultramontane ideal espoused by some Acadian clergy was never achievable.

The series of five books by Vetta LaPointe Faulds was created as a heritage project that combines family genealogies with the memories of descendants still living in the coastal communities that skirt the Bay of Chaleur. Whimsical paintings, based on family photographs, are reimagined as idyllic landscapes of the past, contributing to that wider sense of nostalgia for a simpler time that is promoted throughout the Maritimes. Indeed, there is a painting of the very house that haunted Babette, which was bought from a local family by the Collège du Sacré-Coeur in 1942 and destroyed by fire in 1970. In that brief period, Eudist Fathers[35] used the home for religious retreats, and it corresponds with the period in which the Filles de Jésus were active in the region. Their histories and stories are not explored in the books. Rather, settler genealogies are combined with the recollections of their descendants, and the regional landscapes celebrate settler heritage and achievements, including the establishment of local mills and industries, which are no longer there. When I recently visited friends in the region, they referred to the author simply as Vetta, although she no longer lives along the bay. Collections of her books sat on their shelves and coffee tables, and some hung her paintings, or reproductions of her artwork, on their walls, especially if a landscape featured their family homestead. These artworks are pastoral representations of villages carved out of the wilderness generations ago and underlie notions of going "up home," "down home," or "over home" that root settlers and their descendants to the landscape. As Edward Casey (2002) notes, "in the practice of landscape painting region is a privileged, nonsubsumable domain in which natural presences, things and people and places, coinhere" (2002: 74). LaPointe Faulds' landscapes belong to a folkloric sensibility, wedding a people to the land. As always, such representations involve erasures.[36]

Regional Mi'kmaq communities are only referenced obliquely, through a recounting of Mi'kmaq legend, or by acknowledging Heron Island as the ancient burial ground of the Listuguj, ancestors of contemporary Mi'kmaq Nations (see volume 3, *Six Villages and an Island*). The corresponding artwork situates the Mi'kmaq in the distant past by imagining a temporary summer encampment along a shoreline at the very edge of wilderness (LaPointe Faulds 2005: 110–19). Occasionally, you catch a glimpse of the probable Indigenous roots of an individual, such as the well-respected local midwife Mary Ida (LaBillois) Murchie, whose maiden name suggests she is Indigenous (ibid. 2005: 72–3). Indeed, what the collected genealogies make evident is that the ethnic communities along the bay are deeply entwined. The inland settlements that were the subject of my interest are only mentioned in passing. For instance, the efforts of an individual from one of the settlements who contributed to life in the wider diocese or region might be mentioned. But for the most part, these portraits of life are cobbled together from family-centred village life along the shores of the bay, as the title of the series would suggest.

So, in the following chapter, the focus is on those who are only glimpsed at the edges of LaPointe Faulds' narrative. It concerns the period that begins during New Brunswick's Great Depression and ends with the "Equal Opportunity" years of the 1960s. The stories are told and recorded in the 1990s, first from the point of view of the Filles de Jésus, who built a school in a poor inland settlement, and then from Rita, who attended that school. I interviewed Rita a year after visiting the women religious in a quiet suburb of Saint John, where she was living with her second husband in a comfortable bungalow.

# Chapter Three

# Clothing of Piety, Clothing of Poverty: Object Lessons and the Poverty Narratives of Women[1]

> When places are actively sensed, the physical landscape becomes wedded to the landscape of the mind, to the roving imagination, and where the mind may lead is anybody's guess.
>
> Keith Basso, *Wisdom Sits in Places*[2]

I had been in the field for a year and a half before I headed south, with some trepidation, to visit the women religious who, in the 1940s, founded the small local school that both Babette and her mother Rita attended as children. The trees were stripped bare, and the sky was overcast. Although I have always welcomed the stark landscapes and stillness of November, on that morning the countryside was cast in decidedly gothic shades of grey, only to be broken, here and there, by the naked red of dogwood stems. It was the perfect backdrop for my brooding thoughts, which had come increasingly to dwell on a past I imagined to be oppressively religious and darkly disturbing. Sombre nuns and angry priests skirted the rural roads of my imagination.

As discussed in the previous chapter, a pall hung over the history of the Roman Catholic Church in the Atlantic region of Canada in the 1990s. Stories of endemic abuse, particularly the abuse of vulnerable children, cast a long shadow over the church. The previous winter the CBC had aired a number of television dramas in which both priests and nuns in traditional habits were featured in the darkest imagery imaginable.[3] The unfolding scandals at both the Mount Cashel Orphanage in Newfoundland, which was run by Roman Catholic Christian Brothers, and the thoroughly secular Kingsclear Training School for Boys in New Brunswick, fuelled the unease.[4] A sensibility I came to think of as Maritime Gothic crept into everyday talk and personal life history narratives. People spoke of the past as a dark place where predatory priests roamed the countryside and uncharitable nuns harshly disciplined school children. Nothing I had heard over the past year or so prepared me for my visit to Moncton and the mother house of the Filles de Jésus, the religious congregation that built schools throughout much of the French-speaking region of New Brunswick in the early twentieth century, especially along the Acadian Peninsula and northeastern shore. In these regions, extreme poverty had destroyed the earlier secular school system, which was dependent on the ability of local school boards to collect a school tax to pay for teachers. In Moncton, I met and interviewed three elderly women religious, all long retired from active service. Two of them were among the three intrepid sisters who founded the school in the 1940s, just as the Second World War was coming to an end. Off and on, all three of them returned to live and work in the settlement's convent school until and beyond its secularization in the 1960s.

These women religious belong to a congregation that originated in Brittany, France, but "the political events in France from 1902 onwards prompted hundreds of sisters to leave their country of origin because they were no longer allowed to teach in the schools."[5] The political program and laws of laïcité in France made it impossible for religious sisters to wear the habit and give religious instruction in schools, and so early in the twentieth century they emigrated to French-speaking parts of the world.[6] When speaking to the sisters, they referred to that historical period, quite simply, as "the persecution," reminding me that the question of religious garb in France, in particular the veiling of women, was as contentious for Roman Catholicism in the last century as it is for Islam in this century. In the 1960s, the schools the congregation built in New Brunswick would, once again, be appropriated and secularized by the state. But this process of secularization was understood very differently, as the sisters I interviewed welcomed the new provincial interventions, which they considered long overdue. Under the banner of "equal opportunity," the Acadian premier Louis Robichaud centralized the system of taxation and funding for education, so that money flowed into the coffers of the impoverished rural schools in northern New Brunswick for the first time.[7] When I spoke to Sister Anne, who was principal of the settlement convent school during the transition, she exclaimed, clasping her hands together, "My, it was the abundance; we were rich."

There are several ironic twists here, or perhaps they merely appear ironic because we have been taught to think of secularization as the logical end goal within a system of modern educational reform. But in New Brunswick, the political events that led to the "equal opportunity" years were anything but straightforward, and upset such simplified trajectories. The events underscore Asad's argument that theories of modernization, which assume that a secular worldview belongs to modernity while a religious worldview belongs to a premodern past, tend to miss the more complex nuances of social and cultural change, which must be examined within a particular historical context (2003: 181–201).

Obviously, such a radical change in perspective on the part of women religious concerning two distinct secularization programs, first in France and then in the Canadian province of New Brunswick, demands other forms of analyses, for despite a change in attitude toward the secularization of schools, the Filles de Jésus remain Roman Catholic women religious. They did not abandon their faith when they moved from the old world to the new; nor did they alter their mission, which was (and still is) to serve the poor and needy by educating them and attending to their spiritual and social needs. But when they moved into the Maritimes in the early twentieth century they encountered new forms of religious and secular practice, and new political realities that shaped the relationship between the two.[8] Further, the young Acadian women who found their vocation within the congregation brought with them working-class and ethno-nationalist values shaped by particular political struggles in which debates over language, religion, and education were central.[9] Such politics had been shaped in part by a Protestant elite, descendants of English Loyalists, who secularized schools shortly after Confederation to undermine the authority and political aspirations of Roman Catholic clergy. As Wilbur notes, "This meant that New Brunswick's Roman Catholic citizens entered Confederation without constitutional protection for their separate schools" (1989: 7). This completely disadvantaged impoverished Roman Catholic Irish immigrants and especially French-speaking Acadians in the province, who could not afford to participate in a system of education they were required to fund out of their own pockets. It was the inability of so many to pay school taxes and retain teachers that eventually led to a loosening of strictures against religious forms of education, as various Roman Catholic orders were willing to build and subsidize schools in the poorest regions of the province.[10]

It was such circumstances that brought the Filles de Jésus to the settlement in the 1940s. The settlement became a parish in 1941, and the Filles de Jésus established a convent and school in 1944. The secular school had been closed for the better part of two decades, as families had been unable to pay the school tax and retain a teacher for more than a week or so, here and there. Indeed, many of the religious schools in New Brunswick emerged from the failures of the secular state. The sisters of the Filles de Jésus adapted the school's curriculum to meet the needs of children who were mostly Roman Catholics of mixed heritage, often spoke both English and French with a smattering of Irish, and had received little or no previous education. Daily, they strived to provide the children with a proper Roman Catholic *formation*, a formation closely tied to the ideals of the Acadian clergy and Acadian nationalism.

What most surprised me when I met the sisters was how their rendering of the past differed from the one I found circulating on the North Shore, one that suggested new ways of looking at the past and the present. Not only was I led to reconsider the abuse narratives I had so quickly assumed to be the underlying feature of life in the settlement, but I also had to reconsider categories I so readily imposed on the social world I was attempting to understand, categories such as ethnic and national identities and the working class, which I had assumed belonged to distinctly secular struggles. The Filles de Jésus identified as Roman Catholic, Acadian, and working-class in very particular ways. If their religious identity was linked partly to an understanding of religious persecution in France in the early twentieth century, their national and ethnic identity was rooted even more deeply in the past to the British expulsion of the Acadians in 1755 – Le Grande Dérangement – and the historical struggles of those who returned to resettle on marginal lands in New Brunswick after 1764.

I argue that the stories that follow, as told by women religious who worked in the settlement's convent school from the 1940s into the 1960s, challenge and complicate stories of secularization in New Brunswick. The sister's decidedly gendered and working-class depictions of their labour and struggles stand in sharp contrast to those I heard while in the settlements in the 1990s. In doing so, their vivid narratives move us away from an understanding of the Catholic Church as a decaying and corrupt monolithic religious institution, as found in the gothic, toward an analysis of working-class Acadian sisters, who were once a visible and active moral presence on the North Shore. The following account draws attention to the ways the women religious experienced radical social and historical shifts, both in terms of the provincial program of Equal Opportunity that secularized the schools they built, and in terms of the changes to their religious lives, wrought by the Second Vatican Council. It is against this backdrop of sweeping reforms to education and religious practice that I try to make sense of the collective hostility toward the church that surfaced in 1990s, when it became clear that such reformations – transformative as they were – failed to deliver all that they had once promised, or if they did, they did so unevenly. And I do so in two ways: first, by paying close attention to the objects that flit through accounts of the past to capture the social and material conditions of the times; second, by noting the prevalence of the tiny word *so*, that adverb and conjunction which punctuates the sisters' oral recollections. Together, tangible memories and this narrative propensity and reliance on the word *so*, participate "in the dissimulation of both historicality and, even more so, of deeper levels of temporality" (Ricoeur 1980: 171). And so, the women religious flag a different sort of reckoning with the past than that found in the previous chapter, creating a sense of historical realism that clarifies and justifies an unfolding of events in the settlement school and in the settlement more broadly. While the gothic and realism produce entirely different temporalities and alternative sensibilities, both ways of remembering and reckoning with the past remain rooted in the preoccupations of the ethnographic present of the 1990s in New Brunswick, a time when recovered memories and accusations of abuse were ascendant.[11] So, I want to first give a sense of life in the small school – that was once a convent school – when I worked there as a substitute teacher in the early 1990s.

**The 1990s: Troubled Lessons**

The second winter I was in the field, I taught a Grade 3 class in the settlement school for six weeks. It was a harrowing experience as the children spent their days running amok. I had agreed to substitute for a teacher who, I was told, suffered a nervous breakdown. I was one of the few people in the area with sufficient education *and* a willingness to work in the settlement school, which suffered a reputation as a difficult school. For the six weeks leading up to the Christmas holidays, I worked to gain control of an unruly and riotous group of children. In an effort to bring the classroom under control without shouting at the top of my lungs, I took the suggestion of another teacher, and would simply raise my hand and wait for students to notice and raise their own hands, turning their attention to me. It worked brilliantly until a visiting parent sneered at her child and laughed out loud, completely undermining my authority. Often a physical brawl would break out and as I tried to pull the children apart and off the floor, they would cuss each other out, using colourful invective, "cock-sucking son of a whoremaster" being a favoured expletive.

So, I attempted a lesson recommended by my older sister, a veteran primary school teacher. The exercise was supposed to build mutual respect and instil compassion among the students. For the month of December, each child was given the task of being a secret angel to a fellow classmate, whose name was drawn from a hat. Students were asked to bestow special gifts of kindness upon that classmate. Children would have an opportunity to guess the identity of their special angel in a celebration prior to leaving school for the Christmas holiday. Most children took the task very seriously. As students quickly figured out the identity of their special angel, new bonds were created and there was a marked improvement in classroom behaviour. However, one child adamantly refused to participate. In trying to reason with the obstinate boy after class, I was told, "My mother says to just get in there and take my part (in a fight or argument). So, I don't have to do anything I don't want to." Nothing in my previous education had prepared me for the challenges of teaching in a primary school like this.

One of the things I found most disruptive were the daily visits of their parents, who did not hesitate to intrude into the quotidian routines and lessons of my classroom, whether to serve an impromptu Christmas feast, to monitor their children's progress and/or "rights," or simply to stand on the other side of the door to eavesdrop and check out the new teacher. I was never asked or informed ahead of time of such visits, but parental activities and concerns trumped mine at every turn, as, I must concede, they often should. But it is difficult to proceed with a math lesson when a turkey is being carved by a parent who wants to do something special for her son's class. My lessons fell on deaf ears.

Father Henri, the parish priest, dropped by one day to announce that catechism classes would be held for children after school, in the parish hall next door, to prepare them for Confirmation. The school had been a secular institution since the 1960s, but because the Roman Catholic Church had built the school, certain accommodations[12] were made for the parish priest, who had worked in the area for decades. He stood in the doorway shaking his head in disbelief. "How" he asked, "will these children ever survive without a proper *formation*?" Father Henri was concerned for the intellectual and spiritual welfare of children in need of a proper *formation*, which he always pronounced *en français*, although we spoke only English in class. The implication was that these children would benefit from some old-fashioned Catholic moral instruction and discipline, and despite my own quasi-secular and Protestant upbringing, I found myself nodding my head in agreement. For instance, I was told I could not even rest my hand on a child's shoulder to calm them, as parents would come to threaten the school with a lawsuit. It had already happened. By the 1990s, the idea of discipline had been reduced to only its punitive aspects. Whether students and parents acted on their threats or not, teachers were terrified.

Another day, I stood with a fellow teacher, an ex-nun who had been teaching there since the early 1960s when it was still a convent school run by the Filles de Jésus, as children filed by. We watched in horror as one of the parents drove a beat-up old Buick into the schoolyard and proceeded to do "wheelies" on the icy playground. It was 8:30 am and he was "pissed," according to the students passing by. Eventually, a young girl jumped from the car laughing and ran into the school, where the ex-nun stood sternly in front of her and informed her that her father was in violation of school property. I felt a terrible pang in my heart as the smile was wiped from her face, for I had never seen her smile before. She was a dejected child, the same child the stubborn boy had refused to sit beside, or to bond with as a secret angel. It seemed unbearable to me that she should be held accountable for the sins of the father. Later, I found her crying as she straddled the second-floor banister, threatening to throw herself off. I spoke to the principal, and she called for the regional school therapist, but it would be months before anyone would be able to see her. As teachers, we felt utterly helpless, as we were expected to maintain a "healthy and orderly environment" (according to the unsympathetic regional supervisor of schools who dropped in to scold us) in a community that granted us little moral authority or respect. Apparently, at some point in the past, such authority had been so abused that the bonds of trust had been irrevocably lost.

As I have already mentioned, the settlement school, like all other Catholic schools in New Brunswick, was secularized in the 1960s, but some of the teachers, and most of the parents of the children I was failing to educate, recalled its convent origins. And so, the parents told me they would not allow their children to be subjected to the same abusive forms of education they experienced at the hands of Catholic priests and nuns. In the eyes of the parents, the Roman Catholic Church, and the schools they operated had failed to protect children, and all were now held accountable for the sins of the past. Even small acts of charity, such as giving a young boy lip balm for his cold sore, were rejected as condescending slights to the family. Parents wanted to protect *their* children's *self-esteem and rights*, notions that replace the older concern for a Roman Catholic moral *formation*, in which sacrifices for the good of the community were accentuated. This shift is "indicative of a new world" in which people "no longer speak the same language" (Williams 1983: 11). As Ben Highmore notes, when Williams speaks of people no longer speaking the same language, he "seems to be claiming that at the level of intuitive life (the world of cultural reflexes, the world of meaning that is nearest at hand) something has fundamentally altered" (Highmore 2017: 26).

In the previous chapter, people from the North Shore of New Brunswick recalled Catholic priests and nuns dressed in their traditional habits and the ritual trappings of religious observances as ephemeral and ghostly presences. Daily conversations and the life-history narratives I collected were riddled with references to frightful priests and sisters in long dark robes. Babette's grandmother Ernestine recalled an event in her youth in which visiting religious brothers knocked on their doors late on All Hallow's Eve to round up members of the community to go to the graveyard. Once there, the brothers admonished the men for pilfering timber from Crown land, and young women for indulging in sexual perversions involving bedposts. They were to seek the forgiveness of the saints and their ancestors. Ernestine thought the brothers were nuts, but she also found these religious rituals frightening. Middle-aged people recalled countless humiliations in the convent school, as fingernails were inspected for dirt and hair scrutinized for lice. The nuns cut Rita's long red braids off, which she resents to this day. Younger adults, like Babette, were haunted by spectral figures, sinister objects, and feverish nightmares from which recovered memories were culled, suggestive of things vaguely understood that, nevertheless, haunt the present. These are the doubles found in gothic narratives that endlessly pursue culpability, producing a temporality from which there is no escape.

But in what follows, I turn to the recollections of teaching sisters, who speak of religious apparel and sacred objects in an entirely different register, alongside commonplace *things* that are embedded in gritty quotidian practice. Together, these objects relate to both the sacred and profane worlds of their daily lives, which are woven together seamlessly, and create a sense of remembered time. I argue that the distinction between the strange or illusive objects of the gothic and the tangible objects that have concrete points of reference in the world, as found in the sisters' narratives, create an alternative temporality. A distinct sense of time and place lend their accounts a greater sense of historicity, a rootedness in time and landscape, such as that found in the regional fiction of David Adams Richards. However, the sisters' stories belonged to an historical period quickly becoming unintelligible, or sensible, to many in the ethnographic present of the 1990s.

Indeed, this enormous cultural shift from a predominantly Roman Catholic to a secular worldview produces much of the tension that surfaces in the fiction of David Adams Richards. The *felt* friction in his novels between those who leave the region to pursue academic careers, and the misunderstood devotees and innocents who embrace a Roman Catholic worldview, becomes intelligible within this historical context. In my view, it is no accident that David Adams Richards' realist fiction abounds with maligned and even persecuted religious figures, strangely reversing and mirroring that found in the gothic. For instance, in *The Lost Highway* (2007), the simple faith of Amy, a young girl who finds comfort in the scriptures, is contrasted with the desolate floundering of Alex, who left the priesthood under mysterious circumstances, to "wander the world" (2), and later was ousted from university, where he was pursuing his doctorate in Aristotelian ethics: "All had floundered" (166). Alex returns home to the Miramichi to teach a course on Aristotelian ethics at a community college, where the promises of higher education are rewarded with only precarious employment and bafflement on the part of Alex's family and friends. Alex blames his great-uncle James for his unhappiness, and his evolving resentments and spite fuel the very ordinary tragedy that unfolds, following Alex's determination to prevent his Uncle James from cashing in a lottery ticket. The two moral universes that collide in this novel reiterate the very provincial history that is explored here ethnographically.

## The Filles de Jésus Remember Their Time in the Settlement

As I pulled up to the mother house of the Filles de Jésus in Moncton, I could not help but be impressed by the large brick convent, and the grounds which occupied an entire city block. I rang the bell, and a sister opened the front entrance for me and led me to an utterly spotless sitting room, which was comfortable, but had a decidedly institutional feel to it. I tried to imagine living my life in such a sterile place. At one time the convent had clearly housed a large and active community, but by the 1990s numbers had dwindled to a small community of retired sisters. I had written to the congregation asking to meet with those who had taught at the settlement convent school. Two of the sisters I interviewed were original founders of the school, and before leaving I would be taken to an upper floor – that had been turned into a hospital ward – to meet the woman who had been the Mother Superior at that time. She was frail and suffered from advanced stages of dementia. The other sisters spoke lovingly to her, explaining that I had come to ask them about the convent school in the settlement. A beatific smile spread across her face, and the other sisters clasped her hands. Together they sang "Jingle Bells" for her. The warmth the sisters effused soon melted the institutional chill I had initially felt.

We met first as a group that included the four sisters I would interview. There was some initial querying about my project. I was asked if I knew a particular person of whom they were clearly wary. I did not, but learned later that such a person had approached the police with accusations of abuse in the past. The sisters were being cautious. Once it was determined my questions were strictly concerned with making sense of their past, the sisters were extremely engaging and spoke openly about their memories of life up north at the convent school in the small settlement. On the first day, I conducted two lengthy interviews. The first was with two of the three founders, Sisters Ruth and Hélène (both in their eighties); later, we were joined by Sister Anne (in her seventies), who worked at the school during the time of secularization. Then, on the following morning, I spoke alone with Sister Ruth. Over the years she taught in many of the convent schools in the region. I also spent a few hours with an elderly sister who worked as archivist for the order, who was a proud Acadian nationalist, and the only one to couch her responses in a form of religious prose that felt arcane.[13]

As they explained, late in the summer of 1944, three Roman Catholic Sisters, members of the congregation of the Filles de Jésus, journeyed to the small settlement that lay deep within the woods on the fringe of Crown lands. The local parish priest noted that few of his parishioners could read or write, so the sisters went to this particular settlement at his bidding. The priest had already tried, but failed, to find lay teachers willing to work there. Lay teachers told him they were afraid of the people who lived there. According to Sister Ruth: "They had such a bad reputation; nobody wanted to go there." When the sisters arrived in the settlement, the convent was not quite finished. So, Father (the parish priest) gave them the upper floor of the rectory for their own needs, and they taught in the church basement, around the furnace, for the first several weeks. When they opened the doors of the new school, over 150 children, all entering Grade 1, appeared. Sister Ruth explained, "So, we allowed them to begin school at age seven and they could come after that for as long as they cared to. With such numbers, even the cook (Sister Hélène) had to become a teacher and we hired a lay teacher too." According to the sisters, the poverty was obvious, "When we came in '44 there were only shacks; clean, but it was poverty." Sister Ruth was certainly no stranger to poverty, as she was born and grew up on the Acadian Coast. As she said, "Poverty was nothing new. Everybody was poor."

Still, the poverty she experienced in the isolated settlement felt different. In the small Acadian villages in which she had previously worked, people traditionally combined farming, fishing, and work in the woods for their livelihood.[14] The Acadian clergy not only built churches, but they also helped to establish schools and hospitals. These institutions fostered a sense of Acadian identity and community. But in the settlement, which had been established in the 1860s for landless poor when the timber industry collapsed, there was just grinding poverty. The settlers were of Acadian, French-Canadian, Irish, Scottish, and Mi'kmaq ancestry and belonged to the drifting unemployed who had become a constant drain on the small towns that provided them relief. So, the province sold them land for homesteading. However, the land was unsuitable for agriculture and the settlers lacked investment capital, and so the lumberjacks and their families remained dependent on scarce wages from work in the woods (Parenteau 1994a, 1994b).

The teaching sisters quickly realized it would be pointless to ask the local school trustee to go door to door to collect a school tax none could afford, even if they were willing to pay. Sister Ruth continued:

> So, we taught for nothing because they were too poor to pay us. The sisters from the convent (in the nearby mill town) sent us our clothing and food. We used money from our congregation to build the school and provide for our needs. We are not rich, but because we are a religious order, we could borrow money. We felt that in time we would be able to collect the school tax from the parishioners. We had already established convents in places throughout New Brunswick and Nova Scotia, so we pooled our resources.

Here, "so" punctuates the oral history narrative in a way that is suggestive of responsiveness to a situation; an ethics of care is immediately established as the governing principle of actions taken by the sisters in the convent school. An awareness of the settlers' poverty and concern for their welfare governs decision-making and sacrifices on their part. Also, we get a brief glimpse of the organizational reach of the Filles de Jésus in the region and their commitment to building self-sustaining Roman Catholic rural communities based on the principles of Roman Catholic subsidiarity, which meshed seamlessly with powerful ultramontane beliefs that had long sustained the traditional Acadian community in the Maritimes. Note the hopeful assumption that "in time" the parishioners would be able to contribute to maintaining the convent school.

Apparently, the presence of the sisters in the settlement had an immediate and positive effect on the moral comportment of the children. For one night, about a month after they had first arrived, the convent doorbell rang. Sister Ruth giggled as she recalled their fright:

> And we were wondering, who could this be? At the time we were afraid, as it was already after dark. Sister Superior came to get me; so, she felt I had more experience. Well, she said, "Will you come with me?" So, together we went to answer the door and it was a travelling salesman! He said, "Ladies, I want to congratulate you." And we were wondering, "Why?" At the time it was after ten o'clock, or at least nine-thirty, at night.

He said, "I used to be so afraid coming here because you never knew if someone would throw a rock as you passed by. But tonight, as I passed along the road, boys were tipping their caps and saying, "Goodnight, sir.' "Everybody was saying, "Hi sir." There is such a change." So.

*So*, Sister Ruth joins a frightened Mother Superior, because she entered the congregation later in life and has some experience of the wider world, beyond the convent doors. In this tiny passage we get an inkling of the fear and vulnerability the young sisters must have felt in those first few days in the settlement. We see them as young women religious, not as formidable nuns. *So*, as in "there you go," or "what do you make of that?" A concluding *so*, suggesting that the meaning of this story is self-evident. "But," Sister Ruth hastens to add, "the people were good. I think they behaved that way before we went there because they knew others scorned them and laughed at them. They thought they were good for nothing and … Ah well – one might as well act that way if that is what people think." It was obvious, when speaking to the sisters so many years later, that they looked back at their time in the settlement with great fondness. After all, they were recalling the adventures of their youth and they had, as young women religious, overcome their fears to accomplish small miracles. But clearly the times had been very tough, which they conveyed through reminiscing about various objects, objects they understood viscerally, objects that recalled a sensate world. They could not afford wax for their floors, so they gathered the stubs of leftover church candles, which they mixed with kerosene to make polish. When they found the children were unwilling to remove their boots at the door, for shame of others seeing their threadbare socks, or lack thereof, they fashioned slippers out of bits of felt, which the children could slip over their boots. All day long the children scooted across the floors, polishing them until they sparkled. The sisters chuckled as they recalled the children shaking the sand and dust from the felt skates at the end of the school day, before returning them to the wooden box that stood by the front door. Their recollections evoked certain smells, like kerosene and candle wax, or the feel of grit embedded in thick felt. I could easily imagine the gleeful pleasure of gliding across waxed floors or choking on air filled with chalk dust near the box for the felt skates. The stuff of daily life animated their stories.

It was men and women who were lucky enough to attend the old secular school, more often closed than not, for a couple of months in their lifetime, who sent their children to the convent school in droves, children who wore no socks in their rubber gumboots. And these families found ways to support the work of the sisters, even if they lacked means to pay a school tax. Some brought them firewood, which the boys would help Sister Hélène stack at recess. Others brought them vegetables from their small kitchen gardens, or berries and game from the woods, fish from the rivers, scallops, clams, and mussels from the mudflats on the coast. Sister Hélène recalled how touched she was when a small boy gave her an apple chosen especially for her. These humble gifts and provisions enabled the sisters to carry out their work in the community.

It was the extreme poverty of the Great Depression that created an economy in which goods and labour were primarily concerned with their use value and demarcating the ties that bind (Miller 2001; Spyer 1998). The lumberjacks' sole dependence on work in the woods had made them so vulnerable to the ebbs and flows of capitalist markets, that it was their exclusion from work during the Depression years, rather than their actual exploitation, that led to the emergence of forms of reciprocal exchange that are peripheral to capitalist spheres of exchange. Of course, such survival strategies on the part of the poor are well documented (Stack 1974). What I want to highlight here is how perfectly such livelihood practices fit within a moral economy traditionally valued and supported by the Acadian Roman Catholic clergy in New Brunswick (Thériault 1982: 298).

This moral economy, as I have already noted, combined traditional Acadian values rooted in agrarian practices and religious principles of mutual aid and community. The idea of subsidiarity, or mutual aid sustained by corporate communities (religious and otherwise) that could mediate the soul-destroying poles of the grasping individual and liberal state, came to dominate Catholic social philosophy throughout the Depression and war years.[15] It received its first explicit papal formulation in Pius XI's *Quadragesimo anno* in 1931 (Chaplin 1993: 175). The sisters who went to work in this simple convent school in the 1940s were committed to the ideals of mutual aid and the survival of the Acadian community, and so they adapted the school's curriculum to meet the needs of illiterate children who were predominantly Roman Catholics of mostly Acadian and Irish mixed heritage. The children communicated in a lilting French-English patois inflected with Irish idioms, and they were quick to respond to instruction that was given in both English and French. Daily, the sisters worked to provide the children with a very particular Acadian Roman Catholic *formation*, which valued working the land and a simple faith in God. As such, the labours of the sisters were recognized and richly rewarded, for they found the children hard-working and industrious. It appears that the Depression years had been perfect for "creating the conditions within which obedient wills are created" (Asad 1993: 125), as evidenced in the peddler's observations, and recalled by sister Ruth:

> So, by the end of the first year some of our pupils were ready to enter Grade 4. The majority were in Grades 2 and 3, but the truly exceptional students were already in Grade 4. So, the next year I took that class and worked very hard with them. They were in Grade 6 by the end of the year! By the end of our third year there, some of my brightest pupils [and she lists them by name] had picked up some work in Grade 8. They were really very, very bright. At the end of the three years, we sent them to college, in Bathurst and Chatham. They went on to St. Xavier and St. Thomas Universities. One became a civil engineer, another a banker in Montreal.

*So*, again signalling a responsiveness to the situation at hand; this time adapting the curriculum and allowing students to skip grades to achieve their full potential. Sister Ruth stayed at the school for four years before taking an appointment up the coast at the Eel River Indian Day School.[16] She assured me that the sister who took her place in the settlement school continued her work, ordering a correspondence course from the Fredericton Normal School, which enabled the children to complete Grade 10. When Sister Ruth returned to the settlement two years later, many of her previous students were ready to leave school. The brightest male students did not follow their fathers into the woods. A few girls even briefly entered the congregation of the Filles de Jésus, although they left the order before taking vows. The exceptional students left the settlement, although many of them kept in touch with the sisters who had taught them. Still, even in this recollection of those first hopeful years in the settlement, one can see already that success led to departure from a rural life, and not its continuity. The ideal of a self-sustaining Roman Catholic and rural Acadian community was already faltering as the students left to study elsewhere and to work in urban areas. As I listened to these accounts of goodwill between the Roman Catholic sisters and parishioners who worked to build the convent school in the 1940s, I could not help but wonder what had happened to leave such a different impression of the past in the memories of the children who attended the school in the 1950s and 1960s.

## The 1950s: Money for Beer and a Teacher's Strike

The province of New Brunswick must have been relieved when the Filles de Jésus agreed to build schools in the poorest region of the province during the Depression and war years, despite a foundational political commitment to secular institutions of education. It was not the first time such an improbable alliance between secular and religious institutions would be created out of economic collapse. Nor would it be the last.[17] And in the early years, the efforts of the sisters seem to have been genuinely appreciated in the settlement. Perhaps it had all been too good to be true and simply could not last. Or maybe the recollections of the sisters had mellowed over time. But all the sisters marked a change for the worse in terms of their relationship with families in the settlement in the years that followed.

As the war came to a close, men returned to the woods to work. Needless to say, most students are not exceptional, and many of the young boys in the settlement left school early to join their fathers and grandfathers in the lumber camps. In 1945, the federal government introduced a universal family allowance tied to compulsory education for children under the age of sixteen: "The long-term financial and social implications for French New Brunswickers, with their tradition-ally larger families, were obvious. For the first time, many wives could look forward to monthly cheques to supplement the often low cash returns the men earned from long hours in the woods or out on the cold waters of the Gulf" (Wilbur 1989: 171).[18] In the same year, a pro-vincial minimum wage was introduced (C. Miller 1993: 315). Still, in the 1950s, wages for lumberjacks in New Brunswick remained among the lowest in the country.[19] André Doucette, minister of industry and reconstruction at that time, revealed companies "were taking advan-tage of a period of readjustment to cut pulp prices to a level … much too low to provide decent wages to producers" (Wilbur 1989: 175). Shockingly, by 1950, "the Liberal member for Restigouche, Louis Label charged that the lumber companies had responded to the new provincial minimum wage by cutting wages 25 to 50 percent" (Wilbur 1989: 176). Conditions on the North Shore remained grim. Still, in the eyes of the sisters, the settlers were no longer destitute and should begin to contribute something toward the school tax. After all, as Sis-ter Anne pointed out, "the men had money for beer when they came home from the woods."

Meanwhile, the sisters were having a very difficult time attracting lay teachers to work in the school, who (unlike the women religious) were unwilling to work for nothing. So, the sisters dipped into their own funds, divvying up the small stipend they received from the province (for use of the convent) to pay the wages of the lay teachers they hired. They were, quite literally, taking the food from their own table to keep the school running. According to Sister Anne, it could not go on like this, and so she approached the Sister Superior with an idea. She proposed that they shut the school down and go on strike:

So, we had to have lay teachers. Then, we weren't paid a wage by the province. It was the school trustee who had to go from door to door to collect taxes, and we were paid with that. I had two teachers from (a nearby mill town), two girls who had their Grade 10, I suppose. The classes were overcrowded, and we had to have those girls. So, they started working in the school in September: No pay. October: No pay; November: No pay. So, we said to (the local school trustees): "You're not starving us." After another month with no pay, I told them [the trustees] it was the Mother Superior who had to provide us with food and clothing. Well, not very much clothing, because at the time we still wore the religious habit. I remember if she (the Mother Superior) got five or ten dollars from the school board, well, it was a celebration.

No, I'm not kidding you.

I told her [the Mother Superior] we were going to lose those teachers, and what were we going to do then? Have students in those classes stay at home? "Well," she said, "we will have to do something." So, I said, "I have one idea, if you'll let me do it." She was my Superior. I was the principal of the school, but she was my Superior. I told her, "I think we should close the school." At that time, we didn't go on strike. Eh? But in the end, the three of us must strike, funnily enough!

Eventually, the three teaching sisters at the small convent school organized a strike to protest the community members' ongoing refusal to pay the provincial school tax, upon which their wages, and those of the lay teachers they hired to help, depended. Sister Anne describes the outcome:

So, I rang the bell and waited for them [the students] to line up at the door. They were fairly obedient. You know? When I rang the bell, they would quietly take their places in line, not a word. And they [the students from the settlement] were the easiest ones to listen [were attentive listeners] always interested in everything. We used to give them behaviour lessons, and they would put what they learned to practice immediately. Oh, it was marvellous. The inspector of schools was always so impressed. He would sit in my class for the whole morning, he enjoyed them so. They were really special students.

Anyways, I had to tell them, that morning, that they couldn't come in. I explained that we couldn't live on air alone. We had teachers there threatening to leave us because they had not been paid in three months. They were to go home and tell their parents we simply had to be paid. We couldn't live like that. Oh my gosh, I could cry now remembering it.

And she did. Tears welled up in her eyes and she placed her hand over her mouth until she gained control. *So,* as in students so bright, so exceptional, so impressive; *So,* the word tumbling out one-after-the-other to explain the reasons for taking an otherwise abhorrent action. And *eh?* And *you know?* Little phrases beseeching understanding, asking me if I understood their predicament.

> The big ones – the older children – started to cry. I felt so badly, but my mind was made up. I said, we all needed at least some money. I was supposed to be paid a hundred dollars a month, and I was the principal of the school. It was hard work. When we were not paid, it was not right, because we had the upkeep of that big house [convent plus school]. We had to heat it, and clean it, and care for it all by ourselves. We certainly could not afford to hire a janitor; we couldn't even support ourselves.
>
> Anyways, the second day, the school trustee came back – I think he was on the road for three days – I'm not so sure now. But, I said, while they are out of school it is better that he goes to all the houses – it took him three days to go to all the houses. And what he collected was enough to pay the girls [lay teachers], and a few of us got a hundred dollars [funds that would be given to the religious community]. But we weren't all paid. There was a huge sum of money that we never even tried to collect, because we knew it was impossible. But those men, people, were working in the woods, were cutting wood. They'd come home over the weekend – and they had a good pay – they'd drink, they'd say, "It's our right!" They were celebrating! We were not celebrating. We had hardly enough to live on. So.

*So,* spoken with such finality, as in "that's the way it was," or "there you go," or "what else could we do, under the circumstances?" I try to imagine the trustees going door to door to urge their desperately poor neighbours to pay school taxes. Were they reminded that the Mother's Allowance could be withheld if their children were not in school? Pure conjecture on my part, as I consider the difficulties the lumberjacks must have faced in coming up with the funds required to support the school. But I am not without sympathy for the young teachers and women religious who went unpaid month after month, another instance of the ways in which the labour of women is devalued,[20] the ways in which appeals to nurturing and caring for children can be turned against women, so much so that forty years after the events described, Sister Anne is brought to tears as she recalls children weeping on the steps of the school.

This account, by a sister who first went to work in the settlement in the 1950s, took me completely by surprise. It was as if I had finally stumbled across working-class and feminist consciousness, but in an unlikely place. Of course, going on strike to protest the inability of miserably poor lumberjacks to pay a school tax is not the same as striking against the owners of production, the large pulp and paper companies that failed to provide lumberjacks with a living wage. The women religious were not demanding that the province tax the large forest companies to support schools and other social services. From our present vantage point it seems horribly misdirected. But it gives some sense of how the sisters *themselves* were beginning to value their own labour *differently*. More importantly, it gives us a sense of a traditional religious value system under tremendous strain, both from within and without (MacDonald 2003a, 2003b; Ebaugh 1993; Smyth 1999, 2007; Wittberg 1994). For the forms of social solidarity and community rooted in a rural economy and a Roman Catholic tradition of subsidiarity were fundamentally at odds with the political and economic realities facing working-class rural workers in New Brunswick at that time. In rural New Brunswick, tax cuts continued to favour the large forestry companies, and not the rural working poor. And while the new federal Family Allowance was especially beneficial for the larger Roman Catholic families of the North Shore, even that became a cause for resentment in the Protestant South (Levine 2020: 171). Caroline Levine notes, "Structures are precisely not emergent – they are what endures over long stretches without much change" (2020: 429), and we can see that the political economy that favoured the large forest interests endured. Nevertheless, one can detect in the sister's narrative an emergent sensibility in which zones of friction are exposed, even if it falls short of imagining new economic arrangements and social relations.

The history of small convent schools in New Brunswick belies the idea that secular times must follow religious times, for in the early twentieth century religious schools were created out of the failures of the secular school system in much of New Brunswick. However, it is also clear that the forms of sociality fostered in those early days in the settlement school were as much dependent on harsh economic realities as on a desire to create an ultramontane Roman Catholic moral order. A mere decade after building the convent school in the settlement, the sisters' re-evaluation of the worth of their own labour, and that of the young women lay teachers they employed, belongs to a new social register, in which women seek proper remuneration for their work in a new postwar economy. The very meaning of *belonging* is actually altered so that the rights to fair pay for the work of women can be expressed. But, as is so often the case, emergent forms of consciousness, as Raymond Williams (1977) explained, can be messy, caught up in older and ongoing value systems and structural formations that inform human action.[21]

According to the women religious, when the men returned to work, they did not find money to support the work of the sisters, but they did have money to purchase beer. The sisters' moral outrage finds its object: Beer, "the demon drink," the destroyer of family and community.

## Object Lessons

According to the sisters, the very men who could not pay the school tax, could, apparently, find money for beer. "They felt it was their right," exclaims Sister Anne. Certainly, the homosociality of life fostered in the lumber camps – where men bunked together in close quarters for extended lengths of time – stands in sharp contrast to the community ethos espoused by the religious sisters, who *also* lived together in close quarters. Just as my old railroad buddies sought relief from the monotony of hard physical labour when they had a few days off, many of the men in the lumber camps returned to the settlement seeking a good time, ready to kick up their heels. Sister Anne felt such behaviour was more than irresponsible; it was disrespectful of the efforts and sacrifices the sisters were making for the community. And so, we have two entirely different, but parallel, communities, in which homosociality produced an entirely oppositional ethos.

In 1954, the sisters staged a tableau for Marian celebrations. Other years they organized dramas and musicals, which attracted the attention of people from other parts of the North Shore, people now willing to drive to the settlement they had previously avoided, to attend what had become regular fundraising events for the school. Every year they would rehearse the children's choir for months in preparation for the provincial musical festival:

> We took part in the music festivals. That was all a part of wanting to take the children out to meet other children and see other places. I remember the first time, the first time we went to the festival. We went early to practise a dance, and when we got there all the others had costumes, you know? So, I thought, we could do that with crepe paper. So, we had lots of crepe paper, really. So, the next time we told the children to bring a slip, or undershirt, or something, so that we could sew the crepe paper on. We'd start at the bottom and just turn them around, tacking on the paper. And it made a nice costume. They were red. It must have been for Christmas.
>
> For the music festival, we prepared dances and choral speeches. Sister Antoinette conducted the choirs. She had four. And I had the rhythmic dance classes. That was way back in '56–57. I think we loaded the children

into cars. There were several people who had cars by then. Anyways, we got there. I don't know how, but we got there.

Sister Hélène fondly recalled the choir mistress:

> I was very fond of her, but she used to come into our classes and say, "Sister, keep on teaching. I'm going to practise those children at the back of the classroom." Those children in Grade 2, now, do you think they wanted to listen to me! Now, I would try anything to avoid that. She would stay an hour and sometimes more. And never ask beforehand. She'd just come: "I want to practise those children!"

The enthusiasm and energy with which the sisters tackled their projects is only too evident. But one cannot help but wonder how it felt as a small child to attend the provincial music festival in a crepe paper costume when the children from other parts of the province wore proper uniforms. If the crepe paper got wet at the water fountain, it would wither and bleed droplets of blood-red ink. Could anything be more humiliating? As Webb Keane notes, material objects are vulnerable to wear and tear, and it is the condition of an object that affects its capacity to signify (2001: 85). And *so*, again, the sisters struggle to respond to circumstances by using the *things* they have at hand, but this time to outfit students in costumes as they travel beyond the community to the provincial music festival. Within such a context, one's deictic perspective, as either the perceiver or the wearer of such a costume, could fundamentally alter one's memories of those colourful costumes. As Carolyn Steedman so poignantly illustrates, clothing is the perfect primer for lessons on class relations. "Changes in the market place, the growth of real income and the proliferation of consumer goods that marked the 1950s, were used by [her] mother to measure out her discontent: there existed a newly expanding and richly endowed material world from which she was denied a place" (1986: 36). Even in the backwoods of New Brunswick, this burgeoning marketplace was made evident through the distribution of the Eaton's and Sears' catalogues. The Sears Canada Wish Book (1953–2016) was especially significant for children, who spent hours poring over the pages of ads for toys and clothing aimed directly at them. While the sisters recalled a transformation in the political and economic fortunes of the province that led to better conditions in terms of funding for schools, wages, and welfare programs, none of the women I interviewed, who had been their students in the 1950–60s, framed their recollections of the period in such terms. Instead, they spoke of frustrated desires. Rita, Babette's mother, recalls:

> I was always stubborn. They say that my grandfather was that stubborn. So, I don't know, maybe I got it there, or, if it was just bred into me because they left me mostly on my own. I always did what I wanted and always got what I wanted, one way or another. The first time I didn't get what I wanted, I was married and had a baby, and I was pregnant with the second one, and I cried. I hid and I cried. I don't know what I wanted, but I remember the feeling. No, it was just some little thing, I think it was a new dress or something I wanted for Christmas. I showed it to my husband in the catalogue. I was only fourteen and I thought he would buy it for me. He sort of babied me, you know, and let me pretty well do what I wanted, which was wrong I suppose. But then I wouldn't have taken an order either. Anyways, I remember he said no. I remember that, and I remember the feeling: I felt my heart, in here, as if it was that full, that I was going to choke, and the feeling that I had because I couldn't get what I wanted. And remember, that I was married and had a baby of my own, and that was the first time, you know, that I remember. Because I had always got what I wanted.

Stylish Rita, always dressed impeccably, worked as a seamstress in the 1990s and could alter second-hand clothes to fit her petite frame perfectly. She knew the value of fine fabrics that draped properly and had turned her love of clothing into a marketable skill. But Rita's path out of dire poverty was far from smooth. Rita left school when she became pregnant at the age of thirteen. She credits her absolute stubbornness for her very survival. In the passage that follows, some of the trauma that she experienced as a young woman – a mere girl really – is revealed, and we can also appreciate how her thwarted desires become attached to, and expressed through, *things*. As Steedman notes, when writing about her own mother's life, "the things ... remain a problem" (1986: 34). This is especially so for a woman like Rita, who not only possesses a keen awareness of how others appear; but recognizes that she too is being observed. Appearing at the music festival in a crunchy red crepe-paper dress as a small girl would have been deeply humiliating, if not traumatizing, for Rita.

> Like me, my first child was spoiled. He thought that he was going to do what he wanted when he wanted. One day I was outside, and I was washing out dirty diapers. And I had two of them on diapers. And my son said, "I want ten cents to get an ice cream." I said, "Wait till Mommy's

finished." Because that meant taking my hands out of the diapers, which I hated doing anyways, going in and washing them two or three times to get the smell and everything off them, giving him the ten cents and then going back and putting my hands back in it. And you know, once my hands were in it, I wanted to finish. But he yelled, "I want it now!" And I heard everything coming down in the house. So, I went in and here he was, naked as a Jay bird. He had chairs all knocked down in the house and was in the process of knocking down the table. I went out and I broke myself a switch and walked back in. "You want to dance? Here, dance with this." And I come at him with a switch. Never, ever, ever took another fit. He was five years old. Never took another one.

He conned me, and … you know? He had that ability. He'd say, "My God Mom, you look tired. I'll do the dishes for you." I'd say, "Ah, he's looking for something." But he found a way to get around everybody. And he was the same [as me]. I mean, he died at fifteen years old and I don't think that child could say at one time, "There is something I wanted, and I didn't get it." He had a Ski-Doo to drive in the winter, and a bicycle. The only jeans he liked were GWGs and he always had … I think I gave away thirteen pair when he was killed. He played hockey, he had the best skates, he had all the hockey equipment he wanted. He had drums, he had a banjo, he had an electric guitar, he had an amplifier. You name it, he had it. He had it all. Anything he wanted, he had. He had the ability to … And I mean, we weren't rich, by any means.

Indeed, they were anything but rich. It is hard to square this litany of consumption with the hard realities of Rita's life, captured in the vivid description of her hands in an outdoor washtub. Filling the tub would have involved carrying pails from a stream to be heated on a wood stove. The drudgery of her young life is expressed in the revulsion she feels for the stench of dirty diapers that lingers on her hands. Still, in this passage, Rita comforts herself by recalling all the *things* she gave her child, the *things* that represented love, belonging, respectability. This is a profound expression of grief for the loss of her firstborn son, who died at the age of fifteen late one night when a carload of drunken teenagers drove into an oncoming truck carrying a load of logs. Rita's sense of being a good and caring mother is keenly linked to her ability to provide the *things* she so often was forced to do without. But the stench of soiled diapers and the switch she cuts continue to haunt her.

It was Christmas Eve – my second son was a baby. He had been born [in] November. We had a terrible winter of snow that year. I didn't have a can of milk, I had nothing. I mean nothing. He [her husband] came out of the woods. I can see him yet. He got out of the car with a case of beer, and he come into the house and he had two dollars. He had been in the woods for I don't know how long, and they'd got paid at Christmas. He had got five dollars. That was his pay: Well, I mean they talked about it. He had it thrown in his face at elections. "Your wife and kids were starving while you were laying under the trees sleeping." You know?

Her husband came out of the woods and spent his paltry wages on beer: Rita's sense of despair and outrage finds the same object as that of the Filles de Jésus. She is acutely aware of what others think of her feckless husband and her resentments are encapsulated in the two-four of beer he carries under his arm. *"You know?"* Rita asks. As did the sisters at the convent, Rita is asking if I can understand the dire circumstances that lead to subsequent actions signalled by the tiny conjunction *so*.

So, for the first time I went to the welfare. Christmas Eve. Mamon came with me. 1961. Welfare had just come out. And it was a man there in the rule. And we went in his house and we sat in the kitchen and Mamon told him. I mean me, being sixteen, and I sat there. You know? And so, Mamon told him, "You know she's got nothing, and she just had a newborn baby. She has one that is eighteen months old and a newborn of a month old. And she has absolutely nothing. So, she needs something." And he said, "Ah wait there a minute. It's Christmas Eve, but I'm not … I need to do some research and get some information. I just don't give out orders like that." Mamon told him I wanted an order for groceries because we had nothing. So, anyways, the man's wife – not a word – she got up, she went upstairs and came down with two suitcases. She said, "I'm leaving." He said, "You're what?" She said, "You there! It's Christmas Eve!" She said, "There's a baby there with two babies and you have the face to say you have to do information?" She said, "Look at them!" You know? I was near to tears. She said, "You're not fit for anybody to stay with. I'm leaving." He pulled out a paper and he wrote an order for groceries for seventy-five dollars.

There is so much going on in this passage, as the Christmas story momentarily bursts upon the scene. Mamon (Ernestine) escorts Rita to the home of the welfare officer, just as once she might have gone to the door of the convent or the manse seeking charity. There, lo and behold, a kind wife compels a bureaucrat to forgo the gathering of information, temporarily reaffirming a Roman Catholic moral order. The newness and oddness of bureaucratic structures to the rural community is made evident in this passage, as there can be no faceless bureaucrat in a place where familiarity governs rural life. They sit not in an office, but at the kitchen table. Still, Rita recognizes fully where power rests, as she notes, "And it was a man there in the rule,",, which is a bit like announcing "It was in the time of King Herod." Rita, who is learning the full extent of patriarchy, expresses grudging admiration for this wife who challenges the "man in the rule," while also abhorring the ways in which her own plight is made so glaringly obvious. Again, Rita is the child/woman fully recognizing that she is under observation: "Look at them!" she recalls the wife saying. The depth of Rita's humiliation is excruciating, and she is "near to tears." She continues:

> So, that was the first time then. And I mean, that was the first time ever, in my life ... I called it begging. I found it awful hard. Like often, then – after that, I mean – I've often had to go through times. Because, as I said, my husband made big money when he worked. He could go and get a job anywhere. But he was a job jumper. He'd work someplace two months and then he'd leave. Three months, and he'd leave. The woods? Forget it.

Steedman (1986) draws our attention to the place of frustrated desires in the lives of working-class people, desires which can become attached to objects that hover out of reach and remain unattainable. She also highlights the contradictory politics that developed in England among some of the chronically disadvantaged, who came to resent the communitarian values embedded in working-class struggles, framed in largely patriarchal terms, in which women were admired for being long-suffering moms making sacrifices for their families. Rita not only rejected the communitarian religious ethos espoused by the Acadian Roman Catholic Church, but she also rejected the family values they espoused, values explored in the following object lesson recalled by Sister Ruth, having to do with religiosity, shame, and honour, but also protection and personal integrity.

The curriculum at the convent school included lessons in religious instruction. Sister Ruth explained:

> We had religious classes and religious retreats, which people would follow very closely. I was teaching a catechism lesson, and I was talking about marriage. And I asked the girls, "Do you know why a girl puts on the veil and a white dress?" And they said, "Isn't it because she is getting married?" And I said, "Well, yes and no." I said, "The white is a sign of purity, and this is why a girl can wear a white dress and put on the veil." And this girl, she became serious. So, after school, she came to me and she said, "Mother can I speak with you?" "Yes," I said, "you're worried, I can see." I never thought it was because of my catechism class.

She said, "You know I'm going with a boyfriend, and he gave me a ring, and this is my engagement ring." She had a diamond. I doubt it was an expensive diamond, but she had a diamond. And she said, "Because he gave me this diamond, now he wants the sex." And she said, "You told us now, that when we get married, that white is a sign of purity, chastity, that we should keep away from it, and have no sexual intercourse before we get married." She said, "Well, what must I do?" I said, "Well it's up to you, the two of you, it's your decision." She said, "I'm not like that, and I want to get married and be able to wear my white veil and white dress." I said, "Speak to your boyfriend and tell him what you want, and what you think." I said, "What happened before you learned this, now forget it, you didn't know." So, she said, "Okay."

So, she came later and told me what happened. And she said to him, "Now, when I get married, I want to be able to wear the white dress and veil." And she said, "That's for marriage, after we're married." So … she said, "What's going to happen?" Well, he took the ring back and she broke it off.

As sisters, we were so naïve. We didn't really know about such things. I had many girls who were forced, or obliged, to get married. And after a few years they were separated. And the boys didn't respect them. If you didn't get that before you got married, you can't get it later. So, he tried again to force her to have relations and she returned the ring and broke it off. She must have been fifteen or sixteen years at the time.

While some might find such moral instruction pious in the extreme, I note Sister Ruth's non-judgmental attitude and concern for this young girl. The wedding dress and veil are not here presented as representations of women's oppression, but rather articles of clothing invested with symbolic potency. The desire to wear the white wedding dress and veil gave the young girl the strength to say "no" to unwanted sexual advances, just as the religious habit had instilled strength in the women religious. In other words, within this context, the wedding dress (and the habit) become signs of empowerment, in this instance giving the girl some control over her future, the very control Rita had lacked. Sister Ruth told me this person wrote to her several years later to tell her she was getting married to the same young man, who, she claimed, "never touched me after that, so I will be able to wear my white dress and veil." The young girl achieved some autonomy and was able to complete her schooling. She gained respectability, as it was understood at the time. Sister Ruth believed that their marriage was stronger because it had a sound moral foundation. The tragedy, according to Sister Ruth, is that few of the girl's peers enjoyed the same, as most left school early when they became pregnant, and many of them faced difficult lives, with few prospects to live otherwise.

What strikes me is how both the Filles de Jésus and Rita must manoeuvre within the patriarchal structures that dominate their lives: at moments resisting, and then again capitulating, all the while strategically seeking a measure of control over their lives. The Filles de Jésus hold a strike to demand wages for women teachers, while giving religious lessons in which they uphold patriarchal family values, even in a place where men are often absent and lack the means to support their families. Rita rejects the communitarian ethos and moral instruction of the Roman Catholic Church, and then repeatedly attaches herself to men who might deliver her from poverty and the burdens of motherhood, the consequence of which was becoming pregnant at thirteen and marrying a man almost twice her age. When her own daughters reached puberty, she took them to a clinic to be put on the pill, a form of contraception that did not become available until 1965, but in Rita's view offered a degree of autonomy that a religious article of clothing – a white wedding dress and veil – could not achieve. While claiming she "wouldn't take an order from anyone," she often, as she says, "had to beg." *So,* the red crepe costume and the wedding dress, the soiled diapers and the GWG jeans, taken together articulate the material and moral conditions of life in the settlement in the 1950s and 960s. And the beer the men consume becomes a rough simulacrum of male working-class desires in nowhere places, desires that threaten the moral order of family and community. These gendered desires are produced in a community where men are often absent, labouring in lumber camps for insufficient wages, and where women are left to care for home and family, whether as mothers or as women religious.

## A Lament

The detailed descriptions of the daily toils of stacking wood, polishing floors, and fashioning felt slippers and crepe-paper dresses for schoolchildren lend veracity to the memories of the religious sisters. These were acts of quotidian piety, ritual performances intended to instil a particular work ethic, a sense of social responsibility and community ethos summed up in Father Henri's understanding of a proper *formation.* Meanwhile, the pathos that saturates Rita's memories of soiled diapers and her longing for a new dress conjure the drudgery of life in the settlement for a young mother married off to a feckless lumberjack as a child. Together, their memories capture life in this rural community during the 1950s and 1960s. They recall a time teetering on the edge of significant change, for both the lumberjacks and their wives, and for the women religious working in the convent school.

The restructuring of New Brunswick's faltering political and economic arrangements under the provincial leadership of Louis Robichaud (serving as premier 1960–70) coincided with the modernization of the Roman Catholic Church during the Second Vatican Council (1962–5). Both spelled the end of a pattern of life in the settlement that was dependent on work for men in lumber camps that left women alone for significant periods to care for home and family. Children attended a convent school built by the Filles de Jésus from the mid-1940s to the mid-1960s. As mechanization evolved in the timber trade over the following decades, the lumberjack was replaced by independent contractors with heavy equipment. Few men in the settlement had the capital to invest in such equipment, and so the men travelled farther afield seeking employment as labourers in other nowhere places. As for the sisters, they too left the community. After the Second Vatican Council, many women religious left life in convents to pursue higher education and vocations that opened to women of the working class for the first time. When the convent school was sold to the province and secularized, the people of the settlement chose English as the language of instruction going forward, which clergy interpreted as a rejection of both their Acadian identity and the Acadian Roman Catholic *formation* the clergy represented. It is, therefore, not surprising that the elderly sisters I interviewed, who remained women religious, lamented the passing of a way of life that they had committed themselves to as young women (Danylwycz 1999; MacDonald 2007).

It was not just Rita who recalled the changing fashions that marked this time of emergent possibilities and changing sensibilities. The sisters were equally attuned to changes in their religious habit. As Elizabeth Smyth notes, "In the years following the Second Vatican Council (1962–65), both the meaning of the vows and the features of religious life changed radically" (2007: 8), and the removal of the religious habit was its most visible manifestation. When I asked the sisters what it was like to remove the traditional religious habit, the clothing that figured so largely in the memories of people I knew in the settlement, they collectively burst into laughter. "My, what a change," exclaimed Sister Elaine. Sister Anna circled her face to indicate a wimple, explaining that, "First we took this part off. The habit came off in stages." Then she recalled that in the settlement, "Sister Antoinette, who was a little original, made an announcement that students should *not* come to the convent that afternoon, because *they were changing*." "Can't you hear her now?" she asked the other sisters. All broke into girlish giggles and before long were bent over with belly laughter, wiping tears from their eyes. It was utterly contagious, and I laughed as hard as they did, sensing the initial embarrassment, the exposure, and the self-consciousness that must have attended that simple act of removing an article of clothing.

Then again, a religious veil is not really a simple piece of clothing at all. When Patricia Wittberg (1994) interviewed one-time women religious, who left religious life in significant numbers after the Second Vatican Council, many claimed that the removal of the religious habit strongly influenced their decision. They not only lost the *thing* that distinguished them from others, but they also lost a sense of enclosure and containment (see also Lester 2005: 146–50). As Sister Anne explained:

> The headdress was changed. We used to have that thing. When I lost that, I lost everything, because I felt so comfortable with it. I was hiding in my chapel. No matter where I would go, I could laugh, and no one would see me. If I was crying, I could do that too. Nobody could see me. My face was way inside. It must have been between 1956 and 1958 that we took off the veil. But we took off the habits in 1968–9, a full year before the others.

This lament for an article of clothing lost is so compelling, for it is also a lament for a time that was quickly slipping away, when many young women along the Acadian Coast and North Shore of New Brunswick embraced a religious vocation (Danylwycz 1999; MacDonald 2007). Like the convent itself, the veil's very materiality provided the protection that enabled these young women to safely carry out their work in the settlement school. The very idea of hiding behind the veil, again, draws attention to ways in which women struggle with the burden of being watched, or observed, in ways that threaten their autonomy. Like Rita, Sister Anne was keenly aware of the gaze of others. But when I asked the sisters if the children had a reaction to the nun's change of clothing, they replied in unison, "No! We had the reaction!" And we ended our initial interview in gales of laughter.

The religious sisters who were asked to remove their habits at the time of the Second Vatican Council remember things very differently from the settlers who bore witness to that change. Similarly, the children who wore the various costumes and slippers that the Filles de Jésus refashioned from various bits and bobs do not share the sisters' fond memories of ingenuity and making do at the convent school. For them there is nothing but the memory of a shameful lack of proper, or fashionable, clothing. Thus, the significance of such objects depends partly on one's position. As a person who wore the religious habit, you might recall a sense of intimate enclosure and safety. As a child paraded about in a red crepe-paper costume, you might recall only discomfort and humiliation. As perceivers, one might recall the forbidding presence of a teaching sister, or a delightful performance involving innocent children in colourful costumes. The inherent properties of clothing are vulnerable, to wear and tear, to historical transformation, and to the dictates of fashion in both religious and secular aspects; and so, the objects capacity for bearing the lode of social meaning and affect is as immense as it is mutable (see Webb Keane 2001: 68–70).[22]

*So, Babette's grandmother tells me she has a lonely nature ...*

In the previous chapter, I focused attention on the work of material objects in articulating the memories of life in a small settlement from the 1940s through to the 1960s, in which the Filles de Jésus built a convent school for the families of poor lumberjacks. Radical historical transformations in terms of religious practice and the postwar economy were at play over the two decades in which the Filles de Jésus were present in the settlement, so that both the women religious who taught in the convent school and the people of the wider community came to value themselves, their labour, and *things*,[23] differently. The dense materiality of religious clothing makes it the perfect marker of a waning Acadian and Roman Catholic moral economy, which briefly flourished in a time of extreme economic deprivation. But the largely agrarian way of life that might support the ideal of a self-sustaining Acadian and Roman Catholic community was never really tenable in this settlement of lumberjacks and their families. The *things* explored in the previous chapter help to articulate the friction between two opposing moral economic visions. One was fostered by the Roman Catholic Church, which valued ideals of sacrifice and subsidiarity for community and family; the other flourished in the lumber camps, in which the evanescent freedoms of precarious wages were celebrated. Both upheld the patriarchal values of the postwar period, and young girls and wives were left isolated and abandoned in this middle-of-nowhere place, where little attention was given to their needs and desires.

The recollections of the elderly Filles de Jésus, and those of Rita, Babette's mother, are peppered with the conjunction *so*, which works to link, explain, and justify their responses to the events in their lives that form their life history narratives. Together, this careful tracking of time unfolding, and the vivid details of the quotidian objects that litter their accounts, lend a dense historical quality that is often found in realism, a form of representation in both the regional literature and artwork that lends a sense of opacity to the social and ecological environments in which people of the region live. But in Rita's life story, a haunting ensnarement clings to the stuff of her childhood. Such distilled moments, preserved in memory, invoke the magic realism of an Alex Colville or a Tom Forrestall painting, in which attention to detail falters on the edge of the surreal. The gothic remains, always, just below the surface of the realism found in these life stories, as in Maritime literature and art. Realism and the gothic produce the two temporalities found in the region, one charting the unfolding of history, the other circling back to entrap people of the region in cycles of attachment to a landscape that breeds melancholia. This filiation between genre and a local sensibility help to reinforce the two dominant temporalities at work in the oral accounts I collected, which permeate the regional milieu and create a strong sense of place.

So, in the next chapter, I turn to the narratives of two elderly women, both born in the early 1920s. In doing so, I want to highlight the brutal political and economic arrangements that shaped life in the settlement from its earliest years. The forest economy of New Brunswick greatly benefited from the large reserves of cheap and illiterate woodsmen found on homesteads created at the turn of the twentieth century. This is a creation story, if you will, in which a nowhere place is established close to a key resource, and a troubled attachment to the land takes root, producing what Babette's grandmother, Ernestine, calls her own "lonely nature."

# Chapter Four

# Landscapes of Memory and a Lonely Nature

As the winter of 1993 settled in, I ventured out to record the life histories of two elderly women who were born, went to school, helped their mothers, married, raised families, and grew old in the small, impoverished settlement that is my primary research site. Ernestine, Babette's grandmother, was one of the women, and the one with whom I had an ongoing relationship. The other was a woman I call Mrs. O'Leary, whose lilting speech was heavily inflected with French and difficult to understand. I leaned in to listen, as much by observing her fluttering hands and animated facial expressions as anything else. Transcribing the recording afterward was a tedious, if not impossible, task, and I relied heavily on my quickly scrawled notes. Nevertheless, the two lengthy oral histories given by Ernestine and Mrs. O'Leary have a familiar arc, and the family histories they shared align with the snippets of history-making I gathered from conversations about the past circulating more broadly in the community. Indeed, there was a local history booklet, created for the community's centennial year, which explained that the settlement had been formed under the Free Grants Act of 1879, but none of the people I interviewed over the course of my fieldwork were aware of the conditions for settlement contained in that Act.

Both Ernestine and Mrs. O'Leary were born in the early 1920s. At my request, they began by telling me about the lives of their parents. They traced their genealogical links to the earliest days of settlement by explaining that their parents had migrated from the Acadian Coast and the Gaspésie, respectively, as their fathers searched for work in logging camps. Eventually, in the early decades following Confederation, they purchased land in the settlement for homesteading. Neither woman understood the broader political reasons for creating the settlement in which they lived. When I interrupted our conversation to share my nerdy knowledge of the historical details contained in the Free Grants Act of 1879, both women looked initially irritated and then became somewhat irate. Ernestine firmly asserted, "Papa bought that land and it stretched from [so-and-so's] place to [such and such] a place." They were offended, for I was drawing attention to historical details that implied the people of the settlement had always been a problem of sorts for the province. Even worse, it appeared that I was suggesting I knew better than they their family history.

It doesn't matter that they misunderstood me: They lacked my interest in the ways in which industry, ethnicity, and class shaped forms of ongoing settlement in New Brunswick. They were vexed, because acknowledging any political messiness concerning the creation of their settlement delegitimized their origin stories, which bent toward more conventional celebratory tales of pioneering hard work and ingenuity, not unlike those told by the Fille de Jésus, or captured in Vetta LaPointe Faulds' five-volume heritage series, *The Way It Was along My Bay* (1995–2010). It is important to remember that while a few communities along the Bay of Chaleur took pride in tracing their roots to the earliest Acadian settlements in the region, the people of this community acknowledged a complex ancestry. Settlement in Canada is a discontinuous and ongoing process involving not only the longue durée of historical and colonial upheavals, but also the ways in which state policy and market fluctuations disturb and contour livelihood practices that attach people to the land in particular ways.

Both women began their lives within the moral economy I addressed in the previous chapter, with an emphasis placed on building an Acadian agrarian and Roman Catholic community. Mrs. O'Leary remained a staunch Roman Catholic, even if Ernestine had no use for the church. More so, they lived within an ongoing political economy in which land ownership as private property is deeply valued and confers a sense of belonging and rights. It is thus not surprising that both women abruptly brought an end to my discussion of the historical contestations over land grants and the building of settlements to reassert control over their family histories. Still, their understanding of the past needs to be interpreted within the context of the political and economic arrangements that governed settlement in the northeastern wedge of New Brunswick in the waning decades of the nineteenth century. The forces that led to the creation of this and other settlements are not neutral: "They unfold with purpose, corresponding to both market forces and state policy" (MacKinnon 2020: 179).

## Landscapes of Memory

Settlements dot the perimeter of New Brunswick's forested interior, the Crown lands that are the cornerstone of its economy. According to William Parenteau, the applicants for land under the Free Grants Act of 1879 "came overwhelmingly from the rural working class of northern New Brunswick, a condition that was largely determined by the exclusion of landholders" (1994a: 187). He writes:

> Coming from the marginal mixed farming areas and the small towns surrounding the Crown lands, most toiled in the lowest occupational level ... For the rural labourer in the northern half of the province, work was strictly seasonal, alternating between the farm, forest, river drive and sawmill, or occasionally including stints in quarrying, fishing, shipping and construction. Remuneration for common labourers in these industries provided for subsistence at best. Few settlers began with sufficient capital to buy necessary stock and equipment to carry themselves while establishing a homestead. Labour Act[1] settlement was the domain of the working poor; it involved placing people with little capital and often no farming experience on land with marginal agricultural potential. (1994a: 187–8)

Under the Labour Act of 1869 and the Free Grants Act of 1879, one hundred acre lots were cut from the perimeter of New Brunswick's Crown lands for settlement purposes, as a means of addressing the growing numbers of jobless workers and destitute families in the province. But the timber on such grants remained the property of large lumber operators, who paid ground rent to the province for a full year after approval of a grant.[2] In this period, the cutting of timber on the part of the settlers was restricted to the ten acres they were required to clear for homesteading.

The lumber operators and the professional foresters who worked for the province were opposed to the creation of settlements near Crown lands, arguing the settlers posed a potential threat to the timber resources and revenues produced for the province. They feared settlers would illegally harvest timber. After all, the land was not suitable for farming and the only thing of any real value were the trees found on the lots. Although the settlers were not experienced farmers, most of the men had worked in – practically grown up in – logging camps and knew how to harvest trees. So, the lumber barons questioned the motives of would-be settlers and did their best to have settlement applications overturned. When that failed, they attempted to clear the timber from the land as quickly as possible in the one-year window they were given.

William Parenteau argues it was "the cumulative gnawing away at the edges of Crown lands" that posed the biggest threat to the large lumber operators in the region (1994a: 197). In their view, the settlers were placed far too closely to accessible timber stands. They argued that even if settlers were honest about their intentions to homestead, they posed a fire risk. So, from the beginning, these settlers were placed in a structurally disadvantaged and adversarial position. While the province attempted to address issues of poverty by creating a new class of independent rural landowners, the conditions of that independence ensured their continual poverty by restricting access to the only resource of value on their properties. As early as 1873, the Surveyor General declared the Labour Act a failure, noting that the grants not only "failed to obtain the end they were expected to fulfil, but they have frequently been made use of by private individuals for the purposes of obtaining timberland" (Parenteau 1994a: 184). In the 1930s, Arthur Lower echoed this sentiment when he despaired of settlers in Quebec and Ontario, where there were similar settlement programs, and those who "may or may not have some remote intention of making a home, but in the event, he always does the same thing, cuts the timber off, having built a shack and perhaps made a little garden, sells it and then moves on" (cited in Parenteau 1994a: 180). But the parents of Mrs. O'Leary and Ernestine did not move on; they stayed on the land and grew roots. They built humble dwellings and had children in a nowhere place tied to the extraction of timber in the late nineteenth and early twentieth centuries.

William Parenteau's study of the administration of the New Brunswick Labour Act and the Free Grants Act reveals a class struggle over the province's forest resources, in which the rural poor appealed to local politicians to intervene on their behalf in both their grant applications and subsequent conflicts with lumber operators. Such patron-client relations were used to win concessions from the administrative arm of the state, even though professional foresters in what was then the Department of Lands and Mines believed "Crown land settlement was contrary to rational and efficient resource use" (1994a: 180).[3] Ironically, the passing of the Forest Fire Act in 1918 "created a new hazard: the intentional lighting of forest fires for employment, especially in the 1920s when the forest industries went into recession; the consequent drop in jobs for loggers prompted some people in the settlements to light fires, in order to take advantage of the additional money that had become available under the new act" (1994a: 191).

It was openly acknowledged in the community where I worked that local men continued well into the twentieth century to set fire to the woods to create employment in times of need. I was told men hired to work on fire-fighting crews crowed about cutting their water hoses to extend employment long enough to collect the stamps, or weeks, required to qualify for unemployment benefits. These were desperate measures in desperate times, as unemployment was rampant in the settlements. Indeed, the creation of tree-planting crews in the ethnographic present of the 1990s was as much about providing seasonal employment that would discourage fire-setting and so protect Crown lands, as it was about reforestation. While clear-cutting is still widely used on Crown lands, the work was highly mechanized by the 1990s, and provided little employment to those in the settlements. Further, the reforestation of the lands is best accomplished by nature, and so these days a small copse is left standing in the middle of a scarred swath of land, or trees are harvested in a checkerboard fashion, to encourage natural propagation. Monocropping of black spruce for pulp mills was never an ecologically sustainable practice, and it is hard to say what the long-term effects of using the pesticides needed to protect the stands will entail for the environment in the long run. It was devastating for salmon and birds in the short term, and more recently has been blamed for the rapid spread of forest fires, as climate change has turned the stands of black spruce into the fuel that feeds the fires.

Nevertheless, the employment of tree-planting crews in the 1990s protected the forests in other ways, by discouraging fire-setting, pillaging of firewood, or the selective theft of coveted hardwoods, such as bird's-eye maple, for resale to high-end cabinetmakers. One person in the community sold such precious hardwoods to American makers of luxury yachts. Another concern was the spread of illegal pot farms on Crown lands. I interviewed a woman whose husband waged a war against the rural planning district for placing a streetlamp along the road beside his home. She told me it violated his freedoms, as he had not granted permission to place the streetlight on his property. Others told me he was growing marijuana in the woods behind his property and preferred to work his illegal trade under the cover of darkness. But his wife carefully framed the entire discussion in libertarian ideals of freedom to pursue a way of life outside of government interference. So, while seasonal make-work programs for the poor in rural New Brunswick provided the bare minimum that allowed some people to remain in their rural communities, others pursued ventures in the underground economy. Here again, the division of labour was highly gendered. My friend Joan's planting crew was almost entirely made up of younger women. While some men continued to find work in the trades that often took them away from home for stints of time, others pursued illicit means of making a living. Such gendered livelihood arrangements in rural settlements were a long time in the making, rooted in the very landscape of the northeastern woodlands of New Brunswick.

So, as the Department of Lands and Mines moved to consolidate and rationalize its procedures after the First World War, fault lines opened on many fronts. Lumber barons, professional foresters, sawmill operators, the heavily subsidized pulp and paper industry, local politicians, and settlers vied for control of the woods. These political struggles concerning the control of Crown lands shaped the very landscape in which Ernestine and Mrs. O'Leary dwell, a dwelling infused with feelings and emotions attached to clusters of homes found along a tangle of roads that lie inland from the coastal villages of the North Shore of New Brunswick, where the scrubby alders and poplar that quickly propagate on denuded lands skirt homesteads that had sprung up over the generations, as original lots were divided up for their children to build homes. Dirt roads and tow paths meander into the woods that abut their properties, near the forests that were historically essential to their livelihood practices. This landscape was created out of a welter of relationships and toil in an environment that would not bend to the aspirations of those who once imagined agrarian settlements could be built there. In that sense, it is not unlike the abandoned farmland next to the "Bridge to Nowhere" where my family would gather to picnic in the southern part of the province in the 1950s and 1960s. But on this land up north, other ways of being at home in the woodlands of New Brunswick took hold. As Tim Ingold notes, "Environments, since they continually come into being in the process of our lives – since we shape them as they shape us – are themselves fundamentally historical" (2000: 20).

Tim Ingold asks us to adopt a dwelling perspective, "according to which the forms people build, whether in the imagination or on the ground, only arise within the current of their life activities" (2000: 154). He argues that "[human] children, like the young of many other species, grow up in environments furnished by the work of previous generations, and as they do so they come literally to carry the forms of their dwelling in their bodies – in specific skills, sensibilities and dispositions" (2000: 187). Remembering the rugged woodsmen of his youth, the Maritime poet, Alden Nowlan, observes:

These are the men who live by killing trees –
their bones are ironwood, their muscles steel,
their faces whetstones and their hands conceal
claws hard as peavy hooks: anatomies
sectioned like the man in the Zodiac.

These are the trees: alive, the sluggish light
stationed in their moist hearts; they do not fight
the axe-blade, though they'll break the axeman's back
and look benevolent. The centuries
have made a violent marriage here, the men
wedded by violation to the trees,
so they reflect each other, taking in
strange qualities. The men assume at length
the stubborn stance of trees, their dogged strength.[4]

The "men wedded by violence to the trees" might belong to what Hilary Cunningham-Scharper considers an "ecogothic" landscape, one "attuned to the spaces of 'dark nature,'"[5] where the trees will "break the axeman's back and look benevolent." On the one hand, this confirms Margaret Atwood's observation that "Canadian writers as a whole do not trust Nature, they are always suspecting some dirty trick" (1972: 59), but it also goes further in drawing attention to forms of dwelling in which livelihood and landscape alter one's very nature, "so they reflect each other, taking in strange qualities. The men assume at length the stubborn stance of trees." I am arguing that industrial forestry in the region produced a peculiar and uncomfortable human-nature sensibility, in which "whatever sinister lurks in nature lurks also in us."[6]

The regional poet Fred Cogswell, a friend and mentor of Alden Nowlan's, observed that "Alden was a brilliant misfit in a community where the only measure of a man was how he handled an axe, a drink, or a fight" (Cogswell 1986). And although these poets are descendants of those waves of English settlers that moved into the region and worked on privately owned woodlots, they share certain affinities with the predominantly Acadian and Irish men who went to work as loggers on Crown lands. Cogswell explores the forms of dwelling rooted in the woods of New Brunswick:

Before it takes air in greener shoots
A seed is nurtured by surrounding soil
And patterned by whatever streams can coil
Where worms and borers worked their slow pursuits;
And through it wills to grow a crown that fruits
In skies where lightnings break and thunders clap,
It can't escape the source that feeds its sap:
No tree belies its soil, outgrows its roots.
Not soft the soil where we took root together;
It grew not giants but the stunted strong,

Toughened by suns and bleak wintry weather
To grow up slow and to endure for long;
We have not gained to any breadth or length,
And all our beauty is stubborn strength.[7]

The *Stunted Strong* (Cogswell 2004) observes the beauty and harshness of the natural environment that takes root in the very character of the people who populate Cogswell's poetry. In his dedication in the reissue of *The Stunted Strong* in 2004, Robert Gibbs notes the "illimitable dreams and thwarting limitations of the human condition" to which Cogswell's work repeatedly returns as he explores the lives of those living in rural New Brunswick. According to Cogswell, "The rural world of the Maritime Provinces exacted different roles from the sexes; it enforced those differences by public opinion and by a considerable degree of sexual segregation" and the "result of these restrictions, enforced from childhood, was a basic dichotomy between the sexes that was never more than partly bridged, even by marriage" (Cogswell 1986: 206).

This chapter briefly ponders the sense and sensibility of two women tied to men "who killed trees" for a living in the twentieth century, daughters who would become wives of lumberjacks in northeastern New Brunswick. As noted in the previous chapter, the men of the settlement were often absent from home, working away in the woods. Alden Nowlan, who endured his own childhood in a nowhere place he would later refer to as Desolation Creek,[8] wrote with particular sensitivity about the women wedded to such men. He noted, "Child brides weren't terribly rare" (Bartlett 2017: 10). His own mother, like Ernestine's daughter Rita, was married off as a young girl to a man twice her age and suffered terrible loneliness and despair. Still, both Nowlan and Cogswell observe the women who populate their poetry from that very distance created by forms of dwelling that segregated men from women in isolated communities in the twentieth century. It is, perhaps, Antonine Maillet's *La Sagoine*, a play about a fictional scrubwoman from the Acadian Coast, that best captures the timbre of the voices of the women of the settlements: "Oh yeah, I was young once. That was in my youth. Young and pretty, just like the others ... But them days are gone now, just like you all'll be gone one day too" (Maillet 1979: 21).[9] Ernestine and Mrs. O'Leary spoke to me in English, but their mother tongue is French, and their voices have that distinctive inflection that marks them as coming from this settlement in Restigouche County. The women share, with the fictional Acadian scrubwoman, a penetrating bluntness that captures the realities of life in the world they inherited. In the following, Ernestine speaks of her very own lonely nature, which I want to explore as a particular form of dwelling created by settlers on the edge of New Brunswick's Crown lands.

## A Lonely Nature

The life histories of the two women moved from the realm of family origins in the settlement to recollections of childhood, which focused almost entirely on time spent in a one-room schoolhouse in the late 1920s and early 1930s. The women recalled trudging along snow-packed towpaths to reach a snow-covered schoolhouse. In the depths of the Great Depression (which in the Maritimes began in the 1920s),[10] their mothers fashioned clothes from flour bags and packed them lunches in salvaged lard pails. At school, the children placed their pails on the wood stove and all morning the aroma of lunch mingled with the fug of wet mittens. They were taught reading, writing, and arithmetic, and they recalled their teachers drilling them in math and literacy skills. They described in joyful detail lining up at the door when the bell rang, spelling bees, and other activities. Beyond these descriptions of school-life, they said very little about their childhood years.

These recollections of school days in this period are very familiar to me, as I was raised on them.[11] My parents attended rural schools in New Brunswick in the same period and two of my paternal aunts left home as teenagers, having completed Grade 9 and a year at the Normal School in Fredericton, to assume teaching posts in mixed farming and logging villages in the southern part of the province. As a child, my mother's descriptions of attending classes in a one-room schoolhouse merged with the portrayal of rural Maritime life found in Lucy Maud Montgomery's *Anne of Green Gables* (1908). I devoured the Anne books and was convinced I would have been happier had I been able to attend such a school. The other strong impression left by the books I read and my mother's ruminations on her past is that of an ennobling and character-building poverty. My mother and her brother, who were sent to live with their grandparents after their mother became ill, were paid a small remittance to stock the school woodpile and clean the outhouse. And if some of the more fortunate children in their village pitied them, my mother claims to have learned that hard work never killed anyone. In the telling, the difference in descriptions of hard times, as told by my relatives who lived on farms along the various tributaries of the Saint John River, and those of these women from northern New Brunswick, seemed to be of degree, rather than of kind, the difference between going to school in hand-me-downs and going to school in sackcloth.

You might, therefore, imagine my bewilderment when, later, I pulled out school attendance records at the provincial archives in Fredericton and discovered that the two women I spent hours interviewing had in fact spent precious little time in school. Most years there were no records of attendance to be found at all, and for the years in which there were records, the school appeared to be open for only a few months in the early autumn. This puts the very proud claim of perfect school attendance made by Mrs. O'Leary in a rather different light. Further, I discovered the two women had not even gone to the same school, although I had assumed that they did. Babette's grandmother, Ernestine, had, in fact, lived on the border of a neighbouring settlement, and been sent to that school, although it was some distance from her childhood home. Certainly, it had been difficult to square the fond memories of going to school with Mrs. O'Leary's and Ernestine's modest educational achievement: Grades 3 and 2 respectively. Suddenly, these recollections of happy school days took on a different cast; their few days in school had indeed been precious.

That first winter up north, I would often drop in to visit Ernestine. I would find her rocking and roasting beside the wood stove in her meticulously maintained and brightly painted lavender kitchen. I recorded her life story over a series of cold and bitter days mid-winter. Although I had dutifully prepared a questionnaire, it was obvious she found my line of questioning disruptive and I soon grew silent. Her story was told only when she was ready and its richness and historical significance far exceed anything my point-blank questions were likely to elicit. The following conversation followed my visit to the archive; Ernestine is trying to clear up some of my earlier misunderstandings.

> I was born in 1922 and I was young, eight years old, when I started school [1930]. And I quit at eleven [1933]. Now eleven, that's when the Depression was bad. Mamon said, "You got enough schooling to read and write." She said, "You need a scribbler. You need a pencil." Mamon said, "You have enough schooling." I used to like school. I remember the teacher used to put our work on the board and that we'd copy it and then we'd do it. And then she'd come and check it. What was right and what was wrong. And then she'd have us line up at the door and we'd go in. Everyday we'd go a little further. And I remember sometimes she'd have a spelling match.
>
> We lived two and a half miles from the school. They wouldn't take me at the [local settlement] school. It would have been closer. But the trustee came and said that we belonged to the other settlement and there were too many children in the other school. Yes, I used to like school. [I interrupt with a question about language of instruction, which was English.]

No, I didn't speak much English before I went to school. A little bit, but not much. Lots of things I didn't know in English. Because I used to go [pause]. There was a girl, she didn't live far from us and she was English, eh? And she was at home and she was lonesome, eh? There were no other kids. And she wanted me to go down and play with her. So, that was before I went to school. So, this day she promised me, if I'd go down [to her place] she'd give me some nice apples, because they had a nice apple tree. But papa took us to dig clams and I couldn't go. So, the next day she was mad at me and I explained, "I went with my father to pick roosters." She started to laugh. And Clifford [her brother] said, "You don't know what they call them in English?" "Well," I said, "No." In French, we say "coque." And so, he says to me, "clams."

So, here, the singular Maritime "settler affect," found in the Anne novels and my mother's childhood memories, in which the children of rural communities attend schools and are indoctrinated into the project of Canadian settlement and nationhood, begins to fray. Ernestine's desire to go to school is completely thwarted, for lack of a pencil, for lack of an eraser. Rob Shields (2017) draws attention to Anne's "biographical chronotope," in which the orphan struggles to belong to Green Gables and eventually "advances into a predestined future built on the inheritance of the British imperial values with only the local affordances of place and her imagination as resources to support personal agency" (520). Shields defines "settler affect as exaggerated attachment to place identities grafted onto colonial places" (519), and in the oral histories of these women from the North Shore, one comes to appreciate the nuances of Maritime settler affect. Life in the backwoods grafts a different sense of attachment to the nation for those who have not inherited British imperial values and privileges; but it is no less felt.

Ernestine's understanding of her parents' decision to pull her out of school when she was eleven years old is rendered in terms that a child might understand. A small child is unlikely to have understood the closing of schools because they were too poor to pay a school tax. From the early 1860s onward district supervisors travelled to schoolhouses throughout the province of New Brunswick. If they were lucky, they would reach the schools in the backwoods settlements of Restigouche County once a year, usually in the early autumn before snow made the roads impassable. More often than not, on reaching the settlements, the superintendent would discover that the schools had been closed for most of the previous year. He would then try to meet with the school trustees (always men), but they were frequently away working in the woods. There was always the problem of procuring a suitable teacher willing to work in the settlement schools. Even uncertified teachers were unwilling to accept the substandard living conditions, assuming a place to live could be found at all. As the Depression wore on – and the possibility of making a living in the woods evaporated into thin air – it was the inability to collect the school tax and pay teachers that closed schools throughout the region. In the parish of Durham, where Mrs. O'Leary and Ernestine grew up, the schools were closed more than they were open – sometimes for five years at a stretch.

The district superintendents who travelled to schools throughout the region worked tirelessly and the records of their visitations are reveal-ing. They understood the grinding poverty and the social conditions that prevailed and wrote to the Department of Education in Fredericton about the challenges they faced. Despite their interventions, little in the way of supports to address the needs of these communities was forthcoming. If anything, they were scolded for their failure to make progress in the backwoods settlements. Still, they worked to find solutions. As the Second World War approached, and there was an uptick in employment for lum-berjacks, their efforts met with some success. But the settlement I speak of remained stubbornly impoverished and the settlers seem to have given up on the prospects of ever reopening the school, although the need was great as there were estimated to be over a hundred children in the district, which made it the largest rural district in the region. This was the lay of the land when the Filles de Jésus arrived in 1944 to build a convent school for the community, as all means of supporting a secular school were lacking.

In my view, Mrs. O'Leary's and Ernestine's obvious nostalgia for their early schooldays reflects a longing for an education and a childhood that were all too brief. It is notable that memories of childhood appear to cease once Ernestine leaves school at the age of eleven. Indeed, her preschool memory provides the only hint as to what a child's life in the settlements must have been like most of the time. Children helped their parents dig clams, pick berries, and chop and pile wood. They had no books to read, and rarely went off to visit and play with other children. It is the sort of childhood that would cultivate a "lonely nature"; as the poet Cogswell notes, a child "can't escape the source that feeds its sap."

Ernestine paused her childhood memories to reflect upon the char-acter of her parents:

> I was born Catholic. I don't go much anymore. My Mamon. Poor Mamon used to go to church. If she wasn't sick, she didn't miss church. Espe-cially after they built the church here. Mamon, she didn't drink, she didn't smoke. You know? The women were good then. I remember that. Good living. When I was young both Papa and Mamon would go to church.

These parents could not pay the provincial school tax or provide their children with a pen and scribbler, but when able found ways to travel out to the bay to attend church. Within Vetta LaPointe Faulds' series, *The Way It Was along the Bay*, you catch glimpses of faithful people from the inland settlements participating in the religious life of coastal dioceses, and these same people would have helped build the Roman Catholic church that was established in the settlement in the early 1940s, when Ernestine was already a young mother herself. She recalls:

There would be confessions and receivings, and in the summer, they had what they called retreats. One summer, after I was married, we had a big retreat, and the Holy Fathers were here for over two weeks. That's what we called them. They were really horrible with the long beards, and the long brown dresses. Yes. The Holy Father would pass our houses and call us to come to hear them preach. First, the Holy Father called all the men to come in the afternoon. Then he came for the women at night. Another time he took the older children, and then the little children. You know? He didn't want them all together. And then he used to preach. Oh my! He told us all about the sins. He said things that you never heard about, things that couldn't be done.

I remember my poor sister and how she laughed. Yes, she laughed. "You!" he said. "You don't have to laugh there." He said, "Maybe you think I don't know who you are, but I know who you are." He didn't know her from the man in the moon. He was telling us what were sins, and he said that it was a sin for women to have sex with the bedpost. The bedpost! Upon my soul to God. If you had sex with the bedpost. How could a woman ever? Can you imagine? But I didn't laugh because they scared me to death. I remember they called us all into the graveyard at night. This is a long time ago. I had only two children then. "Go into the graveyard and kneel down," they told us. "All of you who have parents lying here, call them." We all kneeled down there, in the graveyard, and we were calling our fathers, mothers, brothers, anyone who was dead. We were scared to death. Not just me. Everybody was scared. I remember my sister and I were crying. It was pitch dark at night.

Then the Father said that all the men that had cut pulp – you know – he said they were stealing and would go to hell. Well! It turned out some fool went to confession and told. Well, I mean, Holy Father also said that it was a sin to smoke and so-and-so there was scared because the Father caught them and got after them. But nothing happened. He was just saying those things. There were a lot of people said it was crazy. And they said if they had another one [religious retreat] they wouldn't go.

We know both the Filles de Jésus and Eudist Fathers were active in the region at that time. Ernestine's God-fearing parents would surely have felt compelled to do the bidding of visiting Fathers, who, according to sensible Sister Ruth, would periodically hold religious retreats she personally found outlandish. Ernestine's depiction of the gathering held on All Hallow's Eve is startling and reveals the paradoxical conditions that contoured ways of living in the settlement at that time. Ernestine found the very idea of segregating children from parents outrageous; there were few secrets in families that lived on top of each other in their tiny shacks. Even *good* Roman Catholic parents were frequently forced to scrounge about on Crown lands to meet their family's needs, as every child would know. The parishioners' incredulous dismissal of the Fathers' authority on such matters is frank, offering a strong dose of reality concerning the ability to make ends meet in a landscape shaped by social and economic policies that from the beginning necessitated breaking the law. Ernestine recalls settlers easily dismissing the clergy's condemnation of such livelihood pursuits, in which most were engaged. She shrugged her shoulders; the Fathers were fools, people had to survive, make a living. She continued:

> Now the priests around here were not like that. They were different. But there were a couple of wicked ones. They had wicked tempers. Strict. There was one: I didn't go around him too much. He would get something cross. That man used to tramp the roads at night to see what was going on. I remember he slapped one of my sister's daughters. She was going out with the man, who later became her husband, and he caught them. I suppose she was sixteen. He was a wicked priest.
>
> When my daughter was young, I took her to a movie at the school there, and he plainly told me straight up and down, "Why don't you stay home with that kid?" They hurt you so bad. I didn't care for him. Rita was only two years old. A friend had to take me home. We only got to see a movie once a year and I had to go home. Mostly every man up here used to work in the woods in the winter. Most times it was just women and children out here, and a few old men. But I never thought to move. I have a lonely nature. I don't go out much. I used to go to church, and I'd go to house parties and visit my sisters. But I had a nervous breakdown and now I don't go out much.

The invective summoned against the church when Ernestine recalls the religious retreat, or visits from priests tramping the roads at night and poking their noses in places they did not belong, was fierce. She made no bones about her feelings of resentment toward a church she found morally intrusive and judgmental. On matters of child-rearing and sexuality, however, Ernestine internalized a sense of shame that was at times unbearable. Having been publicly slandered and humiliated by the priest who questioned her parenting abilities when she took her toddler to a movie, Ernestine's sense of social isolation (at home with a growing family while her husband is at work in the woods) is made evident. The priest's moral outrage and his imposition of child-rearing practices belong to a moral economy from which Ernestine is largely excluded. After a nervous breakdown, Ernestine's lonely nature unfolds, for "no tree belies its soil, outgrows its roots."

The difficult political and economic formations that altered the landscape of the northeastern woodlands shaped the lives of both Mrs. O'Leary and Ernestine. Their sense of belonging sprung from their forebears having purchased land and lived in the settlement for several generations. Over time, the original hundred-acre lots were split up so that the settlers' children could build their own humble homes, often little more than shacks. In the 1960s, Father Henri – the carpenter priest – helped many of the families secure Canadian Housing mortgages, and the shacks were replaced by simple houses he helped them build. For a long time – over a century – survival remained precariously dependent on men finding work in the woods, although by the 1990s, that possibility had largely disappeared, as mechanization radically reduced the numbers of labourers needed to harvest timber.

To some extent the stories of the two women conform to more generic narratives of Canadian settlement,[12] in which settlers laboured to conquer the elements through back-breaking toil to establish homesteads and community. As such, they could easily admit to humble beginnings, even lives spent in crippling poverty. But anything that might sully their claims to the land was roundly rejected.

In other ways, the elderly women's stories might be interpreted as the quintessentially Canadian "poverty narratives of women" discussed by Roxanne Rimstead (2001). She argues that careful analysis of such narratives can reveal the "remnants of nation" that highlight "the stories and voices cooling in the shadow of the dominant imaginary, not by idealizing coalition or essentializing difference, but by highlighting class interests and class tensions as significant aspects of identity" (2001: 285). As the snippets of Ernestine's life story make evident, these women's voices can be full of contradiction. At times, a peculiar cussedness bordering on outright disdain entered her narrative. She was frequently wary of those who flitted through her life, and of neighbours who could not be trusted to mind their own business. A lifetime of making-do and getting-by too often involved secrecy. Ernestine's lonely nature developed as a form of dwelling in a landscape in which the "stunted strong" survived and endured.

*So, Babette invites friends and family to a party ...*

In this final chapter, a few people from "up north" journey to the provincial capital of New Brunswick, where Babette has relocated in search of work and to live with the woman with whom she has recently fallen in love. She has invited a few of her cousins to visit for the weekend. The cousins grew up in a place where most nearby neighbours are relatives of some sort, the grandchildren of women like Ernestine and Mrs. O'Leary. Together, they attended the local primary school in the settlement during the period of its secularization in the late 1960s, and then rode the bus that took them to the regional high school. Eventually they left the North Shore in pursuit of higher education, or to look for work, although the cousins returned to the settlement when things did not work out elsewhere. They are my contemporaries and throughout the 1980s and 1990s, this pattern of leaving and returning to our Maritime homes is something we shared. I had recently moved back to Fredericton, my hometown, to teach in the anthropology department at the university for a stint while beginning work on my doctoral thesis.

Babette invited all of us to attend a murder mystery party she was hosting. I explore the evening of the party as a proto-event, an example of ritualized play that develops spontaneously among people who know each other well and that exposes deeply felt tensions that are both personal and structural.[13] So, this chapter is the bookend to the first chapter, in which the unfolding of events related to the giving of so-called *Christmy* presents lays bare workplace contradictions that created friction among men working far from home on an isolated railway siding in the Rocky Mountains. In this chapter, I explore the place of laughter and crying in solidifying moments of uncomfortable recognition for those who have known each other all their lives, those who have sprung from the same unforgiving soil, which has, nevertheless, fostered their sense of belonging, or *being at home*. Highlighted in both instances, working far from home and being unemployed at home are the vulnerabilities of human beings caught in relationships and circumstances not entirely of their making, to which they respond with considerable ingenuity and imagination.

At the murder mystery party, the lingering effects of childhood trauma explode upon the scene, producing that gothic sense of entrapment that we explored in previous chapters. But here the gothic breaks into another genre, that of the detective story, which seeks to resolve issues by exposing an underlying crime to be methodically addressed. Cheryl Mattingly (2010: 105) considers the gothic to be a breach narrative, in the sense that it interrupts a narrative that seeks to flatten and control the story. The detective seeks to uncover a crime through the application of scientific method and logic, and so controls the outcome of the story. But at the party, the clues and prompts given to the participants could not contain them and their responses, both proving to be unpredictable. The unpredictability of human action, as Mattingly and others point out, is often at the heart of the ethical dilemmas we encounter and the general messiness of human life.[14]

After the party, the action moves to Halifax, the largest metropole in the Maritimes, where both I and Babette again relocated in the mid-1990s. On this occasion, I have been asked by Babette to host a tea party for her parents, her mother and stepfather, who have come to visit her. Here Babette turns her love of detection to the field of medicine. Again, science and medicine are unable to contain the narrative, as it twists into accusation and disbelief on the part of the audience, and exposes the raw emotions of those who share a painful history. Both parties, the murder mystery party and the tea party, address the ethical entailments involved in caring for kin and friends from a fragile community.

The following chapter, "Unravelling," also reflects on some of the messier consequences of doing anthropology at home. I highlight some of the ethical and moral dilemmas that marked the relationships I formed with people who became both close friends and the subjects of my discourse. While I believe such relationships can be a source of profound pleasure as well as difficulty regardless of where one carries out one's fieldwork, when one does fieldwork close to home it can be especially hard to bridge the expectations that evolve over the course of intensive ethnographic research, and the afterwards that must inevitably follow. The events outlined in this chapter chronicle the end of a key ethnographic relationship with a woman I counted as a close friend for over twenty years, a relationship that began to unravel when I returned to the Maritimes. Fieldwork is utterly dependent on an ability to create and maintain reciprocity and goodwill across a sea of differences. For me, the end of fieldwork had nothing to do with leaving the field site and everything to do with the loss of friendship with the woman I call Babette.

Babette remains a gifted storyteller. I sometimes catch glimpses of her on online platforms, where she continues to refashion her life story for the consumption of different scholars. Her ability to find new audiences is not surprising. While we were friends, it was impossible to get any purchase on her take on reality, which evaporated with every visit – both in the so-called field and long afterwards. Babette continually produced fresh renditions of her life story. On the other hand, the underlying patterning of her stories, the labyrinthine layers revealed over the years, and the cubbyholes into which she could slip and hide, taught me everything about the problems of overly literalist forms of interpretation in social research. Babette's search for her own past in the horrific is contoured by Maritime gothic, but her attempts to twist the gothic into the language of science and detection, whether through the therapeutic discourse of recovered memories, or the medical language of diagnosis, reveal an ongoing struggle to find a specialist who might offer some relief from the afterlives of the trauma she experienced as a child. Still, there is always an audience for a good storyteller, and she deserves to be heard.

So, in the following chapter, I try to tease apart the many threads that began to unravel at the murder mystery party: the unravelling of vulnerable individuals, friendships, and the ethnographic pact. The very idea of being a reliable first-hand witness that underpins the ethnographic project falters when others who were participants or present at the time are unhappy with your take on events. Betrayals entailed in the messiness of carrying out ethnographic research and then writing for an academic audience haunt me, and I struggle with issues of translation and analysis that are sometimes at such odds with the desires and motives of our interlocuters, who we know will read our work.

# Chapter Five

# Unravelling

## An Invitation

The invitation arrived in the mail six months prior to the event.[1] My company was requested at a murder mystery party, which was to be held in my hometown, the better to accommodate my schedule, and to pre-empt my declining. My return to the Maritimes in 1995 had unexpectedly removed the distance I sought for writing about people on the North Shore of New Brunswick. Throughout the spring and summer of that year, I never knew when Babette, the woman who had introduced me to the region, would arrive in town seeking my company and eclipsing the geographic and psychological borders I tried to erect between my life and hers. Although I attempted to keep our worlds separate, she refused to comply. Babette never forgets that we share the same world, albeit unequally.

For years Babette has been adapting murder mystery plays she finds on the Internet, to be performed on or around Halloween. She does not read novels, but she does watch television and surf the net. She and others her age often told me that television brought modernity and the world to their neck of the woods in the 1960s and 1970s, or, as they would put it, dragged them out of the dark ages. It was a time of radical cultural, social, and economic restructuring in northeastern New Brunswick. Schools were secularized, the social welfare system was centralized, the forest industry was mechanized, and a mine-mill-smelter complex was developed in the region, all of which generated new sources of provincial wealth, and to some extent redressed regional economic disparity (cf. Stanley 1993). For these children of the 1960s, born into rural poverty at a time of massive capitalist expansion, television is the marker of a significant social and cultural shift, felt if not understood, and a source of a particular quality of social experience.

As avid viewers of television, Babette and her friends seemed especially drawn to two genres, science fiction and the detective story,
although several sitcoms, like *The Brady Bunch*, also figured large. At
times their interest in these shows seemed to me to verge on the fanati-
cal, if not downright insane. From childhood onward, Babette kept
meticulous files of her favourite movie stars and collected all manner of
Star Trek memorabilia, which she could spend hours organizing. Still,
such eccentricities, shared by many people, pale beside the delusional
behaviour of her cousin, who told me he received a message through
the television instructing him to translate the transcripts of *Space: 99* into
ancient Greek. He eventually left the North Shore to attend a Maritime
university where he studied classical languages, winning a scholarship
for graduate studies. But his ambition to complete the translations of
*Space: 99* met with rejection and he felt scorned. He took his funding
and returned to the settlement, outraged that the university then asked
him to return the funds, which had already been spent. If television
brought the world into the homes of my friends, it was a world so alien
that the notions of "real" and "fantasy" that pervade the dominant
modernist (read bourgeois) sensibility collapsed.

Certainly, Babette's play, *The Last Train to Paris*,[2] and its enactment,
playfully illustrate some of the fascination with partying and play that
could momentarily lift the participants out of the mundane world of
work (a phenomenon also seen among the rail gangs, as described earlier) or, more often than not, lack of work, which could create a dreadful
sense of being stuck, of being in a rut. So, on the evening of the murder mystery party, we were invited to check hard realities at the door
and enter a state of play. On this point, Don Handelman writes: "West-
erners commonly identify the ideation of play with the make-believe,
with artifice and frivolity, and with the impossibilities of fantasy – and,
enamoured of cognitive dualism, compare this unserious ideation with
its opposite of the 'serious', whose apex is the sacrality of 'truth'. Sacred
truth and frivolous falsehood are among the extreme binary opposites
of our modern conceptual universe" (1998: 63).

Included in my invitation to the murder mystery party were liner
notes with brief biographical sketches of the characters in Babette's
play, an all-too-familiar take on Agatha Christie whodunits, including
ones written for murder mystery parties. While a few character parts
in Babette's rendition were up for grabs, most had been specifically
created for the friends and family members whose participation in the
evening's event Babette had requested. Her cousins Ann and Jacqueline were cast, respectively, as Madame Renard, a mysterious woman
of questionable identity, and Amelia Aire-Art (Amelia Earhart), an

American pilot who mysteriously disappeared in 1937. Amelia Aire-Art resurfaces on the last train to Paris as a prisoner of war under the watchful eye of A. Tuff Sickler (Adolf Hitler), described in the notes as "odd, moody, and easily angered (ooh, just like André)." André, the student of ancient languages, was cast in this part. Non-family members were drawn from her circle of women friends. An ex-lover was cast as Marguerite "Mar" Layna (Marlene Dietrich), her current lover as Mr. Lemmingway (Hemingway). Another friend was cast as Gabrielle Colette, described as an author of erotica rumoured to have slept with over two thousand men and women. I was cast as Hagatha Skitzy (Dame Agatha Christie), while Babette cast herself as Mr. Ine Stein (Albert Einstein).

The biographical sketch prepared for me was incredibly detailed. Beyond the obvious, that I was to play the part of a writer of detective novels, I was told that Hagatha Skitzy was born to the upper classes, and that she disappeared briefly in 1926, only to be found eleven days later, the "apparent victim of amnesia." Eventually, Hagatha Skitzy would publish "Ten Little Niggers" which would be adapted later for American publication as "Ten Little Indians." Touché. We had all been viciously typecast. Concealed in the biographical sketches of the characters were messages for friends and family, some less subtle than others, alluding to the tensions that underscored our relationships with each other. Certainly, there was a warning for the disappearing anthropologist who would forget her friends to become a writer of thinly disguised nasty essays. The summer Babette wrote her murder mystery I wrote an essay that explored the life histories of three generations of women in her family, an essay in which her own story of the recovery of repressed memory played a significant part (D. Young 1996). Not only did she resent my sympathetic interpretation of her mother's and grandmother's life stories (she nursed grudges toward both women), she was in the process of continual reinterpretation as to the significance of her lapses of memory and the unruliness of her thoughts and interpretations. That I had captured a mere moment in that process and congealed it in the amber of an essay was annoying to her. She resented the finality of the ethnographic present. Clearly an act of contrition was in order, and I agreed to accept the invitation and to play the part of Hagatha Skitzy. In the spirit of Victor Turner, I crossed over the threshold into the realm of play and tried to go with the flow (Turner 1982: 55–9).

The idea of play is most certainly within post-structuralism's métier, for play is a place where fluidity and indeterminacy of meaning abound. Don Handelman (drawing on the insights of Gregory Bateson) explores the paradoxical border between serious reality and play, where *play* annunciates an "enigmatic realm that is not nothing, and yet is nothing real" (1998: 69). Of course, this paradoxical border between *reality* and *play* threatens to dissolve with the insights of post-structuralism. Nevertheless, I know of few who would choose to live their lives under the highly destabilizing conditions of constant flux. Most of us experience life *as if* its order was natural, and the forms of that order (our various realities) are assumed as the counterpoint to play. Turner argued (as do others)[3] that the "idiosyncratic, quirky" symbols found in liminoid states of play contained critical subversive potential, for liminoid phenomena tend to "develop apart from the central economic and political processes, along the margins, in the interfaces and interstices of central and servicing institutions – they are plural, fragmentary, and experimental in character" (1982: 54). But whereas liminality leads to transformation and/or social reproduction in ritual, Handelman suggests that continual instability – a feeling of being betwixt and between— can, under extreme conditions of alienation and anomie, "shatter its cultural buffers and instead concentrate in quotidian contexts" where its impact can be "searing and destructive" (Handelman 1998: 66). Thus Turner (1982) and Handelman (1998) suggest directions for exploring the links between narrative and structures of feeling as acted out in situations of play. In this instance, Babette and her friends are simultaneously consumers and creators of stories; they have been shaped by, and given shape to, particular narrative forms in which the stock characters of whodunits are playfully set free, or, perhaps more to the point, freed from the set, creating dizzying possibilities for the embodiment of identities and subversion of narrative, in what Mattingly (2010) has described as breach narratives.

## Liminoid Thresholds: Deadly Play on
*The Last Train to Paris*

I arrived at 7:00 pm, my costume tucked into a little blue suitcase I had inherited from my grandmother. Putting the attire together had been a simple affair. I went to my closet and chose a conservative gathered skirt and white blouse, which I wore with a pair of brown service shoes that were exactly like the ones my grandmother used to wear. The ease with which I was able to dress the part was somewhat discomfiting, especially as I noted the elaborate preparations and care expended by others on wardrobe and props. I was dressed and ready in ten minutes, but it took several hours for others to assume their new identities. Some were dyeing their hair or attaching fake facial hair; others were squeezing themselves into dresses with daring décolletage. André, the only man invited to the party, transformed himself into a dead ringer for a

Nazi SS officer. Hysterical laughter was spilling out of various rooms as people primped and raucously joked in thick German, French, American, and British accents. Even under normal circumstances, my friends can switch from their schooled voices to the dialect of the community from which they come without skipping a beat. Copious amounts of alcohol were consumed. By the time we were ready to begin, I was ready to go home.

At about 10:00 pm we were ushered into the basement, which had been transformed into the dining car of a European train. Babette asked for silence, assumed a heavy North Shore accent, and ushered in the play with the following story from up home:

> BABETTE: Let me begin the way I always do, with a story from up home there. I remember the time I was walking slash-ways through the back field to Mamon's, when Rita there, next door, yelled from her window: "That was quite a party you had there last night Babette." I yelled back, "What are you hollerin' about? I didn't have no party." Rita says, "Don't try to deceive me Babette, I saw you going with a case of two-four."
> Then, out of nowhere, Mamon yells from her window: "You don't know what you're talking about Rita, that case of twenty-four was for me."

According to Babette, this story, with which she begins every murder mystery party, makes it evident that "nothing is as it seems, and no one can be sure who is really who." But in beginning our journey on *The Last Train to Paris* with a story from "up home," she also reminds us of the place from which she, and several of the participants, come. The ethos of northern New Brunswick permeates the evening.

**ACTION:** Monsieur Tattel Thael (Tattletale), the conductor of the train, has been murdered during a blackout, as the train passed through a tunnel. When the lights come back on, he is found with a knife pierced through his heart. One of the eight guests in the dining car must be the murderer. We are each handed little booklets, designed specifically for our individual characters, and instructed to reveal clues, as prompted, step by step, throughout the evening. As actors, we have no idea what the others are up to. Only Babette (Ine Stein) knows the intricacies of the plot. We must respond as best we can to accusations as they arise, willy-nilly, throughout the evening. Only the murderer will know who he or she is. We each turn the first page. I discover I am the murderer of Monsieur Tattle Thael.

Detective/anthropologist kills the tattletale/key informant. Bit by bit my duplicity will be revealed. I take a stiff drink. Still, I cannot possibly catch up to the others in the room, who by this time are piss drunk. The play drags on, scene by scene, until four in the morning. With every passing hour, the performances deteriorate further into spectacles of debauchery, grief, rage, and hysterical laughter. I play my part to the bitter end, with stiff upper lip and haughty all-knowing colonial mannerisms and pretensions. I remain steadfastly proper as those about me fall apart. For instance, at one point late in the evening it is revealed that Amelia Aire-Art's (Jacqueline's) body is covered in bruises. She reveals that she has been forced into acts of sadomasochism with the cruel German officer (André). As whips and other S&M paraphernalia are lashed about the room, Amelia (Jacqueline) suddenly turns on me, and begins to scream: "You fuckin bitch. You think you're so much better than the rest of us, with your proper upbringing, your snotty education." She begins to sob and appears to be completely unhinged. I am suddenly at a loss. I do not know if she is still acting and merely following the prompts in her script, or if we have slipped out of play. Is this a playful nip, or a bite?[4] Uncertain, but certainly not prepared to face this desperate rage head on, I stick to the script. I tell her to pull herself together. I mutter to others about the vulgarity of such displays. Ine Stein (Babette) is laughing so hard she can hardly stand up and I'm afraid she is going to be sick. Meanwhile, the Nazi (André) is suggestively pawing his cousins Madame Renard (Ann) and Amelia (Jacqueline). Lemmingway is busy videotaping the entire drama and we are all stumbling over wires and extension cords. Then, in a fit of pique, Ine Stein (Babette) attacks A. Tuff Sickler (André). She calls him a goddamned male chauvinist pig and begins to pound him with her fists. Others quickly intervene and pull her off him before he can violently respond. Again, I have no idea if we are still in the realm of play. André may be many things, but he is not typically a hetero-normative male chauvinist in his day-to-day life, although he certainly has dark moods and is playing the part well. There is a lot of gender-bending potency on display, and the highly charged suggestions of sexual behaviour, in the form of touching and gestures, are beginning to make me feel like an adolescent caught in an uncomfortable situation from which she does not know how to politely escape. Those of us sober enough to think at all begin to rush the play along. Finally, feeling unbelievably raw and exhausted, I confess at the top of my lungs: "I did it, I'm the murderer."

**CUT:** Everybody was drawn up short. I had completely silenced the room. Babette (Ine Stein) looked long and hard at me and said, "Geez, Donna, you ruined it. They're supposed to figure it out on their own." I apologized: *mea culpa, mea culpa*. An uptight spoiler of tales am I. And then we began to laugh, laughing until tears streamed down our faces. We hugged each other and said what fun it had been. But Jacqueline

(Amelia) could not stop crying and kept grabbing my arm to tell me we needed to talk. She was so, so drunk. Finally, as the sun began to rise, my taxi arrived, and I escaped with a full-blown headache and a feeling of despondency that lasted a long time.

It was the last time I saw Jacqueline. A year and a half later she placed her shoes neatly on the side of a cliff and threw herself into the Bay of Fundy. She had gone to visit her sister Ann in Nova Scotia. Following Jacqueline's suicide, Ann returned to live again in the settlement, where she took her dead sister's boyfriend as a lover. Grief, I imagine, forged a bond between them. André remained in the settlement, living in his parents' home, and working at the fire hall in the summer months. He complained bitterly about the ways in which his mission in life had been derailed, and plotted revenge against an institution he felt had failed him. Babette lost her job in Fredericton, having falsified her credentials, and moved back to the settlement to live with her grandmother for a spell. She complained that her hateful supervisor, who also came from up north, had it in for her from the moment he learned she grew up in the much-maligned settlement. Her grandmother, a longtime abuser of over-the-counter and prescription medications, overdosed on antidepressants prescribed for Babette, and then kicked Babette out. Eventually, Babette showed up at my door in Halifax, with not a penny to her name and nowhere to go. All of which proves, in my estimation, that it is easier to playfully set stock characters free from a predictable narrative than it is to free oneself from the circumstances into which you were born.

As children, we were warned that if you laugh too hard in the morning, you'll cry before nightfall. Regret and grief can quickly follow for those who play too hard, suggesting there is a heavy price to be paid for losing control of your deportment, your senses, your emotions. In the months that followed the murder mystery party, things began to unravel for the cousins from the North Shore settlement. Babette not only lost employment and a home, but was also devasted by the death of her cousin Jacqueline, whom she loved dearly. She sank deeply into clinical depression. Everything began to unravel.

## Social Drama as an Act of Purgation

In the last two decades of the twentieth century, much attention was given to the ironic construction of identity, as if one could, through consumption and play, subvert the ways in which region, class, and gender inscribe subjectivity. Living on the postmodern "road to nowhere," we were advised to "lighten up" (Hebdige 1988: 241). Certainly, there are some richly ironic moves in Babette's play suggesting a postmodern sensibility. After all, the detective writer, the quintessential modernist spinner of tales, is found guilty of several crimes, which include racism, elitism, snobbery, and arrogance. Against these crimes, murder seems almost trifling. In this regard, Babette's play undermines the authority of the traditional detective of modernist fiction. The extent to which I, as anthropologist, became the butt of this ironic twist to an old modernist story is, I think, hilarious, at least in retrospect. But this is a superficial reading of irony[5] that does not attend to the ways in which this play was acted out, or to the underlying currents that fed the narrative and occasionally gave way to flooding emotions.[6]

What I witnessed at the murder mystery party was more than simple playfulness and irony; here love and anger, desire and frustration, along with deep resentment and spite, engulfed the narrative and unfolding drama. Any postmodern desire to write oneself into a story, thus assuming a fresh identity, was undermined by the rude intrusion of past lives and tropes hell-bent on destroying the pretence that such a thing could be achieved, even in imagination. Babette's story from up home, with which the drama commenced, had already situated the drama within the landscape of her ancestors, reminding us that identities are not infinitely pliable, for they are formed in early childhood and in ideology. Mattingly notes, "Even our most intimate and personal practices reflect our human historicity, our situatedness in social time … Narrative (or drama) is such an important candidate for a theory of practice because it can challenge the hegemony of structural accounts precisely by highlighting the unfinished, idiosyncratic, unpredictable, suspenseful qualities of life" (2010: 44). Like a puppeteer, Babette knew how to pull our various strings, but she was as likely to become overwrought by forces she set into action as anyone else. As the evening wore on, the very idea of discoverable truth through detached objectivity, central to the modernist genre of detective fiction, imploded, releasing the sister narratives of accusation and blame. When Jacqueline lit into me, it was a dramatic moment "at odds with the scene, generating all sorts of Trouble," one that I attempted to resolve through confession (Mattingly 2010: 46). The social drama we produced depended on our abilities to caricature ourselves in ways that revealed self-loathing and self-pretension. As our own vulnerabilities were exposed, we risked becoming insensitive to the vulnerabilities of others. A disturbing nastiness was afoot. If the evening had a structure of feeling, it was one of rancour, which was given free rein at the party.

In the Maritimes, we say to each other, "better to laugh than to cry." Often, when in the company of my friends from the settlement, we laugh outrageously at what amounts to our own weaknesses, or the misery of others. Gallows humour cements friendships, speaks to the absurd unfairness of the situations we confront in our day-to-day lives. My friends from the settlement rudely throw pity back in the faces of those who would claim to help them, for they are proud. They say, "I wouldn't give them the pleasure of seeing me cry." And when their children are bullied at school, they say to them, "You get in there and take your part, you just take your part." And so, on this evening of the murder mystery party, we entered the fray. I learned this: That pettiness, even cruelty, can build a solidarity of sorts. In this regard, I am reminded of yet another poem penned by Alden Nolan, called "The Back Biters":[7]

Two housewives, friends
for years, are uttering malice
against a third
who is friend to both.
At the office
there are those who can scarcely hide
their restlessness
when a companion
delays his departure
and thus postpones
their parade of his weaknesses.
Pettiness, I use to say.
Even vileness.
Now I think I know better.
It is a purgation.
that permits us to be
a little gentler
when we face
one another again, perhaps even
in its own strange way
an act of love.

The murder mystery party felt to me like just such an act or purgation, a ritual ordeal intended to cleanse our morbid social emotions. But turned inward, as in the case of the melancholic, this rough acrimony and flagellation can produce despair and rancour, and both can destroy. My reading of rancour, as the structure of feeling found in *The Last Train to Paris* at Babette's party, bears a close resemblance to Ross Chambers' reading of melancholy as a major form of oppositional poetics in early modernist fiction (1991: 102–74). Chambers considers melancholy as *other*, if close cousin, to irony, in that a sense of dispossession and an awareness of the unendingly drifting are among the symptoms of melancholia to whose oppositional function Freud pointed when he noted that the complaints of melancholics are accusations (1991). You are overwhelmed by your predicament, and others are to blame.

## Drowning in the Past

Jacqueline was the first and only member of her immediate family to obtain a university education. In the 1980s she completed a bachelor's degree in industrial arts at the Faculty of Education, breaking through class and gender barriers simultaneously. She then married a soldier and moved to Germany, where he was posted. In Germany, she taught school on the base and joined the women's ice-hockey team. The team won tournaments, and she was thrilled, the happiest she had ever been. Then one day she returned home to find her husband in bed with her best friend. She returned to the Maritimes looking hollowed out, defeated. She tried to find work, but there were no teaching positions available. She began to have nightmares and increasingly she was haunted by memories of her childhood, memories of sexual abuse and neglect. But Jacqueline's sister Ann refused to believe the stories and did her best to silence and dispute the claims of abuse by an older family member. Jacqueline sank deeper and deeper into depression and grew quiet. In the end, she set herself adrift.

This pathetically thin description of Jacqueline's life is culled from the memories of her cousins, who were struggling to make sense of her suicide. Had Jacqueline found the words to tell her own story it probably would have taken a series of unexpected turns, as various memories interrupted her train of thought and images of things past and present collided. There were things she wanted to tell me, but I never saw her again. Whether or not the act of narrating one's story can set one free is certainly beyond the scope of this analysis. But to the extent that storytelling is an intercommunicative event linking speakers to listeners, the unspeakable, like suicide, destroys the potential for making sense. As storytellers, human beings become subjects, albeit subjects in process, subjects in conflict. Not only are stories, like memories, predicated on the present:[8] "Personal interpretations of past time – the stories that people tell themselves in order to explain how they got to the place they currently inhabit – are often in deep and ambiguous conflict with the official interpretative devices of a culture" (Steedman 1995: 6).

Jacqueline should have been one of the lucky ones, as she was among the very few from the settlement to complete high school, let alone university. According to the myths of equal opportunity that abounded in her youth she could be anything she wanted if she just studied and worked hard. I try to imagine what it must have been like for Jacqueline to return, broken, to her family home in the rural settlement of her youth, where there was no employment, and to the landscape that recalled a troubled childhood. Haunted, she left the settlement to visit her sister Ann, the very sister who refused to take her accusations of abuse seriously. Things just got worse. There is a horrible circularity to this story, where a young woman throws herself into the very waters that once carried her ancestors to these shores, severing all ties to a troubled past.

## In a New Millennium

A decade after beginning research in northeastern New Brunswick, Babette, her mother, and her stepfather came to my house in Halifax for tea. We ate fresh strawberries on biscuits with lots of whipped cream. It was the Canada Day long weekend in a new millennium. Babette's parents had travelled from their home in New Brunswick to visit her in Halifax. They had no idea she had recently been diagnosed with multiple sclerosis (MS), and she had organized this outing to tell them so. Her mother seemed to sense something unpleasant in the offing and appeared wary. Her stepfather clearly resented being dragged to my house on this holiday weekend. I was feeling impatient. Why did Babette have to make such a production out of everything? And why was my presence required? It all seemed unnecessary and cruel. I urged her to cut to the chase, to say what she had to say.

Babette's voice faltered as she told them about her disease. As always, and in keeping with her character, she had done her research on the Internet and believed she could trace the exact origins of her present predicament. She retains a modernist turn of mind. According to her, the sources of her disease were exposure to mercury and vitamin D deficiency as a child. "Mom, remember when Daddy used to bring mercury home from the fertilizer plant so we could play with it? You would put the bucket of mercury in the middle of the floor, and it would entertain us for hours." Rita, Babette's mother, looked uncertain, but was determined to be agreeable. After all, she was a guest in my home. "Yes, I think so," she ventured. Babette carried on: "And you never made us drink milk, because you didn't like it when you were little. Do you remember that?" Rita nodded, tentatively, as if wondering where this line of questioning was headed. Joe, her husband, could suppress his hostility no longer. "Oh, for god's sake, Babette, how do you know you have MS? Is this a lifestyle disease? Look at you: If you just lost some weight and got a job, you'd be fine." If Babette believed holding this meeting at my house would curb Joe's tongue, she was mistaken. Did she seek an anthropologist as witness? Or had she simply sought the moral support of a friend? Certainly, she had placed her mother in an awkward situation. Rita tried to run interference between her husband and daughter, while appearing the good guest, the good wife, the good mother, all in that moment, in this family, mutually exclusive categories. And in the end, to diffuse the situation, she would have to admit neglect as a parent who had allowed her children to play with mercury and refused them vitamin-rich milk. I am confident such ironies were lost on those present.

In a huff, Joe went outside to smoke. From my window, I caught him scowling at my drooping peonies and sunny English buttercups. Unlike us, he was not born in the Maritimes, or, for that matter, in Canada. We, the women, ended the visit by gossiping about people and things "up home," by which we refer to the small settlement in the northeastern corner of New Brunswick from which Babette and her mother come, and in which I conducted ethnographic fieldwork for the better part of two and a half years in the early 1990s. We exchanged recipes and laughed until our sides hurt. But the repartee constantly threatened to dissolve into accusations of blame, complaining and lamenting, stubborn refusals, and tight-jawed resignation. That night, Rita went back to her daughter's apartment and scrubbed floors until one in the morning, but still, she could not sleep. The next day she took her daughter shopping, a typical response from this woman who cares deeply about sartorial stylishness and prides herself on never shedding a tear. Eventually the gloves would come off and acrimonious phone calls and recriminations between mother and daughter would continue throughout the summer and fall, ruining yet another family Christmas.

For me, one particularly disturbing idea attended the fallout of my tea party. At the core of the arguments waged between Babette and her mother over the following months was Rita's wish to talk to Babette's doctor, and Babette's refusal to grant permission. Rita phoned me to complain that her daughter had been a hypochondriac from the time she was a small child. She found Babette's story fishy, and she knew I had a tender heart and did not want me to worry needlessly. According to Babette, her mother was meddling in her life. I countered that I thought Rita was deeply concerned and that her request to talk to her doctor was reasonable. Further, I argued, the doctor would put an end to her mother's suspicion that she was making the whole thing up. Babette said I didn't understand how spiteful her mother could be and that Rita would convince the doctor his diagnosis was wrong. I asked how that was possible; were the tests not conclusive? Babette told me that when it came to her mother, anything was possible; I should not underestimate her. I dropped the subject and have not broached it since, but seeds of doubt had been planted in my mind.

I am still trying to figure out why I should have found such doubts about the *real* state of my friend's health troubling in the least, for I thought myself beyond this obsession with literal truth. I grasp the significance of the distinction between illness and disease, and as an anthropologist attend to the former rather than the latter (Kleinman et al. 1997; Antze and Lambek 1996; Lambek and Antze 2003). My chief concern is with the interpretation of culturally mediated narratives of self-understanding. Indeed, I credit Babette and her relations with having taught me much about narrative truth[9] and have learned – admittedly, with a good deal of effort – to adopt an ethnographically informed ironic sensibility as I listen to and analyse their stories and talk. By this I mean the deliberate attempt to achieve a degree of respectful detachment, to be sensitive to contradictory and contentious takes on the subject of truth, so as not to succumb to absolute certainties that would diminish the experiences of some while elevating those of others. I try to withhold judgment and not to take sides, for I firmly believe we all make our realities out of language and are subject to its whims and fancy.

But the tea party and the conversations that followed threatened to undermine this hard-won sensibility. When I began fieldwork in the early 1990s, Babette was undergoing therapy, and we spent a considerable amount of time discussing her recovered memories of sexual and satanic abuse, explored earlier in this book. As noted, I even went so far as to help her search the shoreline for a cave where she believed we would find the skeletal remains of sacrificed babies. I was even, at that time, open to the idea that such recovered memories might help to explain her nightmares and depression. The ethnographic encounter is predicated on such openness, and suspicions like Babette's were prevalent at the time. While in the field, Babette gave me her journal to read, which she said I could treat as a life history. Several years later she would come to my office and record another life history, radically altering her interpretation of her life to erase the ritual abuse stories. We had both come to think about such things differently, especially as the press began to write about the "false memories" that had ruined the lives of innocent people who had been falsely accused of horrendous abuse.

So, at the tea party, she began again to rearrange the events of her life history, considering fresh ideas. But this time I began to suspect Babette of a degree of calculation and outright dishonesty that went beyond the subtleties of shifting narrative truths.

By the time of my tea party, I had known Babette and her mother Rita for many years. In the mid-1980s, in the years following my return from out west, having bolted from my life as a railway cook, we all lived in the same dark and mouldy rooming house, in the foggy end of a working-class neighbourhood in the port city of Saint John. I had gone there to work for an NGO researching problems of illiteracy.[10] Babette's mother and her children had recently moved from "up home" to escape a situation of domestic violence. Babette's older brother and girlfriend shared the room next to mine; Rita and her two daughters lived in the basement flat. One day I accidentally locked myself out of my room and Babette's brother showed me how my door could easily be opened with a plastic card. On another day, I came home to find Babette sitting in my room with my dog, having climbed the fire escape ladder and entered through the window. She told me she needed a place to escape from her mother, who was furious with her for quitting her job as a chambermaid at a local hotel. Such intrusions into my personal space barely warranted an explanation, let alone an apology. That I met such impudence with relative calm and acceptance is now baffling, but I chalk it up to a combination of an undergraduate training in anthropology and my years of living in a boxcar, which had primed me to accept the ways of others without judgment. I also have a Maritimer's inclination to be reticent in situations that might bring embarrassment to others, something that was instilled in me from an early age. Whatever the reasons, my friendship with Babette took hold, and even after my return to school to pursue graduate studies we kept in touch.

## A Family Quarrel

The summer before my tea party, Babette lay disconsolate for months in my spare bedroom, her few possessions lying in boxes around her bed. She was deeply depressed and had nowhere to go. I made frantic phone calls to social agencies, but no one was willing to take her on. Years before she had done the circuit as a satanic abuse victim, and therapists told me they found her "too needy." Finally, someone belonging to her queer community of friends intervened and found her an apartment in a non-profit public housing building for women only. She put Babette in touch with social services, and she was given meagre social assistance on which to live. Babette struggled to keep her head above water. She knew she could not work; she felt abandoned by her family, and she could not pay for even the bare necessities of life.

Babette went to see her family doctor, who suggested she might be suffering from MS. That winter we spent hours on the phone discussing symptoms and rewriting her history under a new description. Suddenly her old sleep disorders, her inability to hold a job for more than a few months, her difficulties coping with life, were given a sound medical explanation. As well, it was a clinical diagnosis that could erase the need to examine all the less savoury aspects of her life, such as childhood poverty, childhood sexual abuse, a history of failure in school, living with the fear that someone would discover the credentials she listed on her résumé were falsified, her complete disdain for authority, and a quick temper, which led to troubled relations with employers, friends, and family. MS was a godsend. Babette told me it was such a relief to know she was actually very sick, and not insane.[11] And I agreed. I found myself in the ridiculous position of wishing my friend ill health. We both crossed our fingers, hoping tests would get to the bottom of things, and she applied for a disability pension. In the meantime, she decided it was time to break the news to her mother when she came to visit over the long weekend in June.

But, as I have noted, the news of Babette's illness was not so readily embraced by Rita. Initially, I chalked this up to Rita's inability to bear such dreadful news about her daughter's health, but I soon came to understand that her suspicions stemmed from their troubled relationship. At the tea party, the spin that Babette placed on the story of her illness was brand new to me. It placed the blame entirely at Rita's feet. Indeed, the structure of Babette's discovery and disclosure of MS was the same as her earlier discovery and disclosure of satanic and childhood sexual abuse. I began to detect a disturbing repetition in Babette's stories, in which she accused her mother of neglect and abuse and demanded attention and retribution. No wonder Rita's reaction was hostile. No wonder I felt ambivalent, uneasy.

I confess that, had Babette's last story been her first, had I heard the story about the buckets of mercury brought home from the fertilizer plant *before* I heard the story of satanic cults, my interpretation of its significance could have been completely different. For starters, I would have taken it at face value. It alludes to the changes in the regional economy I had been primed to investigate. Taken literally, it so perfectly illustrates the plight of an undereducated and exploited working poor not properly trained to handle toxic chemicals. Such things are common enough. But I no longer think it is the significant point, at least not in this case. Babette's life stories rarely allude to the workplace at all, but illness as a consequence of childhood neglect, in one form or another, is always central to her narrative.

I will probably never know if Babette really has MS. I'm told it is a particularly difficult disease to diagnose in the early stages and I no longer have contact with her. But regardless of the etiology or prognosis of her illness, it speaks to her ability to creatively carve out new spaces from which to speak as a person in need. I can easily celebrate her ability to recast her story in clinical language (especially at a time when the language of repressed memory had been roundly discredited), so that she could access housing and medical attention. However, in drawing attention to the ways in which discursive regimes create subjects worthy of attention, I do not mean to imply that Babette was merely an opportunist, manipulating possibilities for attention. We all live our lives through language and are culturally implicated. She is hardly exceptional in this regard. Socializing in the field frequently involved commiserating over illness and misfortune. As related to me by others, illness was often a pivotal experience in one's life, marking the end of a relationship, the end of the ability to work, the beginning of one form of trouble or another. Often illness would initiate intense scrutiny on the part of the state, as the welfare worker would then begin a series of home visits to process claims for disability insurance or other forms of public assistance. This was an extremely stressful, but oddly hopeful, time for those being "processed" by what Habermas calls the "therapeutocracies" of the welfare state (Habermas 1984: 530–40). If you received a clinical diagnosis for an illness, one might be given just enough to get by. Otherwise, you were out of luck. Such are the meagre needs of the truly desperate.[12]

Still, it was the twist Babette placed on her story that morning at the tea party that made me uneasy. Had I not heard several different versions of Babette's life history, I would have missed its underlying structure and thus would have failed to focus on details I now find suspect. The longer I knew Babette and her family, the less certain I became of anything as factual. I am left with stories, which constantly shift as people struggle to make do and to make sense of their lives and relationships. While I can do little more than trace the historicity of their understanding, its continuities, and breaks, I remain uneasy about the discrepancies in their interpretations of their lives as they dredge the landscapes of memory for the telling bits that explore the unbearable weight of their family's history, shaped as much by an excess of signification as it is by terrible privation.

## A Falling Out

Following the tea party, I began to note an accusatory attitude when Babette called to chat, and I would feel guilty for not having called her first. She seemed increasingly suspicious and querulous when I would turn the discussion away from her present concerns to ask for news of family and friends up home. She grew impatient with me. I believe Babette could sense my disbelief, and we began to grow apart. Initially, I welcomed this distance as I had found it nearly impossible to write about my ethnographic experiences under her increasingly disapproving gaze. When I returned to the Maritimes in the late 1990s, Babette twice relocated to the cities in which I lived and worked. When she moved, unannounced, lock, stock, and barrel, into my home for a summer (the day after my partner went away to do research), I was forced to put my work away and was unable to write at all. I was greatly relieved when she eventually moved out and achieved a measure of independence, which a disability pension from social services eventually secured for her.

I was very surprised when, almost two years later, she began to date a student in the university department in which I taught. Still, I was happy she had met somebody for whom she cared. It was when she began calling me to reveal things about other students, or to report things they said about *me*, that I became concerned. I told her I could not have such conversations and refused any involvement that would include her new partner and friends. Babette made it clear that she resented this, and to an extent I understood her anger. As an anthropologist, I had exploited our friendship to gain a foothold in the community where I conducted fieldwork. Was she not simply reversing the order of things?

Soon after that conversation took place, an essay I had written about Babette's family was read in a class given by a colleague. A day before I was to visit that class to discuss the essay with students, I received a letter from Babette accusing me of unethical practice. She was embarrassed by things she had once said, which were now recorded for posterity and out there in the public domain for her friends to read. I am not unsympathetic. Writing in the ethnographic present is intended to capture a moment in time, but I concede that in doing so we risk leaving the impression that those we write about are forever caught in that time. Meanwhile, we allow ourselves the privilege of afterthought. When our subjects read what we write they must be startled by the fact that our voices are newly altered so as to be measured and thoughtful, while their voices remain raw. It is a betrayal of sorts that has nothing to do with obtaining consent.

Babette also took umbrage with my publishing the essay without seeking her permission and accused me of concealing its publication. It is true that I did not seek her permission to publish, but I did take her, all expenses paid to a conference where I had presented the same essay, long before it was published. At that time, I even asked if she would like to write a rebuttal to be included with the essay. Back then, she claimed to understand my point of view and declined my offer. Still, she was unprepared for what was to come. As was I: I too felt betrayed, for I had not intended to conceal my work and over the years had often spoken to Babette about my changing perspectives. I meet my ethical obligations to those I write about by never revealing their identities. For the most part, I even avoid place names. Sometimes I invent composite characters by merging the details of several people's lives into a single identity. I have even toyed with the idea of splitting Babette into several people, as she has not only changed her story several times, but also suggested different pseudonyms with each retelling. Because Babette's revisionist history became my most perplexing theoretical problem, she remains one person. Despite this writing process, my interpretations are culled from actual events and the stuff of real people's lives. I stray from the strictly factual to protect identities and to clarify the points I hope to make. After all, it is the underlying social and cultural processes that most concern me. However, only the anthropologist, not those of whom she writes, is bound by the conventions of the profession. Unfortunately, Babette had revealed her identity, as a subject of my research, to her new friends. In the past, this had not been a problem, as my ethnographic domain had simply broadened to include those I met through her. Then our worlds collided. Not only did the distance between home and field dissolve into thin air, so did the distinctions between research, teaching, and friendship. The various domains of my profession, typically kept apart, collapsed into each other, raising a series of ethical and practical difficulties seldom acknowledged, let alone discussed, in anthropology.

In confronting this collapse, I came to appreciate anew the ways in which the antinomies that structure the discipline of anthropology grew out of a very specific set of historical conditions in which the relationship between the anthropologist (the writer) and the subject (the other) belonged to very different worlds, worlds separated by cultural, class, ethnic, and/or national borders. Paradoxically, I wish neither to maintain the antinomy between *us* and *them* (which was, and is still, formed by deeply unequal political structures) nor to claim it can be intellectually transcended, either by assuming an ability to overcome my own social positioning and subjectivity or by adopting a theoretical position that would neatly bury contradictions and messiness under a veneer of sociological distance. The possibility of resolving the very real social and cultural disparities that create the gap between self and other – the key antinomy at the heart of our discipline – through a transcendent philosophical manoeuvre seems dishonest to me. I might claim solidarity with Babette, and I sincerely regret the social inequities that shaped our encounter and their demise, but in the end we both felt caught and caught out.[13] I can think of no comforting theoretical or philosophical resolution to our deeply interpersonal conundrum, which came to fruition when I stopped participating (an inter-subjective process) and withdrew to write (an objectifying process).[14] So, instead, I try to be as frank as possible and acknowledge the jarring contradictions and historical and social processes that shaped my encounter with Babette and her family and friends. Babette told me to stop writing about her world, and then disappeared from my life. But beneath the cacophony and discord I do detect patterns, and I am unwilling to be silenced. As it turns out, I'm more like Malinowski than I once thought. As for Babette, she is a storyteller. We share that compulsion. I hope she understands this, even though she may have cause to resent it.

# Notes

## Introduction

1 In Feld and Basso, *Senses of Place* (1996: 87).
2 Briefly, neoliberalism is a philosophy of global economic restructuring, popularized in the Reagan-Thatcher years of the 1980s, that promoted state policies favouring international markets, and by which the social ideals and programs supported by post–Second World War Keynesian economic models were undermined. Neoliberals commonly argued there would be a trickle-down economic effect if the interests of large capital flourished. In Canada, the adoption of neoliberal liberal policies was referred to as the "common sense revolution" and the political rhetoric compared the running of a state to that of a small business or household. In reality, the economic gap between the very wealthy and the poor widened, while government deficits grew larger. There are many good resources available to those who need a primer on this political-economic history and the debates that ensued: Harvey (2005), Steger and Roy (2010), Kotsko (2018).
3 Karen Foster (2017) draws attention to regions and places in rural Atlantic Canada marked for deliberate degrowth. The nowhere places I attend to are not to be confused with what Marc Augé (1995) refers to as the non-places of supermodernity, such as airports, supermarkets, housing estates, and other places of late capitalism through which, he claims, so many pass as atomized and alienated individuals. Indeed, nowhere places are typically at some remove from such non-places.
4 "Less than 11% of Canada's land is held privately; 41% is federal crown land and 48% is provincial crown land." "Surface and subsurface rights to the mineral, energy, forest and water resources may be leased to private enterprise – a very important source of government income in Canada. National and provincial parks, Indian reserves, federal military and

provincial forests are the largest and most visible allocations of crown land." http://www.thecanadianencyclopedia.ca/en/article/crown-land/

5  Indeed, Robert Desjarlais (1997) insists on using the ethnographic past when he writes about life in Boston's homeless shelters from 1990 to 1992, drawing attention to swift changes in housing policies that are a consequence of political rearrangements (see note 1, pages 261–2).

6  See the truly evocative works of Katie Stewart (2007) and Jason Pine (2016).

7  Here, I simply flag the ways in which the academy is as much situated in forms of political economy and hierarchies of value as any other industry, creating opportunities for some, diminishing them for others.

8  In fact, the rail yard had been moved to the outskirts of the city, but none of the professors I spoke to were aware of such things. The movement of industrial lands away from city centres happened rapidly at the end of the last century for various reasons; particular types of work and workers are increasingly rendered invisible in new urban landscapes.

9  Thankfully, there are dedicated scholars helping to keep those memories alive. See the short film directed by Tony Tremblay and Ellen Rose, *The Last Shift: The Story of a Mill Town* (2011). They explain that throughout the first decade of this century international industries bought mills in New Brunswick with the sole purpose of shutting them down "to create scarcity in a market already dominated by them." http://www.stu.ca/lastshift/credits.html

10  See Edmund Bradwin's seminal work *The Bunkhouse Man* ([1928] 1972). Also see Ian Radforth (1987).

11  See Wicken (2012), Parenteau (1994b), and Parenteau and Sandberg (1995).

12  Note how closely this parallels James Ferguson's understanding of globalization in late capitalist times, under neoliberal regimes. He explains globalization this way: "Again, the 'movement of capital' here does not cover the globe; it connects discrete points on it. Capital is globe-hopping, not globe-covering" (2006: 38). He draws attention to the urban enclaves where wealth and power are consolidated.

13  *Subsidiarity* is embedded in Roman Catholic teaching of the early twentieth century and concerns the relationship between individual activity and the body social. See Pope Pius XI's encyclical *Quadragesimo anno* (1931), in which the church responds to German National Socialism (Nazism) and Soviet communism by offering an alternative understanding of community, individuality, and responsibility. https://www.vatican.va/roman_curia/pontifical_councils/justpeace/documents/rc_pc_justpeace_doc_20060526_compendio-dott-soc_en.html#Origin%20and%20meanin. See also Boswell et al. (2010).

14  The New Brunswick Liquor Commission, in Canada's only officially bilingual province.

15  Lisa Stevenson's *Life Beside Itself* (2014) draws attention to Canadian interventions on behalf of Inuit in Northern Canada, who suffered first a tuberculosis epidemic, and then/now a suicide epidemic. Government interventions are especially magnified within this context, but Stevenson's analysis of the paternalistic measures that introduced the law and systems of care according to standardized methods produced a discourse that increasingly distanced itself from the subjects of care. Sarah King (2014) also draws attention to state interventions in the fishery, in ways that pay little heed to local concerns.

16  Over the past decade there have been several works of literary criticism examining the gothic in contemporary Canadian literature. See Justin D. Edwards (2005), Cynthia Sugars and Gerry Turcotte (2009), and Marlene Goldman (2012) as prime examples.

17  See Benjamin (1969: 260–2). See Katie Kilroy-Marac (2019) for discussion of Benjamin's critique of forms of historical time that assume such an uncomplicated unfolding of time, one that inevitably serves the interests of elites. Kilroy-Marac ocuses on Benjamin's notion of the Jetztzeit, a form of "now-time" in which fragments of the past resurface to produce unexpected constellations of past and present at revolutionary moments (2019: 33–8).

18  At the other end of the neoliberal era, people may forget the optimism with which politicians dismantled public programs in favour of shrewd initiatives that were supposed to turn everyone into champions of privatization.

19  Acadians were the first European settlers (circa 1604–54) in what became the Maritimes of Canada and the state of Maine in the United States. When war broke out between the British and French in 1755, they claimed neutrality, which neither the French nor the English accepted. They were subsequently expelled to the Thirteen Colonies. The Cajuns of Louisiana trace their roots to this expulsion, as do those who returned to the region after 1764 to resettle on marginal lands, having lost their rich agricultural land to English Planters (Griffiths 1974; Thériault 1982). The American poet Henry Wadsworth Longfellow's epic poem *Evangeline: A Tale of Acadie* (1847) concerns the deportation of the Acadian people, and has influenced public memory, although its romantic rendering of the Grand Dérangement has been disputed by historians. See Rudin (2009), Griffiths (2005), and MacLeod (2016) for an overview of historical debates on the subject). For a different take on the return to Acadie, see Antonine Maillet's novel *Pélagie* (1982).

20  See Vetta LaPointe Faulds (2005: 110–13) and Carole Spraye (1979). Picaroons are the rogues and rascals who became pirates trolling the Atlantic coast. Picaroons is also the name of a Maritime craft brewery.

Maritime brewers work to keep history alive in the region by carefully evoking the past through the names they give local libations.

21 See Stuart McLean, "With Death Looking Out of Their Eyes: The Spectropoetics of Hunger in Accounts of the Irish Famine" (1999). I was ten years old when my Grade 5 class visited a train that crossed the country to celebrate Canada's Centennial. Each car was dedicated to a different moment in Canada's history, but the only one that left a lasting impression on me represented the hull of a ship lined with bunks of starving and dying Irish immigrants. It was horrifying.

22 I am in good company in making the case for seeing the bigger picture in the dense detail of the case study or exemplar, which has a long history in the ethnographic tradition of anthropology. See Berlant (2007); and the special issue of the *Journal of the Royal Anthropological Institute*, edited by Hørjer and Bandak (2015), who propose "exemplarity in itself as a good and powerful prism for thinking anthropologically, simply because the example excels in exploring the tension between, and the instability of, the specific and the general, the concrete and the abstract, motion and structure, ethnography and theory, and it does so by never fully becoming one or the other" (6).

23 While Williams most concisely theorizes structures of feeling in *Marxism and Literature* (1977), it is his investigation of the ways English literature came to falsely represent the country as a pastoral ideal at a time of considerable upheaval in rural England that most inspires me (*The Country and the City*, 1973).

24 However, I am indebted to social historians who fruitfully use Williams' ideas to contest commonly held views of Atlantic Canada as folksy, premodern, and backwards: Ian McKay (1994), William Parenteau (1994), Daniel Samson (1994), Graeme Wynn (1981), Heidi MacDonald (2003a), and William Wicken (2012). Collectively, their work exposes the long industrial and modern contours of the Maritime countryside. McKay, in particular, examines the ways in which the state produced idyllic landscapes for the tourist industry that fuelled the nostalgia that is the counterpoint to the more frightening stories of rural poverty that seep into Maritime literature and other forms of remembering.

25 The descendants of British Loyalists (my ancestors), fled to what would become New Brunswick after the American Revolution and settled in the southern part of the province, where they gained political dominance over the province, unless, of course, they happened to be Black Loyalists. See the literary works of George Elliott Clarke (2006) and Lawrence Hill (2015) to get a sense of the Black Loyalist experience. For a deeper look at the waves of immigration pre-Confederation, see Philip A. Buckner and John G. Reid (1994).

26  Wilbur argues the first Acadian premier, P.J. Veniot (1923–5), and the second Acadian premier Louis Robichaud (1960–70) were eventually defeated by these companies (Wilbur 1989: 117–33).

27  See Bill Parenteau and James Kenny (2002), Wayne Warry (2007), and William C. Wicken (2012). Sherrie Blakney (2003) pays particular attention to First Nations logging practices on Crown lands during the 1990s following the Sparrow Decision. After I left the field, these rights were again upheld by the Supreme Court in the Marshall Decision of 1999. Sarah King (2014) sensitively discusses the aftermath of violence in the lobster fishery that erupted in Burnt Church at that time.

28  There is an interesting parallel here with the historical claim made by the rural poor in the 1920s that Crown lands should be considered the "people's land" (Parenteau 1994a). The legal struggles of the 1990s concerning the rights of the First Nations to the resources on Crown lands served as a reminder to other rural poor that access to the "commons" had been lost. As King notes, representations of the struggles between First Nations and settler populations conceal this shared concern.

29  Adam Gaudry and Daryl Leroux (2017) are critical of revisionist stances of people in the Maritimes and the Gaspé region of Quebec who claim Métis status on the basis of a "mixed-race" logic, rather than in terms of peoplehood, as in the historical emergence of the Métis as a nation. Katie Macleod (2015) takes a more sympathetic view of Mi'kmaq-Acadian alliances in the present as an emergent political formation. See also Sébastien Malette (2017).

30  Sarah King (2014) observed the same attitude among the descendents of English settlers of Burnt Church.

31  This is the strength of Sarah J. King's *Fishing in Contested Waters: Place and Community in Burnt Church/Espenoopetiji* (2014), which explores the violence that erupted in the lobster fishery on the Miramichi Bay after the Marshall Decision of 1999. The rancour I detected in the early 1990s came to fruition in this violence, but, as King acknowledges, the underlying issues involved complex colonial structures that only obscured concerns held in common by the two communities, in which livelihoods and attachments to place are threatened.

32  I want to thank Thomas Schwarz Wentzer for commenting on an expanded essay on the word *so* given in a panel honouring Michael Lambek's work on the ethical condition. See also Schwarz Wentzer (2014) for his work on the indeterminacy of history and memory.

33  The building of the railway is especially mythic in the Canadian imagination, thanks to popular histories written by Pierre Berton (1970, 1971) and the CBC eight-part series *The National Dream* (produced and directed by James Murray), based on the books, which first aired in 1974.

But it is Gordon Lightfoot's song "Canadian Railroad Trilogy," released in 1967, the year of Canada's centennial, that best captures its mythic qualities.

34 *Goin' Down the Road* was directed and produced by Donald Shehib and released in 1970.

35 This is known as the staples theory, which Harold Innis outlined in the early twentieth century. It argues that Canadian culture, political history, and economy have been decisively shaped by the extraction and export of raw resources. Consequently, the Canadian economy falters when the demand for particular resources dries up.

36 Donna J. Young, "'The Right Way, the Wrong Way and the Railway': Work on a CPR Maintenance of Way Gang," MA thesis, University of New Brunswick, 1989.

37 See Bradwin ([1928] 1972).

## 1. The Evanescent Freedoms of Life on a CPR Rail Gang

1 Perhaps it was no accident that this peculiar notion of the gift developed on this gang, where there was a large contingent of Newfoundlanders, refugees from the collapse of the cod fishery. See both Faris (1973: 62–3) and Sider (1984, 1986: 77–93) for a description and analysis of a *scoff*, a feast made from stolen food.

2 See Marcel Mauss' seminal work on the topic, *The Gift* (1990). Lambek explains: "As 'total social facts' they are at once economic and political, domestic and public, otherworldly and this-worldly, necessary and pleasurable" (2010: 18). See also Meneley (1996). Essentially, a gift economy is all encompassing and ties members of a social group together in chains of reciprocity and obligation. But not all gifts are the same, and so they can operate in diverse ways to reveal both norms and nodes of friction.

3 See Mary Douglas' foreword to the 1990 edition of Marcel Mauss' *The Gift* for a discussion of the very idea of a pure gift, a concept she argues may have clouded Bronisław Malinowski's understanding of the gift, which he found sorely lacking among the Trobrianders, who were involved in complex forms of the Kula exchange. In response to Malinowski, Mauss argued that there was no such thing as a pure gift. Being caught up in the devastating wake of First World War, in which a generation was "sacrificed" in trench warfare, surely influenced Mauss' thought as well. But for an alternative view on sacrifice and the gift, see Lambek (2007) and Shohet (2013).

4 Marshall Sahlins defined "negative reciprocity" as the "attempt to get something for nothing with impunity, the several forms of appropriation, transactions opened and conducted toward net utilitarian advantage.

Indicative ethnographic terms include 'haggling' or 'barter', 'gambling,' 'chicanery,' 'theft,' and other varieties of seizure." He claimed it was the "most impersonal sort of exchange" (1972: 195). See also Evthymios Paedaxiarchis' essay on gambling in a Greek village as an example of negative reciprocity (1999: 158–75).

5 Slang for the Black men of the American South who worked on extra maintenance-of-way gangs, known for their working chants. In Britain, such men were called navvies. There is a delightful episode in the television series *Cranford*, based on Elizabeth Gaskell's nineteenth-century novel, which attends to the hysteria among the good citizens of Cranford when the navvies descend on their town. Lock up your daughters! (BBC/ PBS 2007). See also Ying S. Lee's *Masculinity and the English Working Class: Studies in Victorian Autobiography and Fiction* (2007: 83–4).

6 Mauss explains that the Maori *Hau* is the spirit of things. One is obliged to return gifts because they are animated, "because the thing itself possesses a soul, is of the soul" and "it seeks to return to its place of origin ... an equivalent to replace it" (1990:12).

7 In note 122 of *The Gift* is a fascinating discussion of the etymology of the German term for "gift," which comes from the Greek "dose" (1990: 122). See also Bailey (1971) and Parry (1989).

8 Five years after leaving this gang I returned to a different CPR gang to complete fieldwork for my MA. I did interviews. The men on that gang had, on average, a Grade 8 level of education.

9 I either never knew for sure, or don't recall his crime; I retain a suspicion that it was connected to either assault or rape, but that may say more about my fear of him than anything else.

10 This time predates the bank debit card; no one I knew had a credit card.

11 My understanding of a "good woman" is deeply influenced by Carolyn Kay Steedman's powerful book, *Landscape for a Good Woman: A Story of Two Lives* (1986), in which notions of goodness are caught up in ideas of respectability that shape and curtail the prospects and desires of British working-class women. It nicely points to the ways in which "the good" gets caught up in the making of reputations in the midst of the messiness and unfairness of life.

12 Evthymios Paedaxiarchis observes the same tendency among wives of Greek gamblers, who quickly assume responsibility for family finances (1999: 158–75).

13 A return to this liberal shibboleth, which dominated debates in the 1960s, is hugely problematic. The suggestion that either faith in a bountiful future, or fear of scarcity (limited goods), can account for these patterns of either spending or saving is limited, at best (Day et al. 1999). Still, the patterns of work and consumption discussed in the volume resonate

strongly with my own observations. Some recognition of the part played by the industries that benefit from the labour of the itinerant worker, and analysis of the actual working conditions, could surely temper this overly ideological argument. It seems to me that, the men held very realistic views concerning the unpredictably of work and feared economic forces beyond their control.

14 Schivelbush writes: "We have now clearly stated the two contradictory sides of the same process: on one hand the railroad opened up new spaces not as easily accessible before, on the other hand, it did so by destroying space, namely the space between points." He is expanding on Karl Marx's understanding that behind the railroad's "annihilation of space by time" lay the generative phenomenon of capital" (33).

15 The song "Me and Bobby McGee" was written by Kris Kristofferson and Fred Foster in the late 1960s. The rendition that plays in my head is by Janis Joplin on the album *Pearl* (released in January 1971 by Columbia Records).

16 "Echo Beach," by Martha and Muffins, released in 1980.

17 See Eve Kosofsky Sedgwick's *Between Men* (1985), for an incisive examination of the ways in which women become ploys in games which solidify homosocial relationships between men. Young women learn the hard lessons of patriarchy in many different work environments. Some make their peace with it, others learn ways to resist it, but few can avoid it, even now.

18 My initial attempt to grapple with these family memories can be found in Paul Antze and Michael Lambek's *Tense Past* (1996); what follows here are expanded meditations on the historicity of memory.

19 The following informed my understanding of the debates and continue to inform my analyses of memory: Paul Connerton (1989), Carolyn Kay Steedman (1992), Maurice Halbwachs (1992), Ian Hacking (1995), Paul Antze and Michael Lambek (1996), Michael Lambek and Paul Antze (2003); Thomas Schwartz Wentzer (2014).

## 2. The Family Gothic

1 "Stamps" is the local term for the number of weeks of paid employment required to collect employment insurance benefits. The number of weeks required is determined by regional employment statistics. This number shifts according to changing federal government policies, and the perceived need of maintaining or punishing a seasonal work force.

2 See James Scott (1985). Parenteau (1994a) argues that the historical practice of setting fires on Crown lands in New Brunswick was one of several "weapons of the weak" that led to collective protest on the part of woodsmen and

changes to labour legislation in the province in the 1920s. I am not questioning the link between such practices and outcomes; I do question the reading of such acts as intentionally political, or signs of revolutionary agency. My understanding of such things is closer to that of Hobsbawm, who wrote: "For social banditry, though a protest, is a modest and un-revolutionary protest. It protests not against the fact that peasants are poor and oppressed, but against the fact that they are sometimes excessively poor and oppressed" (cited in Shanin 1987: 339). Historically, changes to the labour laws were brought about to protect the economic interests of the large companies who in the past held 100-year leases on Crown lands in New Brunswick, because the forest industry was the major source of revenue for the provincial economy.

3  I am avoiding citing this source because it would betray the exact location of my field site.

4  See Stanley (1993).

5  The most comprehensive historical resource for understanding the colonial movements of settlers into the region is the two-volume collection of essays, *The Atlantic Region to Confederation*, edited by Philip Buckner and John Reid (1994), and *The Atlantic Provinces in Confederation*, edited by E.R. Forbes and D.A. Muise (1993).

6  The humorous novels that make up Herb Curtis' *The Brennan Siding Trilogy* (1997) concern themselves with relations between locals and wealthy visitors on the Miramichi River. For an understanding of the historical conservation policies that shaped relations between wealthy anglers and disinherited people of the Maliseet First Nations (who became their guides on the Upper Saint John River) and the Mi'kmaq First Nations (who worked as guides on the Restigouche River), see William Parenteau (1998, 2004) and Lynda Jessup (2006). See also Kenny and Parenteau (2014).

7  This extends from a time when one used the leftovers from painting one's fishing dory, sometimes incorporating several colours from multiple tins of paint. The more artistic did so with attention to design and overall effect. In recent times, the homes of the Acadian Coast and North Shore have become as staid as elsewhere in the province.

8  I should note that at this time, for the most part, the only bilingual people in New Brunswick were native French speakers.

9  "Nuns" is the term used in the local vernacular, although women religious is the term used today.By some definitions one is only a nun if one belongs to a contemplative congregation.

10  The educational reforms of the 1960s are explored in greater detail in the following chapter. Essentially, under the banner of "Equal Opportunity," Premier Louis Robichaud's Liberal government secularized the schools and introduced new funding formulas, addressing the wide disparities found in the province. See Della Stanley (1993).

11 The Filles de Jésus, who operated schools throughout the region, explained that it was easier to convince parents to send their children to school once the universal Family Allowance was established in 1944, as children who did not attend school were ineligible for the benefit. Canada's first universal social program was dismantled the year I began fieldwork and was replaced with non-universal tax credits. See Dominque Marshall (2006) for understanding the historical importance of Family Allowance for addressing widespread poverty.

12 In the English translation of Freud's essay, the word "uncanny" is used to translate the German word "unheilich," meaning literally "unhomely," referring to those things considered terrifyingly unfamiliar and strange. The word "heimlich," in one sense, represents its opposite, the homely. But the word "heimlich" has another sense too, in which something is "concealed, kept from sight … withheld from others" (Freud 1955: 223). "Thus, *heimlich* is a word the meaning of which develops in the direction of ambivalence, until it finally coincides with its opposite, *unheimlich*" (Freud 1955: 225).

13 See Susan Lepselter's *The Resonance of Unseen Things: Poetics, Power, Captivity, and UFO's in the American Uncanny* (2016).

14 I should explain that within the Maritimes this is code for Jewish or Syrian immigrants who travelled throughout the region with their wares in the early twentieth century; it is yet another reminder of complex ethnic relations in Maritime history.

15 On later visits to the manse, Father Henri explained that in the 1960s the manse and convent school were made available to an NGO from Chicago that had optimistic plans for making the community sustainable through cooperative handicrafts. It did not end well. Local members were unimpressed when they visited the head offices in the United States and saw photographs of their children dressed in rags beside photographs of poor children from other parts of the world. The NGO workers complained constantly about the local food and they introduced forms of worship that locals did not recognize as Roman Catholic. Eventually they were driven out by the people of the settlement, who angrily tipped over a trailer in which they were holding a meeting. The RCMP were called and the NGO workers were removed by helicopter! It was a very disillusioning moment for the Acadian clergy, who had worked in the settlement since the 1940s, because they had initially welcomed the members of the NGO. They had hoped for the sort of success enjoyed by the Antigonish Cooperative Movement in Nova Scotia (spearheaded by the charismatic Father Moses Coady). According to one of the teachers at the local school, Father Henri had, like the other religious working in the region, learned to be wary of involvement with outsiders.

16 Sybil is the story of a young woman, abused in childhood, who develops multiple personality disorder (Schreiber 1973). It was turned into a film for television (directed by Daniel Petrie) in 1976, at which point the idea of having multiple personalities entered the popular imagination. It is quintessentially gothic in its portrayal of the family.

17 Perhaps because my first fieldwork experience involved living closely with workers on a rail gang, I could not initially get my head around completing fieldwork in a much larger geographical region where some, but not all, people were closely connected.

18 I am not sure if this was accomplished through the British Home Children program, or some other. I do know it was not the happiest of placements.

19 Remembrance Day falls on 11 November, and it marks the Armistice that ended the First World War. It is the day Canadians honour fallen soldiers.

20 Such stores are staples in small communities throughout the Maritimes, where everything from cans of tuna to work boots and plaid shirts, yarn and screwdrivers, can be purchased at discounted prices.

21 The character, "Lucien: New Brunswick's Blue-Collar Philosopher," created and performed by Marshall Button, adopts a North Shore way of speaking, although an Irish lilt and some archaic Irish words are added to the mix in the settlement. The following clip includes a hilarious reference to the phantom ship that haunts the Bay of Chaleur. https://www.youtube.com/watch?v=eFFIb72A0-8

22 To understand this cultural phenomenon historically, see Ian Hacking (1995), Michael Kenny (1986, 1996), and Paul Antze and Michael Lambek (1996).

23 I know that she read several popular books on the subject of recovered memory at this time, including Sylvia Fraser's *My Father's House: A Memoir of Incest and Healing* (1987). Her therapist recommended some of the books she read.

24 Others have noted this slippage. Lambek and Antze argue that when "the literalist interpretation of abuse accusation is applied uncritically, it becomes a kind of 'assault on fantasy'" (1996: xxviii). They note a movement in Freud's thought, away from a concern for getting to the bottom of things, or recovering a *simple* explanation for one's behaviour, and toward an examination of one's attachment to certain memories, which are understood to be metaphorical. Radstone (2000) also draws attention to this ambivalence in Freudian thought and examines the debates it has sparked in fields as diverse as feminist studies, cinema studies, and history. Like Antze and Lambek, she argues that there are complex links between event and fantasy in all memory work. Truth, for these authors, is rarely simple, and can never be reduced to hard facts.

25 Anthropologists, who study witchcraft cross-culturally, quickly understood such phenomena as bearing a close family resemblance to witchcraft accusation. See especially Michael Kenny, in Antze and Lambek (1996: 151–71).
26 As Antze and Lambek note: "The invocation of memory signals association as opposed to disassociation, continuity over discontinuity" (1996: xxv).
27 I have to say, I often found descriptions of the uncleanliness of childhood homes hard to square with the pristine homes of the elderly I visited in the community. But it was a constant theme in stories of young women and was closely tied to a sense of shame linked to poverty.
28 Tom Dunk (1991) earlier observed the same in Northern Ontario and insightfully examined working-class racism within a Canadian regional context. See also Sarah J. King (2014), who explores English hostility toward the Mi'kmaq community in Burnt Church, New Brunswick.
29 The seminal works of Arnold van Gennep and Victor Turner illustrate the need to ritually respond to such dangerous passages. See Eve Sedgwick (1980) for a discussion of the common elements of the gothic that are endlessly repeated.
30 "Now Masters Have No Borders" is the title of the introductory chapter of Herb Wyile's *Anne of Tim Hortons: Globalization and the Reshaping of Atlantic Canada Literature* (2011).
31 See Anna Tsing, Heather Swanson, Elaine Gan, Nils Bubandt, eds., *Arts of Living on a Damaged Planet: Ghosts, Monsters* (2017).
32 See Susan Lepselter's discussion of apophenia, or errors in perception that are actively cultivated in the poetics of captivity found among Americans (2016: 5–8), and her unpacking of the deep anxieties found in settler society.
33 On the idea of narrative truth, see Jerome Bruner (1991). On the relationship between history, narrative and ethics see Michael Lambek (2014), Cheryl Mattingly (2010), and Thomas Schwartz Wentzer (2014).
34 The five-volume heritage series *The Way It Was along My Along My Bay* was published between 1995–2010, after I had completed my doctoral ethnographic research. I was introduced to her work in subsequent visits.
35 Eudist Fathers belong to the Roman Catholic Apostolic Congregation of Jesus and Mary, who arrived in Canada from France 1890. W. Stewart Wallace, ed., *The Encyclopedia of Canada*, vol. 2 (Toronto: University Associates of Canada, 1948), 303.
36 See especially Ian McKay's seminal work, *The Quest of the Folk: Antimodernism and Cultural Selection in Twentieth-Century Nova Scotia* (1994).

### 3. Clothing of Piety, Clothing of Poverty: Object Lessons and the Poverty Narratives of Women

1 An earlier version of this chapter was published in *Ethnos* 73(3): 377–98.
2 In Feld and Basso, *Senses of Place* (1996: 55).

3  The docudrama *The Boys of St. Vincent*, directed by John N. Smith, aired on CBC television in 1992. The trailer aired at regular intervals, contributing to the larger gothic sensibility.

4  "Five Christian Brothers have been convicted of offences at Mount Cashel ranging from buggery to bodily assault causing harm ... Court documents say in 1975 the Christian Brothers tried to avoid the criminal consequences of Mount Cashel abuse by making a bargain with the St. John's police to keep the matter secret" (www.nationalpost.com/home/story.html?f =/stories/2001204/392618.html). "Kingsclear housed young offenders and boys who couldn't fit into foster homes during the 1960s and 70s. Many residents became victims of former guard Karl Toft, who pleaded guilty in 1992 to 34 sexual assaults on 18 children" (http://nb/cbc.ca/regional /servlet/View?filename+nb_kingsclearprobe20040527). Again, there was a whiff of a cover-up and much was made of Toft's political connections and friendship with Richard Hatfield, who was premier of the province when the abuse was taking place.

5  Sister Rita Poirier, "Les Filles de Jésus," http://www.antigonishdiocese .com/LesFilles.html

6  The political struggles that led to their emigration from France are beyond the scope of this book, but Talal Asad's discussion of secularization in Europe and the political program of *laïcité* in France provides some historical context (2003: 165).

7  This restructuring of the tax system rode piggyback on the massive restructuring of the federal tax system that bankrolled large-scale development in New Brunswick. Della Stanley writes: "Canada seemed finally to have found a solution to the incongruity of a national structure that hived the principal industrial and financial resources into two central provinces and yet expected the others to finance from within their borders the growing welfare and developmental costs of a modern industrial state ... By the 1970s the Atlantic governments were obtaining more than a third of their revenues from federal equalization payments, while comparable amounts were transferred into the regional economy through federal social and development programs" (1993: 421). See also Gregory P. Marchildon and Nicole O'Byrne (2013).

8  Although the Filles de Jésus also had a presence in other French-speaking parts of Canada, education is a provincial concern and so the regional histories vary.

9  See the works of Richard Wilbur (1989) and George Stanley (1981, 1988) for a history of the politics of educational reform in New Brunswick.

10  In the little Acadian town of Caraquet, the attempt by the local MLA (member of the legislative assembly) and merchant Robert Young to overturn the election of the local school board of two Acadian men who

refused to pay the school tax led to the infamous Caraquet riots of 1875, considered by some to be the rallying call for a new Acadian political movement (cf. Stanley 1972; Wilbur 1989). In the aftermath of the riots, the government of the day was forced to make several concessions: "The state school system would remain, but in Catholic areas the teachers could be nuns and brothers dressed in their traditional religious habits. The English in Fredericton would have the final say on textbooks, but promised to remove all anti-Catholic biases. Buildings such as convents could be leased to the public school system and no restrictions on their use would be made after school hours" (Wilbur 1989: 38).

11 Notable at the time for addressing this phenomenon was the publication of Ian Hacking's *Rewriting the Soul* (1995) and Paul Antze and Michael Lambek's edited collection, *Tense Past* (1996). Both remain essential reading for those critically engaged with issues of narrative and memory as cultural phenomena.

12 Not that religious accommodations had not been part of my own so-called secular education in the English and Protestant south. I recall beginning some elementary school classes with the Lord's Prayer and Bible passages. My Jewish friends were invited to step outside the room at such times. And the Gideons distributed the King James version of the New Testament to all Grade 5 students in a special ceremony.

13 Although these are pseudonyms, should members of this congregation read this book, they will fondly recognize their sisters, some now departed from this world. They were remarkable women and my two days with them were not only enjoyable, but also illuminating. I have tried to remain faithful to their accounts, which are in large part presented here verbatim. I should also note that, pre–Vatican II, the sisters were known by the names given to them when they took final vows. Many of the people I spoke to in the settlement knew them only by the names they held prior to Vatican II.

14 Perhaps the earliest sustained ethnographic study of settler life in Atlantic Canada is the Stirling County Study, headed by Alexander Leighton and his colleagues at Cornell in the late 1940s. Tellingly, the second volume in that study is entitled *People of Cove and Woodlot: Communities from the Viewpoint of Social Psychiatry* (Hughes et al. 1960). Prior to the Second World War, most people in the Maritimes were rural and most deployed a similar combination of livelihood strategies (See Samson 1994). But Acadians tended to be worse off for both geographical and political reasons, having been forced to settle on the most inhospitable lands for agriculture after the Expulsion of 1758 (see Reid 1987). As an ethnic group, they remained politically weak until the 1960s (see Wilbur 1989 and Daigle 1982).

15 See John Milbank's essay "Against the Resignations of the Age" for a discussion of Christian social philosophy, which spurred a utopian

movement that had a particularly long tradition in France, from where the Filles de Jésus originated (1993: 39). In Canada, it combined with the nationalist ultramontane vision of the church, in which the French language and the church would be the pillars of French survival on the continent. In Quebec, the church held tremendous power prior to the Quiet Revolution. In New Brunswick, similar ideas developed, as the Acadian clergy were concerned for the survival of Acadians as a people. However, French Canadians formed a majority in Quebec, while in New Brunswick the Acadians were a politically disadvantaged minority.

16 Their Indian Day School at Eel River Bar belongs to the Uppi'Ganjig First Nation. It was one of twelve Indian Day Schools operated by the the Roman Catholic Church between 1880 and 1990. While there were no residential schools for Indigenous children in the province, assimilationist policies were similar. Further, the Sussex Vale Indian Academy established by British Loyalists in 1787 is considered a precursor to Canada's residential school system. (Elizabeth Fraser interview with legal historian Nicole O'Bryne, CBC News, 6 June 2021.) See also Martha E. Walls (2011) and Andrea Bear Nicholas (2001).

17 See Jonathan Chaplin (1993) and Douglas Holmes (2000) for a discussion of the influence of Catholic social teaching, especially the idea of subsidiarity, on political debates during the formation of the European Union. Many of the essays in J.S. Boswell et al. (2000) discuss the religious roots of current political discourse and the return to volunteerism for the delivery of social services. I was surprised to learn that it was Pope Pius XI, in 1931, who coined the idea of the "the third way," not Anthony Giddens and Tony Blair!

18 See Dominique Marshall (2006), who highlights the historical importance of the Family Allowance, a universal program tied to compulsory education, which was critical to social change in the province of Quebec. The universal plan was dismantled in 1989 and replaced with tax credits that largely favoured the wealthy.

19 Only the province of Prince Edward Island had lower wages (Wilbur 1989).

20 MacDonald (2003a) likened the exploitation of women religious in Prince Edward Island during the Depression years to the invisible labour of women in the home, which feminist scholars argue props up capitalism and the liberal economic state.

21 In *Marxism and Literature*, Raymond Williams argues that no single epoch "ever in reality exhausts or includes all human practice, human energy, and human intention" (1977: 125; cited in Levine (2020: 425).

22 Others have noted how easily clothing lends itself to social significance and thus to interpretation. See Sahlins (1976: 179–20), Connerton (1989: 6–40), Steedman (1986); and Arthur (1999). Sahlins' exercise in Sasssurean linguistics produces a distinctly cultural, rather than material, point of

view. Critical of this explicit attempt to reject a connection between the significance of clothing and their physical properties, Connerton notes that Sahlins' point of view is decidedly from the "standpoint of the perceiver, and not the wearer." His intervention is pointed: "Clothes were signs. They also constricted" (Connerton 1989: 34–5).

23  My usage is the same as that of James G. Carrier, who writes "I use 'things' in the broad sense, to include material objects, labour and services" (2018: 21).

## 4. Landscapes of Memory and a Lonely Nature

1  The New Brunswick Labour Act of 1869 precedes the Free Grants Act by a decade, but led to similar forms of settlement.

2  As early as 1819, the colonial administration in Fredericton imposed taxes on those cutting timber on Crown lands. The administration recognized that the timber trade was the province's most valuable resource and its greatest potential source of revenue (Sutherland 1994: 253). Since then, the provincial government has maintained control over the Crown lands, which cover much of the province's interior. Gaining access to the resources found there is always deeply political. See Wynn (1981) and Parenteau (1994a) for a history of the timber trade on New Brunswick's Crown lands in the nineteenth and twentieth centuries, respectively. Native claims to timber on Crown lands represent another iteration of this long political struggle for a share of the resources found there. See Wicken (2012), Blakney (2003), and King (2014).

3  State resource management principles are not necessarily concerned with ideas of livelihood for local populations, but with protecting Crown land resources for industry and the extraction of wealth. Sarah King (2014) argues that the Department of Fisheries and Oceans fuelled the tensions that erupted in Burnt Church/Esgenoôpetiji, following the Marshall Decision of 1999, by applying the same logic. (The Marshall Decision of 1999 recognized Indigenous rights to resources on Crown lands as established in the Peace and Friendship Treaties of 1760–1.)

4  Alden Nowlan, *These Are the Men Who Live by Killing Trees* (Bartlett 2017: 98).

5  www.hilaryscharper.com (25 July 2021).

6  Northrop Frye, cited in *The Nature of Canada* (Coates and Wynn 2019: 5).

7  Fred Cogswell, *The Stunted Strong* (2004).

8  Brian Bartlett writes that Alden Nowlan "gave fictitious names to places in Hants County, such as Slough of Despond, the Road to Ruin, and Desolation Creek" (2017: 8). See also Cogswell (1986).

9  Translated by Wayne Grady.

10  See Forbes (1979: 54).

11  See George Peabody, *School Days: The One Room Schools of Maritime Canada* (1992), which is full of sepia-toned photographs of Maritime one-room schoolhouses and the reminiscences of those who attended them. The recollections of the elderly gathered in the book are very close to those of Mrs. O'Leary and Ernestine.

12  The creation of the province of New Brunswick is linked to the dispersal of lands to British Loyalists arriving after the American Revolution at the close of the eighteenth century; throughout the late nineteenth century and early twentieth century there were various land-granting schemes for land close to New Brunswick's rivers.

13  See Don Handelman, *Models and Mirrors: Towards an Anthropology of Public Events* (1990).

14  Consider the theorists of Aristotelian virtue ethics who ethnographically probe the "ordinary ethics" of human action: see Veena Das (2007) and Lambek (2010). The attention to narrative is brilliantly highlighted by Cheryl Mattingly (2010) and Thomas Schwartz Wentzer (2014).

## 5.  Unravelling

1  I have previously taken stabs at analysing the events described in this chapter (D. Young 1999, 2005).

2  I have since found a script for *The Last Train to Paris* on the Internet, available for purchase for use at a murder mystery party. At the time of the party, Babette claimed to be the author of the script. I do not know if she purchased the script, simply ran with the idea, or is indeed the original author, publishing under a pseudonym.

3  M.M. Bakhtin's seminal *Rabelais and His World* (1968) has been especially influential in this regard.

4  "Bateson argued that the passage to play, and the creation of a reality predicated on play, was keyed cognitively to a meta-message that informed persons on how to relate to, and so how to do, this transition ... Among the examples he used to illustrate this paradox was that of the 'bite' and 'playful nip' ... 'These actions [the nip], in which we now engage, do not denote what would be denoted by those actions [the bite] which these actions [the nip] denote'" (Handelman 1998: 68).

5  The very serious notion that we are all caught in webs of signification, an idea to which Clifford Geertz drew our attention, remains fundamental to the insights of cultural anthropology, and my reading of social and cultural worlds. This is a far less flippant understanding of irony, and one to which I adhere.

6  Here I am thinking of irony in terms of the anthropologist's sensitivity to language and wariness of literalist interpretation. Michael Lambek and Paul Antze invited me to participate in a very stimulating panel on illness and irony. See Lambek and Antze (2003). The opportunity to converse

on this subject with Anne Meneley and Renée Sylvain, as they penned
their own essays on this subject, deeply influenced my thinking (Meneley
2003; Sylvain 2005). Theorists of irony who have influenced my thinking
include the philosopher Richard Rorty (1989, 1999), the psychoanalyst Roy
Schafer (1976), and the anthropologist Vincent Crapanzano (1992, 2000,
2001). For a more critical and less sympathetic view of the uses of irony in
anthropology, see David Scott (1992).

7 Bartlett (2017: 232).
8 There is an extensive literature on this subject. See, for instance, Antze and
Lambek (1996) and Roth (1995).
9 See Jerome Bruner (1991) for a discussion of narrative truth.
10 As an aside, the team with which I worked used Statistics Canada's
definition for measuring illiteracy, which includes anyone with less than
a Grade 9 education. By this definition, most of Babette's family would
have qualified as illiterate. It is, in my view, a ridiculously inadequate
measure. The Maritime poet Alden Nolan, who wrote so beautifully of
the rural poor in New Brunswick, once wrote that by this measure he was
Canada's pre-eminent illiterate poet-laureate. Frankly, I can think of many
"illiterates" of my mother's generation who could teach today's university
students a good deal about the basics of good writing.
11 Cheryl Mattingly (2010) explores the difficulties of obtaining a diagnosis
that conforms to objectified criteria and clinical tests that legitimize the
needs of patients, and their suffering more broadly, in *The Paradox of Hope:
Journeys through a Clinical Borderland*.
12 To my mind, Leyton's *Dying Hard: The Ravages of Industrial Carnage* (1975)
best illustrates the tyranny of a "therapeutocracy," although it is a study
that predates the "discursive turn" in anthropology and the influence of
Habermas and Foucault. Perhaps this is why it so nicely avoids arcane
language and focuses instead on the lives of those caught in the most
absurd and appalling circumstances. More recently, Cheryl Mattingly
(2010) thoughtfully examines this paradoxical needing to assess a clinical
diagnosis that will never fully acknowledge the complexities of suffering.
13 As my good friend and colleague Lindsay Dubois likes to remind me,
structure outs every time.
14 Fixing things textually, by means of a practice theory that recognizes the
relationship between the subjective and the objective, deals only with the
conundrums created by our own analytic constructs, and not with our
very practice as ethnographers, in and out of the field. To do fieldwork
is to engage in intersubjective processes and to write is to objectify. The
very separation seems inescapable to me and I'm deeply suspicious of
those who claim to overcome this objectifying process by giving voice to,
or speaking for, others. The key text on practice theory is, of course, by
Bourdieu (1977); Ortner (1984) discusses its deployment in anthropology.

# Works Cited

Antze, Paul, and Michael Lambek, eds. 1996. *Tense Past: Cultural Essays in Trauma and Memory*. New York and London: Routledge.

Archambault, Paul J. 1998. Autobiography and the Search for Transparency. *Symposium: A Quarterly Journal in Modern Literatures* 51(4): pp.: 231–46. Taylor & Francis.

Arthur, Linda B., ed. 1999. *Religion, Dress and the Body*. Oxford and New York: Berg.

Asad, Talal. 1993. *Genealogies of Religion*. Baltimore: Johns Hopkins University Press.

– 2003. *Formations of the Secular: Christianity, Islam, Modernity*. Stanford, CA: Stanford University Press.

Atwood, Margaret, Dennis Lee, Northrop Frye, and Jay Macpherson. 1972. *Survival: A Thematic Guide to Canadian Literature*. Toronto: House of Anansi.

Augé, Marc. 1995. *Non-places: Introduction to an Anthropology of Supermodernity*. Trans. John Howe. London and New York: Verso.

Bailey, F.G. 1971. Gifts and Poison. In *Gifts and Poison*, ed. by F.G. Bailey, 1–25. New York: Schocken.

Bakhtin, M. 1968. *Rabelais and His World*. Translated by Helene Islowsky. Cambridge, MA: MIT Press.

Bartlett, Brian, ed. 2017. *Collected Poems of Alden Nowlan*. Fredericton, NB: Icehouse Poetry, Goose Lane Editions.

Basso, Keith. 1996. *Wisdom Sits in Places: Notes on a Western Apache Landscape*. In Steven Feld and Keith H. Basso, eds., *Senses of Place*. Santa Fe, NM: School of American Research Press.

Bear Nicholas, Andrea. 2001. Canada's Colonial Mission: The Great White Bird. In *Aboriginal Education in Canada: A Study in Decolonization*, ed. K.P. Binda, 9–33. Mississauga, ON: Canadian Educators' Press.

Beaton, Kate. 2022. *Ducks: Two Years in the Oil Sands*. Montreal: Drawn and Quarterly.

Beidelman, T.O. 1989. Agonistic Exchange: Homeric Reciprocity and the Heritage of Simmel and Mauss. *Cultural Anthropology*, 227–59. https://doi.org/10.1525/can.1989.4.3.02a00010

Benjamin, Walter. 1969. Illuminations. New York: Schocken Books.

Berlant, Lauren. 2007. On the Case. *Critical Inquiry* 33: 663–72. https://doi.org/10.1086/521564

– 2011. *Cruel Optimism*. Durham, NC: Duke University Press.

Berton, Pierre. 1970. *The National Dream: Building the Impossible Railway*. Toronto: McClelland and Stewart.

– 1971. *The Last Spike: 1881–1885*. Toronto: McClelland and Stewart.

Blakney, Sherrie. 2003. "Aboriginal Forestry in New Brunswick: Conflicting Paradigms." *Environments* 31(1): 61–78.

Bloch, Maurice, and Jonathan Parry. 1989. Introduction. In *Money and the Morality of Exchange. Money and the Morality of Exchange*, ed. Jonathan Parry and Maurice Bloch, 1–32. Cambridge: Cambridge University Press, pp. 1–32.

Boswell, J.S., et al. 2000. *Catholic Social Thought: Twilight or Renaissance?* Leuven: Leuven University Press.

Botting, Fred. 1996. *Gothic*. London: Routledge.

Bourdieu, Pierre. 1977. *Outline of a Theory of Practice*. Cambridge: Cambridge University Press.

Bradwin, Edmund William. (1928) 1972. *The Bunkhouse Man: A Study of Work and Pay in the Camps of Canada, 1903–1914*. New York: Columbia University Press. Reprint, Toronto: University of Toronto Press.

Bruner, Jerome. 1991. The Narrative Construction of Reality. *Critical Inquiry* 18 (Autumn): 1–21. https://doi.org/10.1086/448619

Buckner, Philip A., and John G. Reid, eds. 1994. *The Atlantic Region to Confederation: A History*. Toronto: University of Toronto Press.

Carrier, James G. 2018. Moral Economy: What's in a Name. *Anthropological Theory* 18(1): 18–35. https://doi.org/10.1177/1463499617735259

Casey, Edward. (1987) 2000. *Remembering: A Phenomenological Study*. Bloomington: Indiana University Press.

– 2002. *Representing Place: Landscape Painting and Maps*. Minneapolis: University of Minnesota Press.

Chambers, R. 1991. *Room for Maneuver: Reading the Oppositional (in) Narrative*. Chicago: University of Chicago Press.

Chaplin, Jonathan. 1993. Subsidiarity and Sphere Sovereignty: Catholic and Reformed Conceptions of the Role of the State. In *Things Old and New: Catholic Social Teaching Revisited*, ed. Francis P. McHugh et al., 175–205. Lanham, MD: University Press of America.

Clarke, George Elliott. 2006. *George and Rue: A Novel*. Toronto: Harper Collins.

Clifford, James. 1988. *The Predicament of Culture*. Cambridge, MA: Harvard University Press.

Coates, Colin M., and Graeme Wynn, eds. 2019. *The Nature of Canada.* Vancouver,: On Point, UBC Press.

Cogswell, Fred. 1986. Alden Nowlan as Regional Atavist. *Studies in Canadian Literature* 11(2).

Connerton, Paul. 1989. *How Societies Remember.* Cambridge: Cambridge University Press.

Crapanzano, Vincent. 1992. *Hermes' Dilemma and Hamlet's Desire: On the Epistemology of Interpretation.* Cambridge, MA: Harvard University Press.

– 2000. *Serving the Word: Literalism in America from the Pulpit to the Bench.* New York: New Press.

– 2001. "The Problem of Context." *American Ethnologist.* Oxford: Blackwell Publishing Ltd. https://doi.org/10.1525/ae.2001.28.1.243

Cronon, William, ed. 1995. *Uncommon Ground: Rethinking the Human Place in Nature.* New York: W W. Norton.

Curtis, Herb. 1997.*The Brennen Siding Trilogy.* Fredericton, NB: Goose Lane.

Daigle, Jean, ed. 1982. *The Acadians of the Maritimes.* Moncton, NB: Centre d'études acadiennes.

Danylwycz, Marta. 1999. *Taking the Veil: An Alternative to Marriage, Motherhood, and Spinsterhood in Quebec, 1840–1920.* Toronto: University of Toronto Press.

Das, Veena. 2007. *Life and Words: Violence and the Descent into the Ordinary.* Berkeley: University of California Press.

Day, Sophie, Evthymios Paedaxiarchis, and Michael Stewart, eds. 1999. *Lilies of the Field: Marginal People Who Live for the Moment.* Boulder, CO: Westview Press.

Desjarlais. Robert R. 1997. *Shelter Blues: Sanity and Selfhood among the Homeless.* 1st ed. Philadelphia: University of Pennsylvania Press.

Donaldson, Allan. 1984. *Paradise Siding.* Fredericton, NB: Fiddlehead Poetry Books and Goose Lane.

Douglas, Mary. 1990. "Foreword." In *The Gift: The Form and Reason for Exchange in Archaic Societies*, by Marcel Mauss, vii–xviii. W.W. Norton.

Dunk, Thomas W. 1991. *It's a Working Man's Town.* Montreal and Kingston: McGill-Queen's University Press.

Dvořák, Marta, and Coral Ann Howells, guest editors. 2006. The Literature of Atlantic Canada. *Canadian Literatures* 188 (Spring): 12–13.

Ebaugh, Helen Rose Fuchs. 1993.*Women in the Vanishing Cloister: Organizational Decline in Catholic Religious Orders in the United States.* New Brunswick, NJ: Rutgers University Press.

Edwards, Justin D. 2005. *Gothic Canada: Reading the Spectre of a National Literature.* Edmonton: University of Alberta Press.

Faris, James C. 1973. *Cat Harbour.* St. John's, NL: ISER, Memorial University.

Feld, Steven, and Keith H. Basso, eds. 1996. *Senses of Place.* Santa Fe, NM: School of American Research Press.

Ferguson, James. 2006. *Global Shadows.* Durham, NC: Duke University Press.

Forbes, Ernest R. 1979. *The Maritime Rights Movement, 1919–1927: A Study in Canadian Regionalism*. Kingston and Montreal: McGill-Queen's University Press.

Forbes, E.R., and D.A. Muise, eds. 1993. *The Atlantic Provinces in Confederation*. Toronto: University of Toronto Press.

Foster, Karen. 2017. "Work Ethic and Degrowth in a Changing Atlantic Canada" *Journal of Political Ecology* 24: 633–43. https://doi.org/10.2458/v24i1.20902

Fraser, Elizabeth. 2021. New Brunswick's Long and Little-Known History of Assimilating Indigenous Children. CBC News, broadcast 6 June.

Fraser, Sylvia. 1987. *My Father's House: A Memoir of Incest and Healing*. Toronto: Collins.

Freud, Sigmund. (1919) 1955. The Uncanny. In *The Standard Edition of the Collected Works*, vol. 17, 217–56. London: Hogarth Press.

Garcia, Angela. 2010. *The Pastoral Clinic: Addiction and Dispossession along the Rio Grande*. 1st ed. Berkeley: University of California Press. https://doi.org/10.1525/9780520947825

Gaudry, Adam, and Darryl Leroux. 2017. White Settler Revisionism and Making Métis Everywhere: The Evocation of Métissage in Quebec and Nova. *Critical Ethnic Studies* 3 (Spring): 116–42. https://doi.org/10.5749/jcritethnstud.3.1.0116

Geertz, Clifford. 1980. Blurred Genres: The Refiguration of Social Thought. *The American Scholar* 49(2): 165–79. http://www.jstor.org/stable/41210607

Goldman, Marlene. 2012. *DisPossession: Haunting in Canadian Fiction*. Montreal and Kingston: McGill-Queen's University Press.

Gordon, Avery F. 1997. *Ghostly Matters: Haunting and the Sociological Imagination*. Minneapolis: University of Minnesota Press.

Griffiths, Naomi. 1974. Acadians in Exile: The Experience of Acadians in British Seaports." *Acadiensis* 4(1): 67–84.

– 1982. Longfellow's Evangeline: The Birth and Acceptance of a Legend. *Acadiensis* 11(2): 28–41. https://doi.org/10.1515/angl.1925.1925.49.153

– 2005. *From Migrant to Acadian: A North American Border People, 1604–1755*. Montreal and Kingston: McGill-Queen's University Press.

Habermas, Jürgen. 1984. *The Theory of Communicative Action*. Vol. 1. Trans. Thomas McCarthy. Boston: Beacon Press

Hacking, Ian. 1995. *Rewriting the Soul*. Princeton, NJ: Princeton University Press.

Halbwachs, Maurice, and Lewis A. Coser. 1992. *On Collective Memory*. Chicago: University of Chicago Press.

Handelman, Don. 1998. *Models and Mirrors: Toward an Anthropology of Public Events*. New York: Berghahn.

Harvey, David. 2005. *A Brief History of Neoliberalism*. Oxford: Oxford University Press.

Hebdige, D. 1988. *Hiding in the Light*. London: Routledge.

Highmore, Ben. 2017. *Cultural Feelings: Mood, Mediation and Cultural Politics*. Abingdon, Oxon; Routledge.

Hill, Lawrence. 2007. *The Book of Negroes*. Toronto: HarperCollins.

Hørjer, Lars, and Andreas Bandak. 2015. "Introduction: The Power of Example." *Journal of the Royal Anthropological Institute*: 1–17. https://doi.org/10.1111/1467-9655.12173

Hughes, Charles C., et al. 1960. *People of Cove and Woodlot: Communities from the Viewpoint of Social Psychiatry*. New York: Basic Books.

Ingold, Tim. 2020. *The Perception of the Environment: Essays on Livelihood, Dwelling, and Skill*. London and New York: Routledge.

Jessup, Lynda. 2006. Landscapes of Sport, Landscapes of Exclusion: The "Sportsman's Paradise" in Late-Nineteenth Century Painting. *Journal of Canadian Studies* 40 (1): 71–123. https://doi.org/10.3138/jcs.40.1.71

Keane, Webb. 2001. Money Is No Object: Materiality, Desire, and Modernity in an Indonesian Society. In *The Empire of Things: Regimes of Value and Material Culture*, ed. Fred Myers, 65–90. Santa Fe, NM: School of American Research Press.

Kenny, James, and Bill Parenteau. 2014. "Each Year the Indians Flexed Their Muscles a Little More": The Maliseet Defence of Aboriginal Fishing Rights on the St. John River, 1945–1990. *Canadian Historical Review* 95(2): 187–216. https://doi.org/10.3138/chr.2312.

Kenny, Michael G. 1986. *The Passion of Ansel Bourne: Multiple Personality in American Culture*. Washington, DC: Smithsonian Institution Press.

– 1996. Trauma, Time, Illness, and Culture: An Anthropological Approach to Traumatic Memory. In *Tense Past: Cultural Essays in Trauma and Memory*, ed. Paul Antze and Michael Lambek, 151–72. New York and London: Routledge: 151–72.

Kilroy-Marac, Katie. 2019. *An Impossible Inheritance: Postcolonial Psychiatry and the Work of Memory in a West African Clinic*. Berkeley: University of California Press. https://doi.org/10.1525/9780520971691

King, Sarah J. (Sarah Jean). 2014. *Fishing in Contested Waters: Place and Community in Burnt Church/Esgenoôpetitj*. Toronto: University of Toronto Press.

Kleinman, Arthur, et al., eds. 1997. *Social Suffering*. Berkeley: University of California Press.

Kotsko, Adam. 2018. *Neoliberalism's Demons: On the Political Theology of Late Capital*. Baltimore: Johns Hopkins University Press.

Kristeva, Julia. (1980) 1997. *Powers of Horror*. In *The Portable Kristeva*, ed. Kelly Oliver. New York: Columbia University Press.

Laidlaw, James. 2000. A Free Gift Makes No Friends. *Journal of the Royal Anthropological Institute* 6: 617–34. https://doi.org/10.1111/1467-9655.00036

Lambek, Michael. 2007. Sacrifice and the Problem of Beginning: Meditations from Sakalava Mythopraxis. *Journal of the Royal Anthropological Institute* 13(1): 19–38. https://doi.org/10.1111/j.1467-9655.2007.00411.x

– 2010. *Ordinary Ethics: Anthropology, Language, and Action*. 1st ed. New York: Fordham University Press.

– 2015. *The Ethical Condition: Essays on Action, Person, and Value.* Chicago: University of Chicago Press.

Lambek, Michael, and Paul Antze, eds. 2003 *Illness and Irony.* New York: Berghahn Books.

LaPointe Faulds, Vetta. 2005. *The Way It Was along My Bay.* Vol. 3, *Six Villages and an Island.* Islandview, NB: Rhyme for Reason.

Laroux, Daryl. 2019. Commentary: "Eastern Métis" Studies and White Settler Colonialism Today. *Aboriginal Policy Studies* 8(1): 104–14. https://doi .org/10.5663/aps.v8i1.29362

Lepselter, Susan. 2016. *The Resonance of Unseen Things: Poetics, Power, Captivity, and UFOs in the American Uncanny.* Ann Arbor: University of Michigan Press.

Leslie, Esther. 2010. Siegfried Kracauer and Walter Benjamin: Memory from Weimar to Hitler. In *Memory: Histories, Theories, Debates,* 1st ed., ed. Susannah Radstone and Bill Schwarz, 123–35. New York: Fordham University Press.

Lester, Rebecca J. 2005. *Jesus in Our Wombs: Embodying Modernity in a Mexican Convent.* Berkeley: University of California Press.

Levine, Caroline. 2020. Raymond Williams, Marxism and Literature (1977). *Public Culture* 32(2): 423–30.

Leyton, Elliot. 1975. *Dying Hard: The Ravages of Industrial Carnage.* Toronto: McClelland and Stewart.

Longfellow, Henry Wadsworth. (1847) 2014. *Evangeline: A Tale of Arcadie.* Fredericton: Goose Lane.

Lower, Arthur. 1936. *Settlement and the Forest Frontier in Eastern Canada.* Toronto: University of Toronto Press.

MacDonald, Heidi 2003a. Doing More with Less: The Sisters of St Martha (PEI) Diminish the Impact of the Great Depression. *Acadiensis* 33(1): 21–63.

– 2003b. Not Mere Victims of Circumstance: The Sisters of Saint Martha of Charlottetown Respond to Social and Religious Change, 1965–85. Unpublished manuscript.

– 2007. Entering the Convent as a Coming of Age in the 1930s. In *Changing Habits: Women Religious Orders in Canada,* ed. Elizabeth M. Smyth, 87–102. Toronto: Novalis.

MacKinnon, Lachlan. 2020. Post-industrial Memoryscapes: Combatting Working-Class Erasure in North America and Europe. In *The Routledge Handbook of Memory and Place,* ed. Sarah De Nardi, Hilary Orange, Steven High, and Eerika Koskinen-Koivisto, 175–84. London and New York: Routledge.

MacKinnon, Lachlan, Sarah De Nardi, Hilary Orange, Eerika Koskinen-Koivisto, and Steven High. 2020. Post-Industrial Memoryscapes: Combatting Working-Class Erasure in North America and Europe. In *The Routledge Handbook of Memory and Place,* 1st ed., 175–84. London and New York: Routledge. https://doi.org/10.4324/9780815354260-21

MacLeod, Katie. 2015. United against Fracking: Opposition to Shale Gas Exploration in Elsipogtog, New Brunswick. https://www.academia.edu/24039956

– 2016. The Unsaid and the Grand Dérangement: An Analysis of Outsider and Regional Interpretations of Acadian History. *Graduate History Review* 5(1): 115–37.

Maillet, Antonine. 1979. *La Sagouine*. Trans. Luis de Cespedes. Toronto: Simon and Pierre.

– 1982. *Pélagie*. Trans. Philip Stratford. Toronto: Doubleday.

Malette, Sébastien. 2017. The Eastern Métis and the "Negationism" of Professor Leroux: "Aiabitawisidjik wi mikakik" (trans. Rémy Biggs). *Trahir* (October): 1–17.

Marchildon, Gregory P., and Nicole C. O'Byrne. 2013. Last Province Aboard: New Brunswick and National Medicare. *Acadiensis* 24(1): 150–67.

Marshall, Dominique. 2006. *The Social Origins of the Welfare State: Quebec Families, Compulsory Education, and Family Allowances, 1940–1955*. Trans. Nicola Doone Danby. Waterloo, ON: Wilfrid Laurier Press.

Mattingly, Cheryl. 2010. *The Paradox of Hope: Journeys through a Clinical Borderland*. Berkeley: University of California Press.

– 2012. Two Virtue Ethics and the Anthropology of Morality. *Anthropological Theory* 12(2): 161–84. https://doi.org/10.1177/1463499612455284

Mauss, Marcel. 1990 *The Gift: Forms and Functions of Exchange in Archaic Societies*. Trans. Ian Cunnison. New York: W.W. Norton.

McKay, Ian. 1994. *The Quest of the Folk: Antimodernism and Cultural Selection in Twentieth-Century Nova Scotia*. Montreal and Kingston: McGill-Queen's University Press.

McLean, Stuart. 1999. "With Death Looking Out of Their Eyes": The Spectropoetics of Hunger in Accounts of the Irish Famine. *Social Analysis* 43(3): 40–67.

Meneley, Anne. 1996. *Tournaments of Value: Sociability and Hierarchy in a Yemeni Town*. Toronto: University of Toronto Press.

– 2003. Scared Sick or Silly? In *Illness and Irony*, ed. Michael Lambek and Paul Antze, 21–39. New York: Berghahn Books.

Milbank, John. 1993. Against the Resignations of the Age. In *Things Old and New: Catholic Social Teaching Revisited*, ed. Francis P. McHugh et al. Lanham, MD: University Press of America.

Miller, Carman. 1993. The 1940s: War and Rehabilitation. In *The Atlantic Provinces in Confederation*, ed. E.R. Forbes and D.A. Muise. Toronto: University of Toronto Press; Fredericton: Acadiensis Press.

Miller, Daniel. 2001. Alienable Gifts and Inalienable Commodities. In *The Empire of Things: Regimes of Value and Material Culture*, ed. Fred Myers, 91–115. Santa Fe, NM: School of American Research Press.

Montgomery, L.M. 1908. Anne of Green Gables. Toronto: McClelland-Bantam.

Northey, Margot. 1976. *The Haunted Wilderness: The Gothic and Grotesque in Canadian Fiction*. Toronto: Toronto University Press.

Ortner, Sherry. 1984. Theory in Anthropology since the Sixties. *Comparative Studies in Society and History* 26: 126–66. https://doi.org/10.1017/s0010417500010811

Paedaxiarchis, Evthymios. 1999. A Contest with Money: Gambling and the Politics of Disinterested Sociality in Aegean Greece. In *Lilies of the Field: Marginal People Who Live for the Moment*, ed. Sophie Day, Evthymios Paedaxiarchis, and Michael Stewart. Boulder, CO: Westview Press.

Parenteau, Bill, and Richard W. Judd. 2005. More Buck for the Bang: Sporting and the Ideology of Fish and Game Management in New England and the Maritime Provinces, 1870–1900. In *New England and the Maritime Provinces: Connections and Comparisons*, ed. Stephen J. Hornsby and John G. Reid, 232–51. Montreal and Kingston: McGill-Queen's University Press.

Parenteau, Bill, and James Kenny. 2002. Survival, Resistance, and the Canadian State: The Transformation of New Brunswick's Native Economy, 1867–1930. *Journal of the Canadian Historical Association* 13(1): 49–71. https://doi.org/10.7202/031153ar

Parenteau, Bill, and L. Anders Sandberg. 1995. Conservation and the Gospel of Economic Nationalism: The Canadian Pulpwood Question in Nova Scotia and New Brunswick, 1918–1925. *Environmental History Review* 19(2): 55–83. https://doi.org/10.2307/3984832

Parenteau, William. 1994a. Settlement and the Forest Frontier Revisited: Class Politics and the Administration of the New Brunswick Labour Act, 1919–1929. In *Contested Countryside: Rural Workers and Modern Society in Atlantic Canada, 1800–1950*, ed. Daniel Samson. Fredericton, NB: Acadiensis Press.

– 1994b. Forest and Society in New Brunswick: The Political Economy of the Forest Industries. PhD diss., University of New Brunswick.

– 1998. "Care, Control and Supervision": Native People in the Canadian Atlantic Salmon Fishery, 1867–1900. *Canadian Historical Review* 79(1): 1–35. https://doi.org/10.3138/chr.79.1.1

– 2004. A "Very Determined Opposition to the Law": Conservation, Angling Leases, and Social Conflict in the Canadian Atlantic Salmon Fishery, 1867–1914. *Environmental History* 9 (July): 436–63. https://doi.org/10.2307/3985768

Parry, Jonathan. 1989. On the Moral Perils of Exchange. In *Money and the Morality of Exchange*, ed. J. Parry and M. Bloch. Cambridge: Cambridge University Press.

Parry, J., and M. Bloch. 1989. *Money and the Morality of Exchange*. Cambridge: Cambridge University Press.

Peabody, George. 1992. *School Days: The One-Room Schools of Maritime Canada*. Fredericton, NB: Goose Lane Editions.

Petrie, Daniel, Dir. 1976. *Sybil*. Lorimar Productions.

Pine, Jason. 2016. Last Chance Incorporated. *Cultural Anthropology* 31(2): 297–318

Power, Thomas P., ed. 1991. *The Irish in Atlantic Canada, 1780–1900*. Fredericton, NB: New Ireland Press.

Radforth, Ian. 1987. *Bush Workers and Bosses: Logging in Northern Ontario 1900–1980*. Toronto: University of Toronto Press.

Radstone, Susannah, ed. 2000. *Memory and Methodology*. Oxford and New York: Berg.

Reid, John G. 1987. *Six Crucial Decades: Times of Change in the History of the Maritimes*. Halifax: Nimbus.

Richards, David Adams. 1976. *Blood Ties*. Ottawa: Oberon Press.

– 2007. *The Lost Highway: A Novel*. San Francisco: MacAdam/Cage.

Ricoeur, Paul. 1980. Narrative Time. *Critical Inquiry* 7(1): 169–90. https://doi .org/10.1086/448093

Ricoeur, Paul, and John Thompson. 1981. *Hermeneutics and the Human Sciences: Essays on Language, Action, and Interpretation*. Cambridge: Cambridge University Press.

Rimstead, Roxanne. 2001. *Remnants of Nation: On Poverty Narratives by Women*. Toronto: University of Toronto Press.

Rorty, Richard. 1989. *Contingency, Irony, and Solidarity*. Cambridge: Cambridge University Press.

– 1999. *Philosophy and Social Hope*. London: Penguin Books.

Roth, M. 1995. *The Ironist's Cage: Memory, Trauma, and the Construction of History*. New York: Columbia University Press.

Rudin, Ronald. 2009. *Remembering and Forgetting in Acadie: A Historian's Journey through Public Memory*. Toronto: University of Toronto Press.

Sahlins, Marshall. 1976. *Culture and Practical Reason*. Chicago: University of Chicago Press.

Samson, Daniel. 1994. *Contested Countryside: Rural Workers and Modern Society in Atlantic Canada, 1800–1950*. Fredericton: Acadiensis Press.

Schafer, Roy. 1976. *A New Language for Psychoanalysis*. New Haven, CT: Yale University Press.

Schivelbusch, Wolfgang. 1986. *The Railway Journey: The Industrialization of Time and Space in the Nineteenth Century*. Berkeley: University of California Press.

Schreiber, Flora Rheta. 1973. *Sybil*. Chicago: Regnery.

Scott, David. 1992. Criticism and Culture: Theory and Post-colonial claims on Anthropological Disciplinarity. *Critique of Anthropology* 12(4): 371–94. https://doi.org/10.1177/0308275x9201200401

Scott, James. 1985. *Weapons of the Weak: Everyday Forms of Peasant Resistance*. New Haven, CT: Yale University Press.

Sedgwick, Eve Kosofsky. 1980. *The Coherence of Gothic Conventions*. New York: Arno Press.

- 1985. *Between Men*. New York: Columbia University Press.
Shanin, Teodor, ed. (1971) 1987. *Peasants and Peasant Societies*. 2nd ed. Oxford and New York: Basil Blackwell.
Shields, Rob. 2017. Lifelong Sorrow: Settler Affect, State and Trauma at *Anne of Green Gables*. *Settler Colonial Studies* (Routledge). https://doi.org/10.1080/2201473x.2017.1388467
Shohet, Merav. 2013. Everyday Sacrifice and Language Socialization in Vietnam: The Power of a Respect Particle. *American Anthropologist* 115(2): 203–17. https://doi.org/10.1111/aman.12004
Sider, G. 1984. Family Fun in Stave Harbour: Custom, History, and Confrontation in Village Newfoundland. In *Interest and Emotion: Essays on the Study of Family and Kinship*, ed. H. Medick and D.W. Sabean, 340–70. Cambridge: Cambridge University Press: 340–370.
- 1986. *Culture and Class in Anthropology and History: A Newfoundland Illustration*. Cambridge: Cambridge University Press.
Smith, Andrew, and William Hughes, eds. 2003. *Empire and the Gothic: The Politics of Genre*. New York: Palgrave Macmillan.
Smyth, E.M. 1999. Professionalization among the Professed. In Challenging Professions: Women and the Professions in English Canada, ed. E. Smyth et al., 234–54. Toronto: University of Toronto Press.
- ed. 2007. *Changing Habits: Women's Religious Orders in Canada*. Ottawa: Novalis.
Spraye, Carole. 1979. *Will O' the Wisp: Folktales and Legends of New Brunswick*. Fredericton, NB: Brunswick Press.
Spyer, Patricia, ed. 1998. *Border Fetishisms: Material Objects in Unstable Spaces*. New York: Routledge.
Stack, Carol B. 1974. *All Our Kin: Strategies for Survival in a Black Community*. New York: Harper & Tow.
Stanley, D. 1993. The Illusions and Realities of Progress. In *The Atlantic Provinces in Confederation*, ed. E.R. Forbes and D.A Muise, 421–59. Toronto: University of Toronto Press.
Stanley, George, F.G. 1972. The Caraquet Riots of 1875. *Acadiensis (Fredericton)* 2(1): 21–38.
- 1981. The Flowering of Acadian Resistance. In *Eastern and Western Perspectives*, ed. D.J. Bercuson and P. Buckner. Toronto: University of Toronto Press.
Steedman, Carolyn. 1986. *Landscape for a Good Woman*. New Brunswick, NJ: Rutgers University Press.
- 1995. *Strange Dislocations: Childhood and the Idea of Human Interiority 1780–1930*. London: Virago Press.
Steger, Manfred B., and Ravi K. Roy. 2010. *Neoliberalism: A Very Short Introduction*. 2nd ed. Oxford: Oxford University Press.
Stewart, Kathleen. 1996. *A Space on the Side of the Road: Cultural Poetics in an "Other" America*. Princeton, NJ: Princeton University Press.

– 2007. *Ordinary Affects*. Durham, NC: Duke University Press.

Sugars, Cynthia, and Gerry Turcotte. 2009. *Unsettled Remains: Canadian Literature and the Postcolonial Gothic*. Waterloo, ON: Wilfrid Laurier Press.

Sutherland, D.A. 1994. 1810–1820: War and Peace. In *The Atlantic Region to Confederation: A History*, ed. P.A. Buckner and J.G. Reid. Toronto: University of Toronto Press.

Sylvain, Renée. 2005. Loyalty and Treachery in the Kalahari. In *Auto-ethnographies: The Anthropology of Academic Practices* ed. Anne Meneley and Donna J. Young, 25–38. Peterborough, ON: Broadview Press.

Taussig, Michael T. 1980. *The Devil and Commodity Fetishism in South America*. Chapel Hill: University of North Carolina Press.

Thériault, Leon. 1982. The Acadianisation of the Catholic Church in Acadia, 1763–1953. In *The Acadians of the Maritimes: Thematic Studies*, ed. Jean Daigle, 47–86. Moncton, NB: Centre d'études acadiennes.

Tremblay, Tony, and Ellen Rose, directors. 2011. *The Last Shift: The Story of a Mill Town*. Fredericton, NB: A Golden Girl Production.

Tsing-Lowenhaupt, Anna, 2015. *The Mushroom at the End of the World: On the Possibility of Life in Capitalist Ruins*. Princeton, NJ: Princeton University Press.

Tsing-Lowenhaupt, Anna, Heather Swanson, Elaine Gen, and Nils Bubandt, eds. 2017. *Arts of Living on a Damaged Planet*. Minneapolis: University of Minnesota Press.

Turner, V. 1982. *From Ritual to Theatre: The Human Seriousness of Play*. New York: Performing Arts Journal Publications.

Walby-Beckett, Moira, screenwriter. 2017. *Anne*. Toronto: Northwood Entertainment and CBC.

Walls, Martha E. 2011. [T]he teacher that cannot understand their language should not be allowed": Colonialism, Resistance, and Female Mi'kmaw Teachers in New Brunswick Day Schools, 1900–1923. *Journal of the Canadian Historical Association* 22(1): 35–67. https://doi .org/10.7202/1008957ar

Warry, Wayne. 2007. *Ending Denial: Understanding Aboriginal Issues*. Peterborough, ON: Broadview Press.

Wentzer, Thomas Schwartz. 2014. "I have seen Königsberg burning": Philosophical Anthropology and the Responsiveness of Historical Experience. *Anthropological Theory* 14(1): 27–8. https://doi .org/10.1177/1463499614521723

Wicken, William C. 2012. *The Colonization of Mi'kmaw Memory and History 1794–1928: The King v. Gabriel Sylliboy*. Toronto: University of Toronto Press.

Wilbur, Richard. 1989. *The Rise of French New Brunswick*. Halifax, NS: Formac Publishing.

Williams, Raymond. 1973. *The Country and the City*. St. Albans, UK: Paladin.

– 1977. *Marxism and Literature*. Oxford: Oxford University Press.

– 1983. *Keywords: A Vocabulary of Culture and Society*. Revised and expanded edition. London: Fontana.

Wittberg, Patricia. 1994. *The Rise and Decline of Catholic Religious Orders. A Social Movement Perspective*. Albany, NY: SUNY Press.

Wyile, Herb. 2011. *Anne of Tim Hortons: Globalization and the Reshaping Atlantic-Canada Literature*. Waterloo, ON: Wilfrid Laurier University Press.

Wynn, Graeme. 1981. *Timber Colony: A Historical Geography of Nineteenth-Century New Brunswick*. Toronto: Unversity of Toronto Press.

Young, Aurele. 1982. The Acadian Economy: History and Development. In *The Acadians of the Maritimes: Thematic Studies*, ed. Jean Daigle, 197–218. Moncton: Centre d'etudes acadiennes.

Young, Donna J. 1996. Remembering Trouble: Three Lives, Three Stories. *Tense Past: Cultural Essays in Trauma and Memory*, ed. Paul Antze and Michael Lambek, 25–44. New York and London: Routledge.

– 1999. Deadly Play: Shifting Identities on the Last Train to Paris. *Social Analysis* 43(3): 26–39.

– 2005. Writing against the Native Point of View. In *Auto-ethnographies: The Anthropology of Academic Practices*, ed. Anne Meneley and Donna J. Young, 203–15. Peterborough, ON: Broadview Press.

– 2008. Clothing of Piety, Clothing of Poverty: Object Lessons in a Convent School. *Ethnos* 7(3): 377–98. https://doi.org/10.1080/00141840802324052

# Index

abandonment: sense of, 4

abjection, 63, 64

academics: opportunities in Canada, 6, 140n7

Acadian clergy. *See* Roman Catholic clergy

Acadians: alliances with Mi'kmaq First Nations, 143n29; cultural and political awakening of, 20; expulsion of, 15, 73, 141n19, 152n14; livelihood practices, 82, 152n14; nationalist movement, 62–3; religious beliefs, 67; roots of, 10–11, 52, 101; values of, 82

Alcool NB Liquor, 9, 140n14

All Hallow's Eve, 77, 114

*Anne of Green Gables* (Montgomery), 109, 111

anthropologist-subject relationships, 135–7

anthropology, 6, 15–16, 25, 26, 136, 142n22, 156n12

Antigonish Cooperative Movement in Nova Scotia, 148n15

Antze, Paul, 146n19, 149n24, 152n11, 155n5

apophenia, 150n32

Archambault, Paul, 23

Asad, Talal, 151n6

Atlantic Canada: attachment to landscape, 18; brewers, 142n20; economic development, 26, 65, 109; equalization payments, 151n7; ethnic relations in, 148n14; ethnographic studies of, 41, 152n14; gender violence, 24; historical studies of, 142n24; in literature, 17, 66; livelihood strategies, 152n14; notion of "up home" in, 65; out-migration from, 24; places of deliberate degrowth, 139n3; population of, 18; preoccupations with the past, 15, 64; present-oriented temporalities, 12; prior to Confederation, 18; relationship to the rest of the nation, 65; rural settlers, 8, 11, 12, 13, 14–15, 20, 24, 106, 108; seasonal labour, 24; unprofitable railways, 41

Atwood, Margaret, 7, 107

Augé, Marc, 139n3

autobiographical pact, 23

Banff National Park, 36

Bay of Chaleur, 15, 63, 68, 102

Beaton, Kate: *Ducks: Two Years in the Oil Sands*, 24

## ANTHROPOLOGICAL HORIZONS

Editor: Michael Lambek, University of Toronto

**Published to date:**